Labor Markets and Business Cycles

CREI Lectures in Macroeconomics

Series Editor: Hans-Joachim Voth

Labor Markets and Business Cycles,
Robert Shimer

Labor Markets and Business Cycles

Robert Shimer

This work is published in association with the
Centre de Recerca en Economia Internacional (CREI)

Princeton University Press
Princeton and Oxford

Published by Princeton University Press,
41 William Street, Princeton, New Jersey 08540

In the United Kingdom: Princeton University Press,
6 Oxford Street, Woodstock, Oxfordshire OX20 1TW

Shimer, Robert.
Labor markets and business cycles / Robert Shimer.
p. cm. - (CREI lectures in macroeconomics)
Includes bibliographical references and index.
ISBN 978-0-691-14022-3 (hardcover : alk. paper)
1. Labor market. 2. Business cycles. I. Title.
HD5706.S445 2009
331.12-dc22 2009047840

British Library Cataloging-in-Publication Data is available

This book has been composed in LucidaBright using TEX

Typeset and copyedited by T&T Productions Ltd, London

Printed on acid-free paper. ∞

press.princeton.edu

Printed in the United States of America

10 9 8 7 6 5 4 3 2 1

Contents

Introduction

The Center for Research in International Economics (CREI) aims to deepen our understanding of the global forces that shape modern economies. CREI was founded in 1994 with support from the Generalitat de Catalunya and Universitat Pompeu Fabra (UPF). It is dedicated to generating research of the highest quality, in all areas of macroeconomics—ranging from growth, international finance, business cycles, the study of labor markets, and monetary economics to trade, development, and international economic history.

The CREI Lectures in Macroeconomics will present new work by young but already distinguished scholars, whose recent contributions have already had a substantial impact on the profession. Authors will be prominent contributors to areas of economics that have attracted a good deal of attention recently. The goal is that scholars delivering the CREI Lectures offer a synthesis of their thinking on one of the key research challenges facing the profession. Books in this series are aimed at graduate students and researchers in macroeconomics, broadly defined.

Preface

The goal of this book is to consolidate, extend, and provide a new perspective on recent research that uses search frictions and wage rigidities to explain the cyclical dynamics of labor markets. Since the working paper versions of Shimer (2005), Hall (2005), and Costain and Reiter (2008) first circulated in 2002 and 2003, there has been a profusion of research in this area, but the underlying question is as old as macroeconomics: why do employment and unemployment fluctuate so much at business cycle frequencies?

Lucas and Rapping's (1969) theory of intertemporal substitution in labor supply is the starting point for any modern analysis of employment fluctuations, including the Real Business Cycle (RBC) model and the New Keynesian model. The key assumption is that workers decide how much to work at each point in time, taking as given the prevailing wage. To the extent that labor supply is elastic, hours of work fluctuate with movements in the wage.

While models based on intertemporal substitution in labor supply are qualitatively consistent with the movement of hours of work over the business cycle, they run into at least two problems. First, in a frictionless environment, the marginal rate of substitution between consumption and leisure should be equal to the marginal product of labor, after adjusting for labor and consumption taxes. When they looked at data, Parkin (1988), Rotemberg and Woodford (1991, 1999), Hall (1997), Mulligan (2002), and Chari et al. (2007) found that this relationship does not hold. In chapter 1, I reaffirm this finding, verifying that there is a wedge between the marginal rate of substitution and the marginal product of labor, the *labor wedge*, and that the wedge varies cyclically. During almost every recession, the labor wedge increases sharply. From the perspective of a frictionless model, there are two ways to interpret this finding: recessions may be times when labor income taxes and consumption taxes rise, discouraging workers from supplying labor; or they may be times when the disutility of work increases. In a reduced-form model, both would dissuade workers from working, causing countercyclical increases in the measured labor wedge. But unfortunately neither possibility is empirically tenable.

The second problem with the frictionless model is that, in an environment where workers can decide how much to work at each point in time, it is possible to generate movements in hours worked but impossible to generate unemployment, i.e., nonemployed workers who would like to work at the prevailing wage. This omission potentially has important implications for welfare, since a worker who cannot find a job at the prevailing wage but would like to have one is, by revealed preference, worse off than if she simply chose not to work at that wage. It potentially also has important consequences for the positive analysis of business cycles, since most cyclical movements in the aggregate number of hours worked are accounted for by movements between employment and unemployment, not by movements in hours worked by employed workers.

Equilibrium search-and-matching models provide an ideal laboratory for understanding unemployment and have been used extensively for this purpose.[1] The models build on the idea that it takes workers time to find a job. Thus a worker entering the labor market or a worker who loses her job necessarily experiences a spell of unemployment. Moreover, unemployed workers are worse off than employed workers because they are unable to work until they find a job. In this sense, search and matching provides a theory of unemployment, not just of nonemployment.

Search-and-matching models also often assume that firms must expend resources in order to find a suitable worker. A matching function determines the number of workers and firms that meet as a function of the unemployment rate and firms' recruiting effort. Fluctuations in the profitability of hiring a worker, possibly due to fluctuations in aggregate productivity, induce fluctuations in recruiting. When firms recruit harder, unemployed workers find jobs faster, pulling down the unemployment rate. Thus search-and-matching models naturally generate movements in unemployment duration, which are an important component of the observed fluctuations in unemployment at business cycle frequencies.

But the question remains whether search-and-matching models are quantitatively consistent with the observed behavior of labor market outcomes. There is a good reason to expect that they are not. Recall that a competitive labor market model cannot explain all of the observed fluctuations in the labor wedge. Viewed through the lens of a frictionless model, recessions look like periods when the labor wedge rises, reducing labor supply.

[1] Important papers in the search-and-matching literature include Lucas and Prescott (1974), Pissarides (1985), and Mortensen and Pissarides (1994). For a thorough textbook treatment of the matching model, see Pissarides (2000).

Now consider introducing a labor adjustment cost into a competitive model, making it costly for firms to increase their employment level. This will directly lower the volatility of employment. Firms will increase employment by less during expansions because hiring is costly. They will also be less willing to reduce employment during recessions in order to avoid future hiring costs, when desired employment returns to normal. Thus hours worked will tend to be more stable over the business cycle when adjustment costs are larger. If real-world data were generated by an economy with labor adjustment costs but an economist ignored the existence of those costs, he would be surprised by how stable observed hours worked were over the business cycle. Measuring the labor wedge with data generated by the economy, he would rationalize this by concluding that the wedge rises during expansions and falls during recessions—exactly the opposite of what we observe in the data.

Search frictions act, at least in part, like a labor adjustment cost, since they imply that it takes unemployed workers time to find a job and it takes firms time to hire workers. If this reduces the volatility of employment, the labor wedge will tend to be positively correlated with employment. Such a model of search frictions will not be useful in explaining the cyclical behavior of labor markets.

The bulk of this book confirms the thrust of this argument. Search frictions do not per se help to explain fluctuations in the labor wedge, but rather they exacerbate the problems of the frictionless model. However, I also argue that subsidiary assumptions, especially alternative assumptions on wage setting, may help to explain why the measured labor wedge is countercyclical and why employment is so volatile.

To understand this last statement, note that in matching models based on Pissarides (1985) and Mortensen and Pissarides (1994), search frictions create a gap between the marginal product of labor and the marginal rate of substitution. This is because workers and firms engage in a time-consuming search for partners before negotiating a wage. Once they have sunk this cost, there is a range of wages at which both prefer to match rather than break up. Loosely speaking, any wage that is larger than the marginal rate of substitution between consumption and leisure but smaller than the marginal product of labor will be mutually preferable to breaking up.

A critical question is how wages are determined. A common assumption in the search-and-matching literature is that the worker and the firm bargain over the gains from trade, splitting the surplus according to the Nash bargaining solution (Nash 1953). In chapter 2, I prove that under this wage-setting assumption, the wage, the marginal rate of substitution, and the marginal product of labor are all proportional to current productivity under particular assumptions on preferences (balanced growth and additive separability between consumption and leisure) and under the assumption that output is produced using only labor. Productivity shocks affect neither the labor wedge nor the (un)employment rate. This neutrality result is inspired by Blanchard and Galí (2006), who reach a similar conclusion in a model where firms face a labor adjustment cost.

In chapter 3, I break this neutrality result in several ways. First, I allow for more general preferences, although I maintain the balanced-growth restriction. The resulting fluctuations are minuscule. Second, I introduce capital into the model. While the resulting framework generates cyclical movement in employment and the labor wedge, it is inconsistent with the data. In particular, I verify that employment is positively correlated with the measured labor wedge in the model, for the reason described above: search frictions dampen fluctuations in employment, which, viewed through the lens of the frictionless model, suggests that expansions are periods when labor tax rates are higher. Third, I consider other shocks, especially reallocation shocks that change the probability of an employed worker becoming unemployed. This has little effect on the results. I conclude that the (counterfactual) positive comovement of the labor wedge and employment is a robust feature of search models when wages are set via Nash bargaining.

Chapter 4 considers an alternative wage-setting procedure that is no less plausible than the Nash bargaining solution and has qualitatively different implications for the behavior of the model. I assume that wages are backward looking. I find that this form of wage rigidity can potentially explain why employment is so volatile even if the elasticity of labor supply is relatively small. If wages do not fall following a negative productivity shock, firms will be reluctant to hire workers, pushing up unemployment duration and the unemployment rate.

This type of wage rigidity is based on ideas first developed in Hall (2005).[2] In a framework similar to Shimer (2005), Hall shows that if wages are rigid, unemployment is extremely sensitive to underlying shocks. He stresses that this type of wage rigidity is not susceptible to the Barro (1977) critique. That is, no matched worker–firm combination would mutually prefer to renegotiate their wage. Similarly, Blanchard and Galí (2006) consider a real-wage rigidity that makes the wage move less than one-for-one with the shock. Firms respond to relatively low wages during booms by creating many new jobs, driving down the unemployment rate. However, this also implies that part of the productivity increase is spent

---

[2] One may also think of this as a modern attempt to integrate search theory with disequilibrium macroeconomics (Barro and Grossman 1971; Benassy 1982; Malinvaud 1977).

on additional job creation. Consumption then increases by less than productivity, generating a countercyclical labor wedge. Gertler and Trigari (2009) reach a similar conclusion in a model with overlapping wage contracts that are not contingent on the path of productivity shocks.

Chapter 5 briefly concludes by summarizing some recent related research and suggesting the directions that future research may take.

I intend for this book to provide a stand-alone treatment of the business cycle properties of search-and-matching models. It should be suitable for advanced graduate students and other researchers familiar with modern recursive methods, for example at the level of Ljungqvist and Sargent (2004). At the same time, the book is far from exhaustive. In particular, I focus exclusively on business cycle issues, neglecting fascinating and important topics, such as cross-country differences in unemployment rates, that many others have addressed using search models. For these issues and others, the textbook treatment in Pissarides (2000) complements this book. Moreover, Pissarides (2000) provides a less technical introduction to search-and-matching models, which may be particularly useful to a reader who is uncomfortable with the history-contingent notation that I use throughout this book.

This book is also not a comprehensive survey of the literature on business cycles and unemployment. I develop one particular model of unemployment, integrating the search-and-matching model with a standard RBC model. I abstract from important, but difficult and controversial, issues like the role of incomplete markets in search models with aggregate fluctuations (Bils et al. 2007; Krusell et al. 2007; Nakajima 2008). Perhaps most importantly, I do not attempt to review the burgeoning literature on the business cycle properties of search models, mentioning only a few papers from which I knowingly borrow ideas.[3] My excuse is that the scope of this project, originally conceived to accompany three lectures at the Centre de Recerca en Economia Internacional (CREI) in June 2008, prevents me from doing so.

I am grateful for the comments I received at CREI during and after those lectures and for CREI's hospitality during the week I spent there. Comments by Jordi Galí, Jaume Ventura, and others had a significant influence on the shape and emphasis of this manuscript. Thijs van Rens, in addition to providing comments during the lectures at CREI,

[3] An inexhaustive reading list would certainly include Yashiv (2006), Krause and Lubik (2007), Mortensen and Nagypál (2007), Rudanko (2009), Farmer and Hollenhorst (2006), Kennan (2006), Rotemberg (2006), Rudanko (2008), and the papers collected in a special issue of the *Scandinavian Journal of Economics* entitled "Macroeconomic Fluctuations and the Labor Market" (2007, volume 107, issue 4).

subsequently used a draft of this book as part of a course and provided me with detailed feedback on the near-final manuscript.

I have taught short series of lectures based on this book at the Massachusetts Institute of Technology, Osaka University, and Study Center Gerzensee. I found that four ninety-minute lectures, one devoted to each of the first four chapters, were sufficient for a thorough overview of the material. Covering all the variants of the models and the related literature takes considerably longer. I appreciate the comments that I received from students at each of those institutions.

I also received detailed feedback from my colleagues at the University of Chicago. Fernando Alvarez's and Robert Lucas's comments were particularly important in revising this book. More broadly, my thinking about the issues in this book was informed by numerous discussions with colleagues at other universities, including Dale Mortensen, Christopher Pissarides, Richard Rogerson, Iván Werning, Randall Wright, and especially Robert Hall.

Katarina Borovickova provided me with fantastic research assistance, replicating all of the algebra and code in this book, thus significantly reducing the number of mistakes in the final manuscript. I am also grateful for the financial support of the National Science Foundation. Finally, I would like to thank Alicia Menendez for her extraordinary patience with me through the research and writing process.

Labor Markets and Business Cycles

1
The Labor Wedge

Throughout this book, I study the interaction of optimizing households and firms in a closed economy. I begin in this chapter by developing a competitive, representative-agent version of the model. The chapter has two objectives. First, I introduce much of the notation that I rely on throughout the book. Because of this, I include details in this chapter that are not really necessary for the second, more substantive objective: I use the model to measure and analyze the behavior of the *labor wedge*, the wedge between the marginal rate of substitution of consumption for leisure and the marginal product of labor. I confirm the well-known result that the labor wedge tends to rise during recessions, so the economy behaves as if there is a countercyclical tax on labor. The remainder of the book explores whether extending the model to incorporate labor market search frictions can explain the behavior of the labor wedge.

I start the chapter by laying out the essential features of the model: optimizing households, optimizing firms, a government that sets taxes and spending, and equilibrium conditions that link the various agents. In section 1.2, I use pieces of the model to derive a static equation that relates hours worked, the consumption–output ratio, and the labor wedge. Section 1.3 discusses how I measure the first two concepts and uses these measures to calculate the implied behavior of the labor wedge in the United States. I establish the main substantive result: that the labor wedge rose strongly during every recession since 1970. I show the robustness of my results to alternative specifications of preferences in section 1.4 and discuss the possibility that the results are driven by preference shocks in section 1.5. I finish the chapter with a brief discussion in section 1.6 on the empirical relationship between the fluctuations in hours, which I analyze here, and fluctuations in employment and unemployment, which are the main topic of subsequent chapters.

1.1 A Representative-Agent Model

I denote time by $t = 0, 1, 2, \ldots$ and the state of the economy at time t by s_t. Let $s^t = \{s_0, s_1, \ldots, s_t\}$ denote the history of the economy and $\Pi(s^t)$

denote the time-0 belief about the probability of observing an arbitrary history s^t through time t. Exogenous variables like aggregate productivity, government spending, and distortionary tax rates may depend on the history s^t. At date 0, there is an initial capital stock $k_0 \equiv k(s^0)$ and an initial stock of government debt $b_0 \equiv b(s^0)$. The capital stock is owned by firms, while households hold the debt and own the firms.

Households

A representative household is infinitely lived and has preferences over history-s^t consumption $c(s^t)$ and history-s^t hours of work $h(s^t)$. To start, I assume that preferences are ordered by the utility function

$$\sum_{t=0}^{\infty} \sum_{s^t} \beta^t \Pi(s^t) \left(\log c(s^t) - \frac{\gamma \varepsilon}{1+\varepsilon} h(s^t)^{(1+\varepsilon)/\varepsilon} \right), \tag{1.1}$$

where $\beta \in (0,1)$ is the discount factor, $\gamma > 0$ measures the disutility of working, and, as I show below, $\varepsilon > 0$ is the Frisch (constant marginal utility of wealth) elasticity of labor supply.

This formulation implies that preferences are additively separable over time and across states of the world. It also implies that preferences are consistent with balanced growth—doubling a household's initial assets and its income in every state of the world doubles its consumption but does not affect its labor supply. This is consistent with the absence of a secular trend in hours worked per household, at least in the United States (Aguiar and Hurst 2007; Ramey and Francis 2009). I maintain both of these assumptions throughout this book. The formulation also imposes that the marginal utility of consumption is independent of the worker's leisure. This restriction is more questionable and so I relax it in section 1.4 below.

The household chooses a sequence for consumption and hours of work to maximize utility subject to a single lifetime budget constraint,

$$a_0 = \sum_{t=0}^{\infty} \sum_{s^t} q_0(s^t)(c(s^t) - (1-\tau(s^t))w(s^t)h(s^t) - T(s^t)). \tag{1.2}$$

The household has initial assets $a_0 = a(s^0)$. In addition, $\tau(s^t)$ is the labor income tax rate, $w(s^t)$ is the hourly wage rate, and $T(s^t)$ is a lump-sum transfer in history s^t, all denominated in contemporaneous units of consumption.[1] Thus $c - (1-\tau)wh - T$ represents consumption in excess of after-tax labor income and transfers, which is discounted back to time 0

[1] One can easily extend the model to include a consumption tax. Then $\tau(s^t)$ measures the total tax wedge: the cost to an employer of providing its worker with one unit of the consumption good.

according to the intertemporal price $q_0(s^t)$. That is, $q_0(s^t)$ represents the cost in history s^0 of purchasing one unit of consumption in history s^t, denominated in units of history-s^0 consumption. Put differently, $q_0(s^t)$ is the history-s^0 price of an Arrow-Debreu security that pays one unit of consumption in history s^t and nothing otherwise. Equation (1.2) states that the household's net purchase of Arrow-Debreu securities in history s^0 must be equal to its initial assets a_0.

It will be useful to define the assets of the household, following history s^t, as

$$a(s^t) = \sum_{t'=t}^{\infty} \sum_{s^{t'}|s^t} q_t(s^{t'})(c(s^{t'}) - (1 - \tau(s^{t'}))w(s^{t'})h(s^{t'}) - T(s^{t'})),$$

where the notation $s^{t'}|s^t$ indicates that the summation is taken over histories $s^{t'}$ that are continuation histories of s^t, i.e., $s^{t'} \equiv \{s^t, s_{t+1}, s_{t+2}, \ldots, s_{t'}\}$ for some states $\{s_{t+1}, s_{t+2}, \ldots, s_{t'}\}$. Then $q_t(s^{t'})$ is the price of a unit of consumption in history $s^{t'} = \{s^t, s_{t+1}, s_{t+2}, \ldots, s_{t'}\}$ paid in units of history-s^t consumption. The absence of arbitrage opportunities requires that $q_0(s^t)q_t(s^{t+1}) = q_0(s^{t+1})$ for all s^t and for all $s^{t+1} \equiv \{s^t, s_{t+1}\}$. Equivalently, the lifetime budget constraint implies a sequence of intertemporal budget constraints,

$$a(s^t) + (1 - \tau(s^t))w(s^t)h(s^t) + T(s^t) = c(s^t) + \sum_{s^{t+1}|s^t} q_t(s^{t+1})a(s^{t+1}), \tag{1.3}$$

so assets plus labor income plus transfers in history s^t is equal to consumption plus purchases of assets in continuation histories s^{t+1}.

Firms

The representative firm owns the capital stock $k_0 = k(s^0)$ and has access to a Cobb-Douglas production function, producing gross output $z(s^t)k(s^t)^\alpha h^d(s^t)^{1-\alpha}$ in history s^t, where $z(s^t)$ is history-contingent total factor productivity,[2] $k(s^t)$ is its capital stock, $h^d(s^t)$ is the labor it demands, and $\alpha \in [0, 1)$ is the capital share of income. A fraction δ of the capital depreciates in production each period, while at the end of period t, the firm purchases any capital that it plans to employ in period $t + 1$. That is, history-$s^{t+1} \equiv \{s^t, s_{t+1}\}$ capital $k(s^{t+1})$ is purchased in history s^t and so must be measurable with respect to s^t. The present value

[2] Although I do not place explicit restrictions on the productivity process, I do assume that a worker's expected utility is finite so her optimization problem is well-behaved. This is ensured if productivity is bounded but is true under substantially weaker conditions, if productivity does not grow too fast.

of the firm's profits is then given by

$$J(s^0, k_0) = \sum_{t=0}^{\infty} \sum_{s^t} q_0(s^t)(z(s^t)k(s^t)^{\alpha}h^d(s^t)^{1-\alpha} + (1-\delta)k(s^t) - k(s^{t+1}) - w(s^t)h^d(s^t)). \quad (1.4)$$

Note that this expression presumes that the firm does not pay any taxes. I do this for notational simplicity alone. In particular, any payroll taxes are rolled into the labor income tax rate τ. The firm chooses the sequences $h^d(s^t)$ and $k(s^{t+1})$ to maximize J.

I can also write the value of the firm's profits from history s^t on as

$$J(s^t, k(s^t)) = \sum_{t'=t}^{\infty} \sum_{s^{t'}|s^t} q_t(s^{t'})(z(s^{t'})k(s^{t'})^{\alpha}h^d(s^{t'})^{1-\alpha} + (1-\delta)k(s^{t'}) - k(s^{t'+1}) - w(s^{t'})h^d(s^{t'})).$$

This implies the recursive equation

$$J(s^t, k(s^t)) = z(s^t)k(s^t)^{\alpha}h^d(s^t)^{1-\alpha} + (1-\delta)k(s^t) - k(s^{t+1}) - w(s^t)h^d(s^t) + \sum_{s^{t+1}|s^t} q_t(s^{t+1})J(s^{t+1}, k(s^{t+1})). \quad (1.5)$$

The value of a firm that starts history s^t with capital $k(s^t)$ comes from current production $z(s^t)k(s^t)^{\alpha}h^d(s^t)^{1-\alpha}$ minus the cost of investment $k(s^{t+1}) - (1-\delta)k(s^t)$ minus labor costs $w(s^t)h^d(s^t)$ plus the value of starting the following period in history $s^{t+1} \equiv \{s^t, s_{t+1}\}$ with $k(\{s^{t+1}\})$ units of capital.

Government

A government sets the path of taxes, transfers, and government debt to fund some spending $g(s^t)$. I assume government spending is wasteful or at least is separable from consumption and leisure in preferences. The government faces a budget constraint in any history s^t,

$$b(s^t) = \sum_{t'=t}^{\infty} \sum_{s^{t'}|s^t} q_t(s^{t'})(\tau(s^{t'})w(s^{t'})h(s^{t'}) - g(s^{t'}) - T(s^{t'})), \quad (1.6)$$

so debt $b(s^t)$ is equal to the present value of future tax receipts in excess of spending and lump-sum transfers. Again, this is equivalent to a sequence of budget constraints of the form

$$b(s^t) + g(s^t) + T(s^t) = \tau(s^t)w(s^t)h(s^t) + \sum_{s^{t+1}|s^t} q_t(s^{t+1})b(s^{t+1}), \quad (1.7)$$

so initial debt plus current spending and transfers is equal to current tax revenue plus new debt issues.

Market Clearing

There are three markets in this economy: the labor market, the capital market, and the goods market. All of them must clear in equilibrium. Labor market clearing dictates that labor supply equals labor demand in all histories, $h(s^t) = h^d(s^t)$. Capital market clearing dictates that household assets are equal to firms' valuation plus government debt, $a(s^t) = J(s^t, k(s^t)) + b(s^t)$. Goods market clearing dictates that output plus undepreciated capital is equal to consumption plus government spending plus next period's capital stock:

$$z(s^t)k(s^t)^{\alpha}h^d(s^t)^{1-\alpha} + (1-\delta)k(s^t) = c(s^t) + g(s^t) + k(s^{t+1}).$$

One can confirm that goods market clearing is implied by the household budget constraint (equation (1.3)), the firm's value function (equation (1.5)), the government budget constraint (equation (1.7)), and capital and labor market clearing. This is an application of Walras's law.

Equilibrium

Given arbitrary paths for government spending $g(s^t)$, taxes $\tau(s^t)$, and government debt $b(s^t)$, an equilibrium consists of paths for consumption $c(s^t)$, labor supply $h(s^t)$, labor demand $h^d(s^t)$, capital $k(s^t)$, assets $a(s^t)$, transfers $T(s^t)$, intertemporal prices $q_0(s^t)$, and the wage rate $w(s^t)$ such that:

- $\{c(s^t)\}$, $\{h(s^t)\}$, and $\{a(s^t)\}$ solve the household's utility-maximization problem, maximizing equation (1.1) subject to the budget constraint (1.2) given $\{q(s^t)\}$, $\{w(s^t)\}$, $\{\tau(s^t)\}$, and $\{T(s^t)\}$;
- $\{h^d(s^t)\}$ and $\{k(s^t)\}$ maximize firms' profits in (1.4) given $\{q_0(s^t)\}$ and $\{w(s^t)\}$;
- the government budget is balanced, so equation (1.6) holds; and
- the labor, capital, and goods markets clear.

1.2 Deriving the Labor Wedge

To see the implications of this model for the labor wedge, I focus on a subset of the equilibrium conditions. First, consider the household's choice of history-s^t consumption and labor supply. These must satisfy the first-order conditions

$$\beta^t \Pi(s^t)\frac{1}{c(s^t)} = \lambda q_0(s^t) \tag{1.8}$$

and

$$\beta^t \Pi(s^t)\gamma h(s^t)^{1/\varepsilon} = \lambda q_0(s^t)(1-\tau(s^t))w(s^t), \tag{1.9}$$

where λ is the Lagrange multiplier on the budget constraint: equation (1.2). Note from the second equation that a one percent increase in the after-tax wage $(1-\tau)w$ raises labor supply h by ε percent, holding fixed the Lagrange multiplier λ and the intertemporal price $q_0(s^t)$. Thus ε is the Frisch elasticity of labor supply, a key parameter in this chapter.

In any history with positive probability, $\Pi(s^t) > 0$, we can eliminate $\lambda q_0(s^t)/\beta^t \Pi(s^t)$ between these equations and solve for the wage:

$$w(s^t) = \frac{\gamma c(s^t) h(s^t)^{1/\varepsilon}}{1-\tau(s^t)}. \tag{1.10}$$

This states that the wage is equal to the tax-adjusted marginal rate of substitution (MRS) between consumption and leisure.

Next turn to the firm's choice of history-s^t labor demand. From equation (1.4), the necessary first-order condition is

$$w(s^t) = (1-\alpha)\frac{y(s^t)}{h^d(s^t)}, \tag{1.11}$$

where $y(s^t) = z(s^t)k(s^t)^{\alpha}h^d(s^t)^{1-\alpha}$ is the firm's gross output. Equation (1.11) states that the wage is equal to the marginal product of labor (MPL).

Eliminate the state-contingent wage between equations (1.10) and (1.11) and impose labor market clearing, $h^d(s^t) = h(s^t)$. Solving for $\tau(s^t)$ gives

$$\tau(s^t) = 1 - \frac{\gamma}{1-\alpha}\frac{c(s^t)}{y(s^t)} h(s^t)^{(1+\varepsilon)/\varepsilon}. \tag{1.12}$$

This static equation explains how the tax rate τ affects the consumption-output ratio c/y and hours worked h.

It is worth stressing that this relationship holds even though productivity, government spending, and distortionary taxes may be time varying or stochastic. Expectations of these changes are all captured by the current consumption-output ratio. For example, if productivity is currently below trend, the consumption-output ratio will be high and, to the extent that labor supply is elastic, labor supply will be low. An increase in government spending without a corresponding change in contemporaneous taxes will tend to reduce the consumption-output ratio and raise hours worked in an offsetting manner.

Prescott (2004) uses a version of equation (1.12) to examine the effect of tax variation over time and across countries on labor supply. More precisely, he uses a slightly different functional form for preferences, with period utility function $\log c + \gamma \log(100 - h)$, where 100 represents the available amount of time per week. He then calibrates γ to match the average number of hours worked across a broad set of countries, $\bar{h} \approx 20$. With this functional form, the Frisch elasticity of labor supply is $100/h - 1$, or about 4 on average. My choice of functional forms brings the issue of the elasticity of labor supply to the forefront of the discussion.

In addition, I focus on a different implication of this equation. Under the hypothesis that business cycle fluctuations are not primarily due to changes in taxes and transfers, I interpret cyclical variation in $\tau(s^t)$ as the labor wedge: the wedge between the MRS and the MPL. More precisely, I measure hours and the consumption–output ratio at quarterly frequencies. By making appropriate assumptions about the disutility of working γ, the capital share α, and the Frisch elasticity of labor supply ε, I back out the labor wedge from equation (1.12). This approach builds upon a substantial body of research, including Parkin (1988), Rotemberg and Woodford (1991, 1999), Hall (1997), Mulligan (2002), and Chari et al. (2007).

1.3 Measurement

To measure the labor wedge for the United States using equation (1.12), I need time series of the consumption–output ratio and hours worked, as well as values for the parameters ε, γ, and α. Nominal consumption and output data are available at quarterly frequencies from the National Income and Product Accounts (see table 1.1.5 therein). Output is gross domestic product, while consumption is personal consumption expenditures on nondurable goods and services.

I focus on the most comprehensive available series on hours: Prescott et al.'s (2008) measure of total hours worked relative to the noninstitutional population with ages between 16 and 64, which has been available quarterly since 1959.[3] This series is based primarily on data originally collected as part of the Current Population Survey (CPS), a monthly survey of households that is used to construct the unemployment rate. The total number of hours worked is equal to the product of the number of civilians at work and the average hours worked by a person at work,[4] plus the number of military personnel, who are assumed to work for

[3] The authors have recently extended their data set back to 1947. The results that I report here are, if anything, stronger in this longer sample.

[4] See www.bls.gov/cps/, series LNU02005053 and LNU02005054, for the monthly data since June 1976. Prescott et al. (2008) obtained earlier data from table A-24 of the Bureau of Labor Statistics publication *Employment and Earnings*.

forty hours per week. The population is equal to the civilian noninstitutional population with ages between 16 and 64 plus the number of military personnel.

I compare the results with those based on a measure of hours paid per adult in the civilian noninstitutional population from the Current Employment Statistics (CES), a monthly survey of business establishments.[5] The main drawback of this survey is that data on hours are unavailable for the government (and military) sector as well as for farm workers, proprietors, unpaid family workers, and supervisors. In addition, the CES measures hours paid rather than hours worked, and thus includes vacation time, sick days, and so on. This series has been available since 1964.

I also use an unpublished series for hours worked constructed by the Bureau of Labor Statistics (BLS) as part of the Major Sector Productivity and Costs program.[6] I again divide this series by the adult noninstitutional population. Although this measure relies primarily on data from the CES, it also uses data from the CPS to estimate the hours worked by workers who are not covered by the establishment survey. It also adjusts the CES data to convert hours paid into hours worked. In principle, the coverage of this series should be similar to that of Prescott et al. (2008).

Rather than take a stand on the Frisch labor supply elasticity ε, I consider a range of possible values and report four of them: $\varepsilon = 0.5, 1, 4$, and ∞. The lowest value is toward the upper range of elasticities for prime-age mens' hours that many microeconomists consider plausible (see Blundell and MaCurdy 1999). The value $\varepsilon = 4$ is in line with the elasticities that macroeconomists frequently use in representative-agent business cycle and growth models. For each value of the elasticity, I set the ratio $\gamma/(1 - \alpha)$ so that the average labor wedge, measured using equation (1.12), is 0.4 from 1959 to 2007, consistent with the tax wedge that Prescott (2004) reports. The results are similar if the average labor wedge is 0.3 or 0.5.

Figure 1.1 shows the implied behavior of the labor wedge using the CPS measure of hours. Two patterns stand out. First, there has been a trend decline in the labor wedge since around 1980. Arguably this reflects underlying movements in labor and consumption taxes. Second, the labor wedge is countercyclical. I indicate National Bureau of Economic Research (NBER) recession dates with gray bands. Regardless of

---

[5] See www.bls.gov/ces/, series CES0500000034.

[6] See www.bls.gov/lpc/, series PRS84006033, for the business sector. The series I use augments this with estimates of hours worked in the government sector. I am grateful to Simona Cociuba for providing me with this data and for clarifying the relationship between the different series for hours.

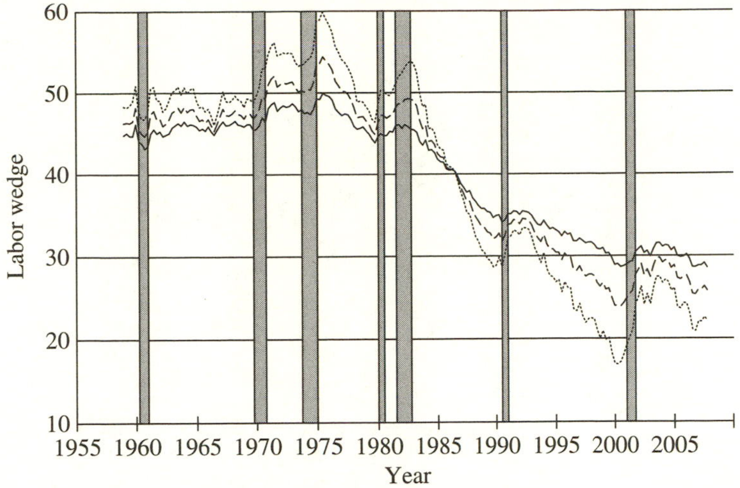

Figure 1.1. The U.S. labor wedge from equation (1.12) using the CPS measure of hours. The solid line shows $\varepsilon = 4$, the dashed line shows $\varepsilon = 1$, and the dotted line shows $\varepsilon = \frac{1}{2}$. In each case, I fix the remaining parameters to ensure that the average labor wedge is 0.40. The gray bands show NBER recession dates.

the elasticity of labor supply, the labor wedge rose during every recession except the first, with more pronounced fluctuations when labor supply is less elastic. This effect does not disappear even when labor supply is infinitely elastic.[7]

To emphasize this pattern, figure 1.2 shows the difference between $\log \tau$ and its trend, where I measure the trend using a Hodrick-Prescott (HP) filter with a standard smoothing parameter: 1,600 for quarterly data. It is easy to see a sharp increase in the labor wedge during every recession except the one in 1960. The magnitude of the implied cycles depends on the elasticity of labor supply. For example, with $\varepsilon = 1$, the period around the 1990 recession is associated with a ten percent increase in the labor wedge relative to trend, while with $\varepsilon = 4$, the increase was almost six percent.[8] Higher values of the labor supply elasticity only slightly dampen the implied fluctuations—even if the Frisch elasticity is infinite, the labor wedge rose by four percent during this time period. Conversely, smaller values of the Frisch elasticity amplify fluctuations in the labor wedge.

[7] Observe that the elasticity of labor supply enters equation (1.12) as $(1 + \varepsilon)/\varepsilon$. This means that an elasticity of 4 and an infinite elasticity have nearly the same effect on the labor wedge.

[8] With $\varepsilon = 1$, the labor wedge was five percent below trend in the third quarter of 1990 and rose to five percent above trend by the second quarter of 1992. With $\varepsilon = 4$, it rose from three percent below trend to three percent above trend during the same period.

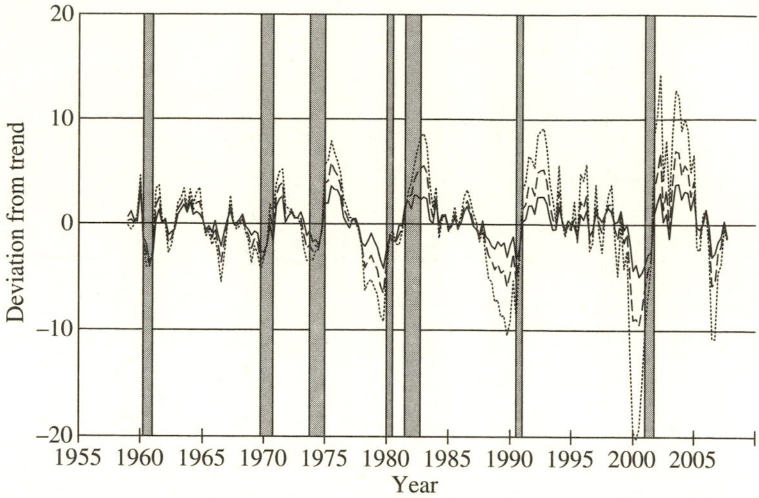

Figure 1.2. Deviation of the labor wedge from log trend, measured as an HP filter with parameter 1,600, using the CPS measure of hours. The solid line shows $\varepsilon = 4$, the dashed line shows $\varepsilon = 1$, and the dotted line shows $\varepsilon = \frac{1}{2}$. In each case, I fix the remaining parameters to ensure that the average labor wedge is 0.40. The gray bands show NBER recession dates.

Figure 1.3 displays the same findings slightly differently, depicting the annual growth rate of the labor wedge. Again, the labor wedge grew during every recession except the first one, in 1960. The magnitude of fluctuations in the growth of the labor wedge depends on the elasticity of labor supply.

Table 1.1 summarizes these results. The first row in the upper part of the table shows the standard deviation of the detrended consumption–output ratio, detrended hours, and the detrended labor wedge for four different labor supply elasticities. When the elasticity is small, the labor wedge is four times more volatile than hours and five times more volatile than the consumption–output ratio, while the relative volatilities of the labor wedge and hours are similar when the elasticity is large. The remaining entries show the contemporaneous correlation between the labor wedge (for different elasticities) and the consumption–output ratio and hours. The correlation with the consumption–output ratio disappears when the elasticity is high enough, but the labor wedge is strongly negatively correlated with hours, regardless of the elasticity of labor supply. The bottom part of the table shows the analogous results for the annual growth rate of the labor wedge, the consumption–output ratio, and hours. They are quantitatively very similar. It looks as if hours growth is negative when the labor income tax rate is rising, regardless of the elasticity of labor supply.

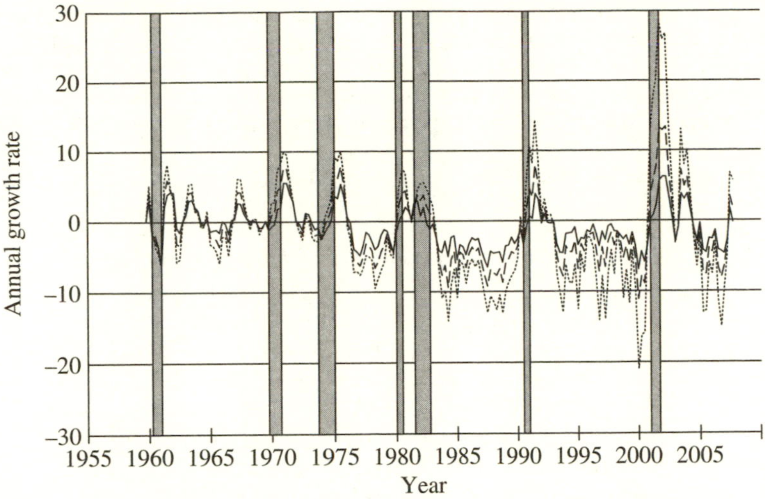

Figure 1.3. Annual growth rate of the labor wedge using the CPS measure of hours. The solid line shows $\varepsilon = 4$, the dashed line shows $\varepsilon = 1$, and the dotted line shows $\varepsilon = \frac{1}{2}$. In each case, I fix the remaining parameters to ensure that the average labor wedge is 0.40. The gray bands show NBER recession dates.

Table 1.1. Comovement of hours, the consumption-output ratio, and the labor wedge τ for four different values of the labor supply elasticity ε using the CPS measure of hours.

(a) All series detrended with HP filter with parameter 1,600

Standard deviations

c/y	h	$\varepsilon = 0.5$	$\varepsilon = 1$	$\varepsilon = 4$	$\varepsilon = \infty$
0.010	0.013	0.055	0.031	0.018	0.014

Correlation matrix

	$\varepsilon = 0.5$	$\varepsilon = 1$	$\varepsilon = 4$	$\varepsilon = \infty$
c/y	0.338	0.278	0.049	−0.131
h	−0.795	−0.835	−0.745	−0.628

(b) Annual growth rates

Standard deviations

c/y	h	$\varepsilon = 0.5$	$\varepsilon = 1$	$\varepsilon = 4$	$\varepsilon = \infty$
0.015	0.018	0.079	0.045	0.027	0.022

Correlation matrix

	$\varepsilon = 0.5$	$\varepsilon = 1$	$\varepsilon = 4$	$\varepsilon = \infty$
c/y	0.256	0.163	−0.088	−0.260
h	−0.803	−0.835	−0.733	−0.617

Table 1.2. Comovement of the labor wedge and hours with labor supply elasticity $\varepsilon = 1$. The first column uses the hour series from Prescott et al. (2008) from 1959 to 2007, constructed primarily from the CPS. The second uses hours data from the CES from 1964 to 2007. The third uses unpublished hours data constructed by the BLS to measure labor productivity from 1959 to the first quarter of 2006.

	CPS	CES	BLS
All series detrended with HP filter with parameter 1,600			
Standard deviation h	0.013	0.018	0.014
Standard deviation τ	0.031	0.049	0.035
Correlation (h, τ)	−0.835	−0.868	−0.883
Annual growth rates			
Standard deviation h	0.018	0.026	0.020
Standard deviation τ	0.045	0.069	0.051
Correlation (h, τ)	−0.835	−0.872	−0.879

There are several different ways to understand these results. Viewed through the lens of a model with a competitive labor market, fluctuations in the labor income tax rate drive fluctuations in hours. If in reality the tax rate is constant, the model underpredicts fluctuations in hours worked at business-cycle frequencies, given the observed time path of the consumption–output ratio. This is an old critique of competitive models of the labor market: such models can only explain part of the cyclical fluctuations in hours worked, particularly when labor is supplied relatively inelastically.

Table 1.2 shows that the main conclusions hold with the alternative measures of hours. I assume that the elasticity of labor supply is $\varepsilon = 1$ and examine how alternative measures of hours affect the behavior of the labor wedge. These other measures raise the volatility of the labor wedge, and by more than they raise the volatility of hours. In addition, the correlation between the two series is, if anything, increased. I find similar results with other values of the labor supply elasticity and so conclude that this result is robust to the exact measure of hours. The competitive model cannot explain all of the movement in hours relative to the consumption–output ratio if the labor income tax rate is constant.

One possible explanation for this pattern is that labor tax rates are in fact countercyclical. This hypothesis has some supporters. For example, in a recent paper, Mertens and Ravn (2008) measure tax shocks using the Romer and Romer (2007) narrative analysis of tax policy. They conclude that tax shocks account for eighteen percent of the variance of output at business cycle frequencies. Perhaps most provocatively, they find that the 1982 recession was caused by workers' anticipation of future tax cuts. Of course, I have shown that expectations of future tax cuts may affect both the consumption-output ratio and the hours worked, but not the labor wedge, so such behavior cannot easily explain the patterns in the data. In any case, most economists seem to be skeptical that tax movements alone can explain the observed variation in the labor wedge.

1.4 Alternative Specification of Preferences

A second possible explanation for the behavior of the labor wedge is that in this model either the MRS or the MPL is misspecified. The specification of the MPL depends only on the assumption of a Cobb-Douglas aggregate production function. Macroeconomists are justifiably reluctant to abandon this assumption because it ensures that the capital and labor shares of national income, as well as the interest rate, are constant, consistent with the Kaldor (1957) growth facts.

The specification of household preferences is also tightly constrained by long-run restrictions.[9] Maintain the assumption that preferences are separable across time and states of the world, but relax the assumption of additive separability between consumption and leisure. To be consistent with balanced growth—the absence of a long-run trend in hours—and a constant Frisch elasticity, preferences over consumption and leisure must be ordered by the utility function

$$\sum_{t=0}^{\infty}\sum_{s^t}\beta^t\Pi(s^t)\frac{c(s^t)^{1-\sigma}(1+(\sigma-1)(\gamma\varepsilon/(1+\varepsilon))h(s^t)^{(1+\varepsilon)/\varepsilon})^{\sigma}-1}{1-\sigma}. \tag{1.13}$$

As before, $\gamma > 0$ parameterizes the disutility of work and $\varepsilon > 0$ is the Frisch labor supply elasticity. The new parameter $\sigma > 0$ determines the substitutability between consumption and leisure. The limit as $\sigma \to 1$

[9] Hall (2009) does not impose balanced-growth preferences, but instead assumes that permanently doubling wages reduces hours worked by fifteen percent, ceteris paribus. Thus income effects outweigh substitution effects in labor supply. He also allows for measurement error in consumption, hours, employment, and productivity. Finally, he allows for rigid wages, as I discuss in section 4.4. These departures jointly lead him to conclude that the labor wedge is in fact relatively small and acyclic. I confirm that such a substantial departure from balanced-growth preferences reduces the correlation between the measured labor wedge and hours worked, but I find that it actually increases the volatility of the measured labor wedge. Moreover, according to the model without balanced-growth preferences, a sharp increase in the labor wedge, roughly from 0 to 0.5, kept hours worked from rising between 1959 and 1973. It is unclear what can explain this secular increase in the labor wedge, except for model misspecification.

nests the separable case in equation (1.1). The case where $\sigma > 1$ is of particular interest, since this implies that the marginal utility of consumption is higher when households work more, consistent with standard models of time allocation (Becker 1965). In any case, utility is increasing and concave in consumption and decreasing and concave in hours of work.

With these preferences, the first-order conditions for consumption and hours are

$$\beta^t \Pi(s^t) c(s^t)^{-\sigma} \left(1 + (\sigma - 1)\frac{\gamma\varepsilon}{1+\varepsilon} h(s^t)^{(1+\varepsilon)/\varepsilon}\right)^{\sigma} = \lambda q_0(s^t),$$

$$\beta^t \Pi(s^t) c(s^t)^{1-\sigma} \left(1 + (\sigma - 1)\frac{\gamma\varepsilon}{1+\varepsilon} h(s^t)^{(1+\varepsilon)/\varepsilon}\right)^{\sigma-1} \sigma\gamma h(s^t)^{1/\varepsilon} = \lambda q_0(s^t)(1 - \tau(s^t)) w(s^t).$$

The Frisch demand system expresses consumption $c(s^t)$ and hours $h(s^t)$ as functions of the Lagrange multiplier λ, the intertemporal price $q_0(s^t)$, and the wage rate $w(s^t)$. Eliminating $c(s^t)$ between the first-order conditions gives

$$\sigma\gamma h(s^t)^{1/\varepsilon} = \left(\frac{\lambda q_0(s^t)}{\beta^t \Pi(s^t)}\right)^{1/\sigma} (1 - \tau(s^t)) w(s^t),$$

so the Frisch elasticity of labor supply—the elasticity of hours with respect to the wage holding fixed the intertemporal price and the Lagrange multiplier—is in fact ε. Moreover, eliminate $\lambda q_0(s^t)/\beta^t \Pi(s^t)$ between the first-order conditions to get

$$w(s^t) = \frac{\sigma\gamma c(s^t) h(s^t)^{1/\varepsilon}}{(1 - \tau(s^t))(1 + (\sigma - 1)(\gamma\varepsilon/(1+\varepsilon)) h(s^t)^{(1+\varepsilon)/\varepsilon})}$$

whenever $\Pi(s^t) > 0$. Eliminate the wage using the firm's first-order condition, equation (1.11), and market clearing, $h(s^t) = h^d(s^t)$. This gives

$$\tau(s^t) = 1 - \frac{\gamma\sigma(c(s^t)/y(s^t)) h(s^t)^{(1+\varepsilon)/\varepsilon}}{(1 - \alpha)(1 + (\sigma - 1)(\gamma\varepsilon/(1+\varepsilon)) h(s^t)^{(1+\varepsilon)/\varepsilon})}. \tag{1.14}$$

This is a modest generalization of equation (1.12). Once again, one needs to know only the consumption-output ratio, hours worked, and the value of four parameters in order to compute the labor wedge.

To understand the quantitative implications of this expression, I use the hours series from Prescott et al. (2008). I fix the labor share at the conventional value of $1 - \alpha = \frac{2}{3}$ and, for different values of the substitutability parameter σ and the elasticity of labor supply ε, I choose the disutility of work parameter γ to ensure an average labor wedge of 0.40.

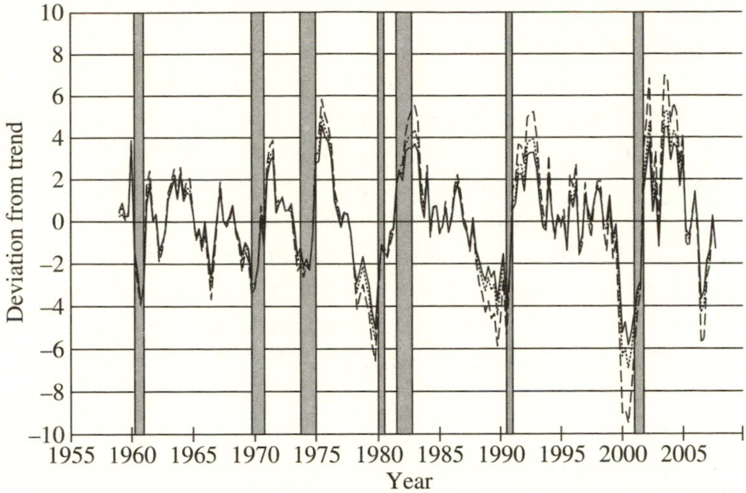

Figure 1.4. The deviation of the labor wedge from log trend, measured as an HP filter with parameter 1,600, using equation (1.14) and the CPS measure of hours. The dashed line shows $\sigma = 1$, the dotted line shows $\sigma = 2$, and the solid line shows $\sigma = 4$. In each case I set $\varepsilon = 1$ and $\alpha = \frac{1}{3}$ and fix the remaining parameter γ to ensure that the average labor wedge is 0.40. The gray bands show NBER recession dates.

Figure 1.4 shows the time series behavior of the labor wedge with the Frisch elasticity fixed at 1. The dashed line corresponds to the limit as σ converges to 1, the additively separable case that I analyzed before, while the remaining two lines show $\sigma = 2$ and $\sigma = 4$. Raising the substitutability between consumption and leisure modestly reduces the magnitude of fluctuations in the labor wedge but does not qualitatively change the results. I do not show the results with a higher elasticity of labor supply, but they too are similar.

Additionally, the microeconomic behavior of the model is unreasonable when σ is much larger than 1. Consider the following thought experiment. Two workers normally work and consume the same amount. One year, however, one is unable to work, for example because of an idiosyncratic shock to the disutility of work γ, while the other continues to work the average number of hours that I observe in the data. With complete markets, the two workers want to keep their marginal utility of consumption λ equal through this episode. How much lower is the consumption of the unemployed worker, c_{u}, than the consumption of the employed worker, c_{e}? The first-order condition for consumption implies that

$$\frac{c_{\mathrm{e}}}{c_{\mathrm{u}}} = 1 + (\sigma - 1)\frac{\gamma\varepsilon}{1+\varepsilon}h^{(1+\varepsilon)/\varepsilon},$$

where h is the number of hours worked by the employed worker. With $\sigma = 1$, consumption is equal for the two workers. With $\varepsilon = 1$ and $\sigma = 1.5$, consumption falls by 13 log points for the unemployed. With $\sigma = 2$, consumption should fall by 20 log points, and with $\sigma = 4$ it should fall by 31 log points.

Are these numbers reasonable? Aguiar and Hurst (2005) provide some guidance. They find that food consumption expenditures drop by about seventeen percent at retirement, accompanied by a fifty-three percent increase in the time spent on food production. This is consistent with values of σ near 2. Much stronger substitutability is inconsistent with the numbers in Aguiar and Hurst (2005) and does not resonate introspectively. In any case, even with infinite substitutability between consumption and leisure, $\sigma \to \infty$, the results do not change appreciably. With the labor supply elasticity fixed at $\varepsilon = 1$, the standard deviation of the annual growth rate of the labor wedge is more than twice the corresponding number for hours and the correlation between the two series is -0.76.

1.5 Preference Shocks

A third theoretical possibility is that the representative agent's disutility of work, γ, is stochastic. This modifies equation (1.12) to read

$$\tau(s^t) = 1 - \frac{\gamma(s^t)}{1-\alpha}\frac{c(s^t)}{y(s^t)}h(s^t)^{(1+\varepsilon)/\varepsilon},$$

where $\gamma(s^t)$ is the history-contingent disutility of work. An economist who ignored variation in the disutility of work would then falsely conclude that there are fluctuations in the labor wedge, even if labor taxes are constant in the data and the model is otherwise correct.

Many recent quantitative macroeconomic models allow for such a preference shock. An unobserved demand shock plays an important role in explaining aggregate fluctuations in Rotemberg and Woodford (1997). They interpret the shock as a combination of a preference shock and a shock to government spending.[10] Erceg et al. (2000) and Smets and Wouters (2003) also have a quantitatively important preference shock in their models of monetary policy. More recently, Galí and Rabanal (2004) find that a preference shock explains fifty-seven percent of the variance

[10] Unlike preference shocks, government spending can be measured and is not strongly correlated with the labor wedge. In any case, the model I have developed here allows for government spending shocks, but these do not affect the labor wedge equation.

of output and seventy percent of the variance of hours in their estimated dynamic stochastic general equilibrium model.[11]

A closely related theoretical possibility is that workers have time-varying market power in labor supply. This is often formalized by assuming that each household is the monopoly supplier of a heterogeneous type of labor and sets the wage to maximize its utility. Recessions are periods when different types of labor are poor substitutes, so households are better able to exploit their market power, reducing hours to drive up wages. A number of recent papers (including Smets and Wouters (2003, 2007)) have emphasized time-varying wage markups as an important source of business cycle shocks. In Smets and Wouters (2007), the wage markup shock accounts for a fifth of the variance in output and over half the variance in inflation at a ten-quarter horizon. Galí et al. (2007) also find an important role for markup fluctuations, but reach a different conclusion. They argue that some other, unspecified, primitive shock causes countercyclical fluctuations in markups, which in turn generates a countercyclical labor wedge.

Like many economists, I have a strong prior belief that the changes in the disutility of labor and changes in wage markups do not drive business cycle fluctuations.[12] Although households may differ in their disutility of work and the disutility may change over time for some households, one would expect those movements to average out in a large economy. Still, the empirical success of preference and markup shocks is revealing. They work because, viewed through the lens of a market-clearing model, recessions look like times when workers choose to supply less labor

---

[11] Galí and Rabanal (2004, p. 271) write that the preference shock can be "interpret[ed] more broadly as a (real) demand shock."

[12] For example, Modigliani (1977, p. 6) writes

> Sargent (1976) has attempted to remedy this fatal flaw by hypothesizing that the persistent and large fluctuations in unemployment reflect merely corresponding swings in the natural rate itself. In other words, what happened to the United States in the 1930's was a severe attack of contagious laziness! I can only say that, despite Sargent's ingenuity, neither I nor, I expect, most others at least of the nonmonetarists' persuasion are quite ready yet to turn over the field of economic fluctuations to the social psychologist.

Mankiw (1989, p. 82) writes

> Alternatively, one could explain the observed pattern without a procyclical real wage by positing that tastes for consumption relative to leisure vary over time. Recessions are then periods of "chronic laziness." As far as I know, no one has seriously proposed this explanation of the business cycle.

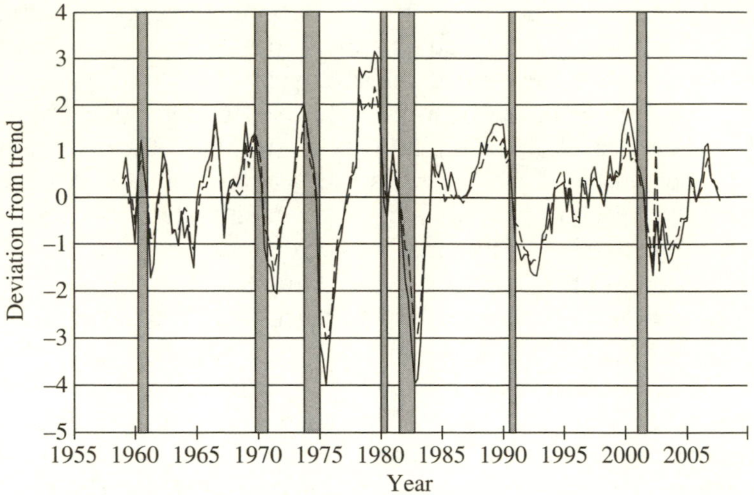

Figure 1.5. Deviation of per capita hours and the e-pop ratio from log trend, measured as an HP filter with parameter 1,600. The solid line shows the deviation of hours from log trend and the dashed line shows the deviation of employment. The gray bands show NBER recession dates.

than is predicted by the model and expansions look like times when they choose to supply more labor.

1.6 From Hours to Unemployment

In the remainder of the book, I explore whether search-and-matching models, based on Pissarides (1985) and Mortensen and Pissarides (1994), can help to explain the behavior of the labor wedge. In doing so, I switch from a focus on the behavior of hours worked to a focus on the behavior of employment and unemployment. This is because search costs introduce a nonconvexity into households' decision problems that emphasizes the binary decision of whether to work, rather than the continuous decision of how many hours to work each week. The data indicate that this focus is, for the most part, appropriate. Figure 1.5 shows that the correlation between the detrended employment-population (e-pop) ratio and the detrended hours per adult is 0.97 and detrended hours are only slightly more volatile than detrended employment, with a relative standard deviation of 1.3.[13] In words, most business cycle frequency fluctuations in hours are accounted for by fluctuations in

[13] I compute hours per member of the noninstitutional population with ages between 16 and 64 using the measure of hours in Prescott et al. (2008). I use their measure of employment as well, and divide by the same population measure.

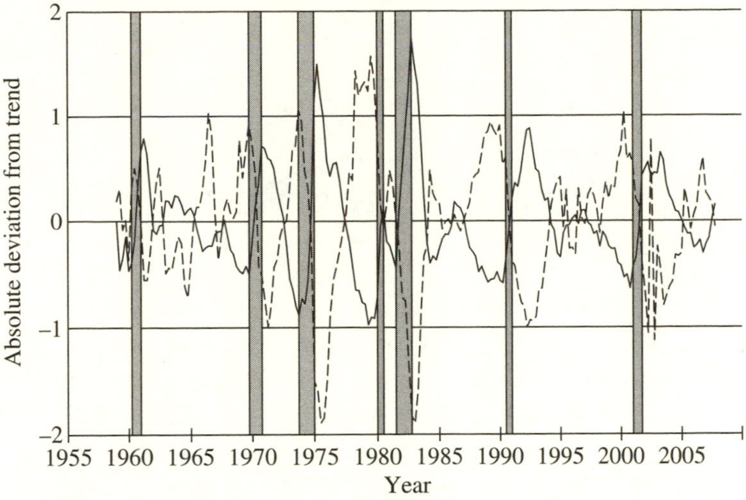

Figure 1.6. Deviation of the e-pop and u-pop ratios from trend, measured as an HP filter with parameter 1,600. The dashed line shows the deviation of the e-pop ratio from trend and the solid line shows the deviation of the u-pop ratio. The gray bands show NBER recession dates.

employment, rather than by fluctuations in the number of hours per employee.

As in many search models, the book also focuses on the margin between employment and unemployment, abstracting away from entry and exit from the labor force. Again, this is empirically reasonable at business cycle frequencies. Figure 1.6 shows that the correlation between the absolute deviation of the e-pop ratio from trend and the absolute deviation of the unemployment-population (u-pop) ratio from trend is −0.90, with a relative standard deviation of 1.4.[14] When employment falls below trend, most of the workers show up as unemployed, rather than dropping out of the labor force.

[14] I use the standard BLS measure of unemployment, based on the CPS.

2

Benchmark Search Model: Neutrality

In this chapter I develop a benchmark search model. A representative firm allocates workers between two activities: production and recruiting. Recruiters enable the firm to attract more workers, while producers generate revenue by creating a consumption good. There is no capital in the model, so production uses only labor and equilibrium savings are zero. Employed workers are periodically hit by shocks that leave them unemployed, while unemployed workers find jobs when they contact a recruiter. Workers' preferences are additively separable over time and between consumption and leisure, and they are consistent with balanced growth. A government levies a labor income tax and rebates the proceeds as a lump sum to households. Finally, wages are set according to the Nash bargaining solution.

I find that aggregate productivity shocks have no effect on employment or the labor wedge, and so are in a sense neutral. Instead, an increase in productivity shows up as a proportional increase in the wage and in consumption. To understand why, suppose that productivity is temporarily above trend and that firms take advantage of this by shifting workers into production. Since there are no savings in equilibrium, this necessarily raises consumption. But workers would like to maintain smooth consumption, which puts downward pressure on interest rates. This makes recruiting, an investment that is costly today but generates revenue in the future, more profitable. With the particular assumption on preferences, firms in fact find it optimal to maintain a constant division of labor between recruiting and production. With a constant number of recruiters, employment is constant. With a constant number of producers, the consumption-output ratio is constant. Thus the model implies that the labor wedge, as measured in equation (1.12), should be constant as well. The benchmark search model is therefore unable to explain the data that I discussed in chapter 1.

I start in section 2.1 with a steady-state version of the model in order to introduce the environment and the notation. Section 2.2 allows for arbitrary productivity shocks, section 2.3 establishes conditions under which the equilibrium solves an associated planner's problem, and section 2.4 shows that the neutrality result is robust to a number of generalizations, including a labor force participation margin and an endogenous choice of hours for employed workers. Loosely speaking, if a version of the model without search frictions does not generate fluctuations in employment or in hours worked, search frictions will not explain why labor market outcomes fluctuate cyclically. Thus this neutrality result is a natural extension of known results in competitive business cycle models.

2.1 Steady State

There are three types of economic actors: households composed of many individuals who consume, search for jobs, and supply labor in order to maximize expected utility subject to a budget constraint; firms, which allocate workers between production and recruiting in order to maximize the expected present value of profits; and a government, which taxes labor earnings and rebates the proceeds to households as a lump sum. There are two technologies: one for matching unemployed workers seeking job openings to recruiters seeking workers and another for producing the consumption good using labor.

Denote time by $t = 0, 1, 2, \ldots$ and assume for now that there are no shocks, so in the notation of the previous chapter, $\Pi(s^t)$ is degenerate.

2.1.1 Firms

A representative firm employs a measure n_0 of workers at time 0. The firm has access to two technologies. The first is a constant-returns-to-scale production technology: each worker who uses the technology produces z units of the consumption good per period. Let ℓ_t denote the measure of producers, i.e., workers who use the production technology in period t. The second is a constant-returns-to-scale recruiting technology: a worker who uses the recruiting technology in period t attracts an average of $\mu(\theta_t)$ unemployed workers to the firm at the start of period $t+1$, where θ_t is the ratio of the measure of recruiters to the measure of unemployed workers in the aggregate economy, hereafter the *recruiter-unemployment ratio*. Let v_t denote the measure of recruiters, i.e., workers who use the recruiting technology in period t.

This implies that $v_t\mu(\theta_t)$ represents the measure of new employment relationships, or matches, in the economy in period t. This is essentially a matching function (Pissarides 1985), but the inputs into matches are unemployed workers and recruiters, rather than unemployed workers and vacant jobs. In particular, the matching function exhibits constant returns to scale and is increasing in both the measure of unemployed workers and the measure of vacancies. Thus I assume that $\mu : \mathbb{R}^+ \to \mathbb{R}^+$ is continuous and nonincreasing with $\lim_{\theta\to 0}\mu(\theta) = \infty$. It will be useful to define $f(\theta) \equiv \theta\mu(\theta)$, which I argue below is the probability that an unemployed worker finds a job. This is nondecreasing and concave, with $f(0) = 0$ and $f(\theta) \leqslant 1$ for all θ, so in particular $\lim_{\theta\to\infty}\mu(\theta) = 0$.

The present value of the firm's profits, discounted back to date 0 and indexed by the initial firm size n_0, is

$$J(0, n_0) = \sum_{t=0}^{\infty} q_0^t(z\ell_t - w_t(\ell_t + v_t)), \tag{2.1}$$

where q_0^t is the price of one unit of consumption at date t, denominated in units of date-0 consumption, and w_t is the wage in units of the contemporaneous consumption good. The firm can freely switch workers between production and recruiting, but total employment $n_t \equiv \ell_t + v_t$ is constrained by past recruiting. That is, n_0 is given, while in any period $t \geqslant 0$,

$$n_{t+1} = v_t\mu(\theta_t) + (1 - x)n_t, \tag{2.2}$$

where $x \in (0, 1)$ is the "employment-exit probability," i.e., the exogenous rate of job separations. Note that since $\lim_{\theta\to 0}\mu(\theta) = \infty$ and μ is continuous, $\mu(\theta) > x$ for small θ. This implies that a firm can always grow by putting enough of its workers into recruiting as long as the recruiter-unemployment ratio is not too large. The firm chooses the sequences $\{\ell_t\}$ and $\{v_t\}$ in order to maximize the present value of profits in equation (2.1), taking as given the constraint on firm growth in equation (2.2), the initial level of employment n_0, the path of prices w_t and q_0^t, and the path of the recruiter-unemployment ratio θ_t.

2.1.2 Households

There is a representative household consisting of a continuum of expected-utility-maximizing, infinitely lived individuals with measure 1. Each household member $i \in [0, 1]$ has time-separable preferences over her consumption c_t^i and her labor supply n_t^i. She may be either employed by a firm ($n_t^i = 1$) or unemployed ($n_t^i = 0$). Her period felicity is $\log c_t^i$ if she is unemployed and $\log c_t^i - \gamma$ if she is employed. She discounts future felicity by a factor $\beta < 1$.

The household allocates total consumption in period t, c_t, in order to maximize the sum of household utility, and so equalizes the marginal utility of consumption across individuals. With additive separability between consumption and leisure, this implies that the household equalizes consumption across individuals, acting as if it has a utility function

$$\sum_{t=0}^{\infty} \beta^t (\log c_t - \gamma n_t), \tag{2.3}$$

where n_t is the fraction of household members who are employed in period t. Effectively, the large household is able to insure its members against all idiosyncratic shocks, mimicking the complete-markets allocation. This approach to finding the complete-markets allocation in search models is due originally to Merz (1995); see Andolfatto (1996) for an alternative approach to modeling complete markets in a search economy.

The household faces two types of constraints. First, there is a single budget constraint, which states that initial assets must equal the difference between the present value of consumption and the present value of after-tax labor income plus transfers:

$$a_0 = \sum_{t=0}^{\infty} q_0^t (c_t - (1-\tau) w_t n_t - T_t). \tag{2.4}$$

The household earns pre-tax income $w_t n_t$, pays a proportional labor income tax τ, receives a lump-sum transfer T_t, and discounts period-t income at the same rate q_0^t as firms.

Second, employment is determined by household members' flow into and out of jobs. Employed workers lose their job with probability x each period, while unemployed workers find a job with probability $f(\theta_t) = \theta_t \mu(\theta_t)$: the product of the recruiter–unemployment ratio and the ratio of matches to recruiters, i.e., the ratio of matches to unemployed workers. Put differently, the number of workers finding jobs, $f(\theta_t)(1-n_t)$, is equal to the number of workers recruited by firms, $\mu(\theta_t) v_t(n_0)$, since $f(\theta) = \theta\mu(\theta)$ and $\theta_t = v_t(n_0)/(1-n_t)$. The household takes n_0 as given and recognizes that

$$n_{t+1} = (1-x) n_t + f(\theta_t)(1-n_t). \tag{2.5}$$

Note that this implies that the household has no direct control over its employment rate. Let $V(0, a_0, n_0)$ denote the time-0 value of maximizing utility in equation (2.3) through a choice of $\{c_t\}$ and $\{n_t\}$, subject to the budget constraint in equation (2.4) and the law of motion for employment in equation (2.5).

2.1.3 Government

The government runs a balanced budget in each period, rebating tax revenue as a lump sum to households:

$$T_t = \tau w_t n_t. \tag{2.6}$$

I assume for now that there is no government spending.

2.1.4 Wages

At the start of each period, each employed worker bargains with her employer over her wage. If bargaining fails, the match breaks up; the worker is unemployed in the current period but has a chance to search for a job, while the firm loses the job. If bargaining succeeds, the worker is paid the pre-tax bargained wage w this period and is deployed by the firm either producing output or recruiting other workers. Moreover, both the worker and the firm anticipate agreeing on the equilibrium wage w_t in any future period t when they are matched. In equilibrium, the bargained wage equals the equilibrium wage in every period.

Rather than write down a particular model of bargaining, I follow Pissarides (1985) and posit that the outcome of bargaining satisfies several reasonable properties and I look at their implications. More precisely, I use the axiomatic Nash bargaining solution (Nash 1953), but relax the symmetry axiom. Let $\tilde{V}_n(t, w)$ denote the marginal utility for a household with the equilibrium level of assets and employment of having a worker employed at a wage w in period t rather than unemployed. Also, let $\tilde{J}_n(t, w)$ denote the marginal profit to a firm with the equilibrium number of employees of employing a worker at w. In both cases, the subscript "n" refers to partial derivatives, to stress that these are marginal values. I compute $\tilde{V}_n$ and $\tilde{J}_n$ in section 2.1.6 below.

Assuming that there are gains from trade (that is, wages w satisfying both $\tilde{V}_n(t, w) \geqslant 0$ and $\tilde{J}_n(t, w) \geqslant 0$), the bargained wage maximizes the asymmetric Nash product:

$$\tilde{V}_n(t, w)^{\phi} \tilde{J}_n(t, w)^{1-\phi}, \tag{2.7}$$

where $\phi \in (0, 1)$ represents workers' bargaining power. If there are no gains from trade, the worker becomes unemployed.

2.1.5 Equilibrium

For an arbitrary tax rate τ, an equilibrium consists of paths for consumption c_t, employment n_t, producers ℓ_t, recruiters v_t, transfers T_t, intertemporal prices q_0^t, the wage rate w_t, and the ratio of recruiters to unemployed workers θ_t such that:

- $\{\ell_t\}$ and $\{v_t\}$ solve firms' profit-maximization problems, maximizing equation (2.1) subject to the law of motion for employment in equation (2.2) given $\{q_0^t\}$, $\{w_t\}$, and $\{\theta_t\}$;
- $\{c_t\}$ and $\{n_t\}$ solve households' utility-maximization problems, maximizing equation (2.3) subject to the budget constraint (equation (2.4)) and the law of motion for employment in equation (2.5) given $\{q_0^t\}$, $\{w_t\}$, $\{\theta_t\}$, and $\{T_t\}$;

- the government budget is balanced, so equation (2.6) holds;
- w_t maximizes the Nash product in equation (2.7) for all t;
- the labor market clears, $n_t = \ell_t + v_t$ for all t; and
- the goods market clears, $z_t \ell_t = c_t$ for all t.

As in the frictionless model, these equations imply that the asset market clears as well.

I look for a steady-state equilibrium where consumption, employment, transfers, wages, and the number of producers and recruiters are all constant, while $q_0^t = \bar{q}^t$ for some $\bar{q} < 1$, so intertemporal prices decline geometrically. Note that for such a steady state to exist, it must be the case that $n_0 = \bar{n}$, where

$$\bar{n} = \frac{f(\bar{\theta})}{f(\bar{\theta}) + x} \tag{2.8}$$

and $\bar{\theta}$ is the steady-state recruiter-unemployment ratio. From equation (2.5), this implies that $n_t = \bar{n}$ for all t. I drop irrelevant time subscripts in what follows.

2.1.6 Characterization

Households

I begin by expressing the household's problem recursively. A household starts a period with assets a and employment n. Suppressing the time argument in the value function, its lifetime utility satisfies

$$V(a,n) = \max_{a'}(\log(a + (1-\tau)\bar{w}n + \bar{T} - \bar{q}a') - \gamma n \\ + \beta V(a', (1-x)n + f(\bar{\theta})(1-n))), \tag{2.9}$$

where $\bar{w}$ is the equilibrium wage and $\bar{T}$ is the equilibrium transfer. The household decides this period how much to save a', determining its state at the start of the next period (a', n'), where $n' = (1-x)n + f(\bar{\theta})(1-n)$ solves equation (2.5). The level of savings determines the consumption available this period via the intertemporal budget constraint: $c = a + (1-\tau)\bar{w}n + \bar{T} - \bar{q}a'$. Together with a natural borrowing limit, which ensures that a household can always service the interest on its debt,

$$a \geqslant -\frac{(1-\tau)\bar{w} + \bar{T}}{1-\bar{q}},$$

this is equivalent to the original household budget constraint in equation (2.4).

The household's behavior is standard. Differentiate the value function with respect to initial assets to get the envelope condition

$$V_a(a,n) = \frac{1}{c},$$

where the subscript denotes a partial derivative and $c = a + (1-\tau)\bar{w}n + \bar{T} - \bar{q}a'$. Moreover, the first-order condition with respect to next period's assets implies that

$$\frac{\bar{q}}{c} = \beta V_a(a',n').$$

In steady state, $a = a' = \bar{a}$ and $n = n' = \bar{n}$, and in particular the marginal value of assets is constant:

$$V_a(a,n) = V_a(a',n').$$

Eliminating V_a between the envelope and first-order conditions then pins down the intertemporal price, $\bar{q} = \beta$. The budget constraint then determines consumption, equal to the annuity value of assets, $(1-\beta)\bar{a}$, plus the after-tax wage times the employment rate, plus the lump-sum transfer. For a household that starts at steady-state employment, $n = \bar{n}$,

$$\bar{c} = (1-\beta)\bar{a} + (1-\tau)\bar{w}\bar{n} + \bar{T}. \tag{2.10}$$

To characterize the wage using the Nash bargaining solution in equation (2.7), I need to compute the marginal value to the household of having a worker employed at $\bar{w}$ rather than unemployed. Differentiating equation (2.9) gives

$$V_n(a,n) = \frac{(1-\tau)\bar{w}}{\bar{c}} - \gamma + \beta(1 - x - f(\bar{\theta}))V_n(a,n). \tag{2.11}$$

Now consider the value of a household that has assets $\bar{a}$, has $\bar{n}$ workers paid $\bar{w}$, and has a small measure, say $\epsilon > 0$, of workers paid an arbitrary wage w this period. All wages revert to $\bar{w}$ next period. Modifying equation (2.9), the value of the household is

$$\begin{aligned}\hat{V}(w,\epsilon) = \max_{a'}(&\log(\bar{a} + (1-\tau)(\epsilon w + \bar{n}\bar{w}) + \bar{T} - \bar{q}a') - \gamma(\bar{n}+\epsilon) \\ &+ \beta V(a', (1-x)(\bar{n}+\epsilon) + f(\bar{\theta})(1-\bar{n}-\epsilon))).\end{aligned}$$

Differentiate this with respect to ϵ and evaluate at $\epsilon = 0$ to get the marginal value of an employed worker at w:

$$\hat{V}_\epsilon(w,0) = \frac{(1-\tau)w}{\bar{c}} - \gamma + \beta(1 - x - f(\bar{\theta}))V_n(\bar{a},\bar{n}) \equiv \tilde{V}_n(w).$$

Combining this with equation (2.11) gives a convenient expression for the marginal value of having a worker employed at w rather than unemployed:

$$\tilde{V}_n(w) = \frac{(1-\tau)(w-\bar{w})}{\bar{c}} + V_n(\bar{a},\bar{n}). \tag{2.12}$$

Recall that $V_n(\bar{a}, \bar{n})$ is the marginal value of having a worker employed at the equilibrium wage rather than unemployed. To this one adds the worker's incremental after-tax income from receiving an arbitrary wage rather than the equilibrium wage, $(1 - \tau)(w - \bar{w})$, multiplied by the marginal utility of income $1/\bar{c}$.

Firms

Next I turn to the firm. It is again useful to express its problem recursively, suppressing time arguments:

$$J(n) = \max_{\nu \in [0,1]} ((z(1 - \nu) - \bar{w})n + \bar{q}J((1 - x + \nu\mu(\bar{\theta}))n)), \tag{2.13}$$

where $\nu = v/(v + l)$ is the share of employees who are recruiters and the size of the firm next period is $n' = (1 - x + \nu\mu(\bar{\theta}))n$. The firm's value function is linear in n, $J(n) = \bar{J}n$ for all n, where

$$\bar{J} = \max_{\nu \in [0,1]} (z(1 - \nu) - \bar{w} + \bar{q}(1 - x + \nu\mu(\bar{\theta}))\bar{J}). \tag{2.14}$$

The value function is linear because a firm that is twice as large as another but devotes the same share of employees to recruiting earns twice as much current profits and is twice as large next period.[1]

Since the objective function in equation (2.14) is linear in ν, the solution is typically extreme: either $\nu = 0$ or $\nu = 1$. The former implies that firms shrink over time with attrition, while the latter implies that there is no production, and so neither is consistent with a steady-state equilibrium. There is an interior solution only if

$$z = \beta\mu(\bar{\theta})\bar{J}, \tag{2.15}$$

where I use $\bar{q} = \beta$. A producer yields output z today, while a recruiter generates $\mu(\bar{\theta})$ additional employees, each valued at $\bar{J}$, tomorrow. For workers to be engaged in both activities, these must be equal.

Eliminate $\bar{J}$ between equations (2.14) and (2.15):

$$z = \beta\mu(\bar{\theta})\frac{z - \bar{w}}{1 - \beta(1 - x)}. \tag{2.16}$$

The left-hand side is the current output of a worker using the production technology. The right-hand side is the expected number of additional workers attracted by a recruiter times the present value of profits produced by those workers if they are all employed in the production technology. If equation (2.16) holds, all firms find any value of $\nu \in [0, 1]$ to be optimal.

[1] I give a formal proof that the firm's value is linear in the stochastic model in section 2.2.

From equation (2.2), employment is constant if

$$\bar{v} = x/\mu(\bar{\theta}). \tag{2.17}$$

More precisely, any individual firm earns the same present value of profits for any choice of $\{v_t\}$; however, in the entire economy, a fraction $\bar{v}$ of all employed workers must be recruiters in any particular period, so as to keep employment constant. Note that since $\bar{v} \in [0,1]$ and $\mu(\theta)$ is nondecreasing, this equation places an upper bound on $\bar{\theta}$: $\mu(\bar{\theta}) \geqslant x$.

Now consider a firm that employs $\bar{n}$ workers at $\bar{w}$ and ϵ workers at w this period. All wages revert to $\bar{w}$ next period. Modifying equation (2.13) slightly, the value of such a firm is

$$\hat{J}(w,\epsilon) = \max_{v}(z(1-v)(\bar{n}+\epsilon) - \bar{w}\bar{n} - w\epsilon + \bar{q}\bar{J}(1-x+v\mu(\bar{\theta}))(\bar{n}+\epsilon)).$$

Differentiate this with respect to ϵ and evaluate at $\epsilon = 0$ to get the marginal value of employing a worker at w:

$$\hat{J}_{\epsilon}(w,0) = z - w + \beta(1-x)\bar{J} \equiv \tilde{J}_n(w).$$

Since $\bar{J} = z - \bar{w} + \beta(1-x)\bar{J}$, I can also express the marginal value of an employee who is paid w as

$$\tilde{J}_n(w) = \bar{w} - w + \bar{J}, \tag{2.18}$$

which is analogous to equation (2.12). The marginal value of employing a worker at an arbitrary wage w this period is the marginal value of employing a worker at the equilibrium wage, $\bar{J}$, plus the wage savings $\bar{w} - w$.

Wage

I next characterize the wage using the Nash bargaining solution in equation (2.7). The necessary first-order condition for the equilibrium wage is

$$\phi\frac{\tilde{V}_n'(\bar{w})}{\tilde{V}_n(\bar{w})} + (1-\phi)\frac{\tilde{J}_n'(\bar{w})}{\tilde{J}_n(\bar{w})} = 0.$$

From equation (2.12), $\tilde{V}_n'(\bar{w}) = (1-\tau)/\bar{c}$ and $\tilde{V}_n(\bar{w}) = V_n(\bar{a},\bar{n})$, while equation (2.18) implies that $\tilde{J}_n'(\bar{w}) = -1$ and $\tilde{J}_n(\bar{w}) = \bar{J}$. Therefore, maximizing the Nash product is equivalent to making the gains from trade proportionate:

$$(1-\phi)V_n(\bar{a},\bar{n})\bar{c} = \phi(1-\tau)\bar{J}. \tag{2.19}$$

To find the equilibrium wage $\bar{w}$, eliminate V_n and $\bar{J}$ using equations (2.11) and (2.15):

$$(1-\phi)\frac{(1-\tau)\bar{w} - \gamma\bar{c}}{1-\beta(1-x-f(\bar{\theta}))} = \phi(1-\tau)\frac{z}{\beta\mu(\bar{\theta})}.$$

Eliminate $1 - \beta(1 - x)$ from the left-hand side using equation (2.16) and simplify:

$$(1-\phi)\frac{(1-\tau)\bar{w} - \gamma\bar{c}}{\mu(\bar{\theta})((z-\bar{w})/z) + f(\bar{\theta})} = \phi(1-\tau)\frac{z}{\mu(\bar{\theta})}.$$

Recalling that $f(\theta) = \theta\mu(\theta)$, solve for the after-tax wage:

$$(1-\tau)\bar{w} = \phi(1-\tau)z(1+\bar{\theta}) + (1-\phi)\gamma\bar{c}. \tag{2.20}$$

The after-tax wage is a weighted average of $(1-\tau)z(1+\bar{\theta})$ and $\gamma\bar{c}$, with the weight on the first term being equal to the bargaining power of workers. If a worker is employed, she can directly produce $(1-\tau)z$ units of after-tax output. In addition, by marginally reducing the unemployment rate, she frees up $\bar{\theta}$ workers to produce output rather than recruit, since $\bar{\theta}$ is the aggregate recruiter–unemployment ratio. That is, these additional workers can produce while keeping the recruiter–unemployment ratio constant. Thus $(1-\tau)z(1+\bar{\theta})$ measures the additional after-tax output generated by moving a worker from unemployment to employment, i.e., the marginal product of labor. The worker captures a fraction ϕ of the MPL. On the other hand, if a worker is employed, she suffers disutility γ. To value this in consumption units, divide by the marginal utility of consumption $1/\bar{c}$. Thus γc is the marginal rate of substitution between consumption and leisure. The worker keeps a fraction $1-\phi$ of the MRS. In a frictionless model, the MRS and the MPL are equal and both are equal to the wage. With search frictions, there are typically gains from trade, so the MPL is larger than the MRS and the wage is a weighted average of the two, with weights determined by bargaining power.

Equation (2.20) states that a worker with higher consumption, or equivalently a lower marginal utility of wealth, is paid a higher wage. This is due to the increase in her threat point when evaluated in consumption-equivalent units. Yet when I solved the household's consumption problem, I implicitly assumed that her wealth does not affect her wage. One possible interpretation is that a firm cannot observe a household's wealth when bargaining. While a worker would like to claim to be rich so as to boost her wage, firms bargain as if they are facing a worker with the representative household's marginal utility of wealth $1/\bar{c}$. Another interpretation is that each firm bargains simultaneously with all its workers and they agree on a common wage. Assuming that households spread their workers across many firms, a single household's decision to save more will not affect the wage that its members receive, eliminating any incentive to distort its savings.

2.1.7 Equilibrium

Five objects completely characterize an equilibrium: consumption $\bar{c}$, employment $\bar{n}$, the wage $\bar{w}$, the recruiter–unemployment ratio $\bar{\theta}$, and the fraction of employed workers who are recruiters $\bar{v}$. I have obtained three relationships between these variables: equation (2.8), which gives the steady-state employment rate; equation (2.16), which gives a condition for an interior solution; and equation (2.20), which determines the wage. To close the model, I use two market-clearing conditions. First, consumption is equal to output:

$$\bar{c} = z\bar{n}(1 - \bar{v}). \tag{2.21}$$

For the representative household, a fraction $\bar{n}$ of workers are employed, and of those, a fraction $1 - \bar{v}$ each produce z units of the consumption good. Second, there are $\bar{v}\bar{n}$ recruiters and $1 - \bar{n}$ unemployed workers, so the ratio of recruiters to unemployed workers is

$$\bar{\theta} = \frac{\bar{v}\bar{n}}{1 - \bar{n}}. \tag{2.22}$$

Given a solution to these five equations, it is easy to solve for any other variable of interest.

To find the equilibrium, first eliminate $\bar{v}$ from equation (2.21) using equation (2.22) and then eliminate $\bar{n}$ using equation (2.8). This implies that consumption is proportional to productivity:

$$\bar{c} = \frac{z(f(\bar{\theta}) - x\bar{\theta})}{f(\bar{\theta}) + x}.$$

Next eliminate $\bar{w}$ from equation (2.16) using equation (2.20) and then eliminate $\bar{c}$ using the preceding equation to obtain an equation in $\bar{\theta}$ alone. One can write this as $\mathcal{T}(\bar{\theta}) = 0$, where

$$\mathcal{T}(\theta) \equiv \frac{\theta(1 - \beta(1 - x))}{\beta f(\theta)} - 1 + \phi(1 + \theta) + \frac{(1 - \phi)\gamma(f(\theta) - x\theta)}{(1 - \tau)(x + f(\theta))}. \tag{2.23}$$

To prove that an equilibrium exists, observe that $\mathcal{T}$ is continuous. Moreover, $\mathcal{T}(0) = -(1 - \phi) < 0$ since, by assumption, $\lim_{\theta \to 0} f(\theta)/\theta = \infty$. On the other hand, $\mathcal{T}(\tilde{\theta}) = (1 - \beta)/(\beta x) + \phi(1 + \tilde{\theta}) > 0$, where $f(\tilde{\theta})/\tilde{\theta} = x$. By the intermediate-value theorem, there must exist a $\bar{\theta} \in (0, \tilde{\theta})$ such that $\mathcal{T}(\bar{\theta}) = 0$. For particular numerical values, it is easy to check whether this equation has a unique solution; indeed, I have not found an example with multiple steady-state equilibria.

An important observation is that productivity z does not appear in equation (2.23) and so the equilibrium ratio of recruiters to unemployed workers is independent of productivity. The key to this result is that income and substitution effects cancel. In an economy with high productivity, workers earn higher wages. The substitution effect makes leisure less attractive, while the income effect makes it more attractive. With these preferences, or balanced-growth preferences more generally, the two effects balance and so there is no change in equilibrium recruiting effort.

For a given value of the ratio of recruiters to unemployed workers $\bar{\theta}$, recover employment $\bar{n}$ from equation (2.8) and then the fraction of employees who are recruiters $\bar{v}$ from equation (2.22), proving both are independent of productivity. Also, use equation (2.21) to find consumption $\bar{c}$ and equation (2.20) to get the wage $\bar{w}$, which are both proportional to productivity. Lastly, one can use equation (2.6) to compute the level of transfers $\bar{T}$.

Finally, one can verify that the household's assets are equal to the value of the jobs that it owns: $\bar{a} = \bar{J}\bar{n}$. Combining the household budget constraint, equation (2.4), and the government budget constraint, equation (2.6), and using $\bar{q} = \beta$ gives

$$\bar{a} = \frac{\bar{c} - \bar{w}\bar{n}}{1 - \beta}.$$

Eliminate $\bar{c}$ using equation (2.21), $\bar{w}$ using equation (2.16), and $\bar{v}$ using equation (2.22):

$$\bar{a} = \frac{z\bar{n}}{1 - \beta}\left(- \frac{\bar{\theta}(1 - \bar{n})}{\bar{n}} + \frac{1 - \beta(1 - x)}{\beta\mu(\bar{\theta})}\right).$$

Finally, note that $(1 - \bar{n})/\bar{n} = x/f(\bar{\theta})$ and $\mu(\bar{\theta}) = f(\bar{\theta})/\bar{\theta}$. This gives $\bar{a} = z\bar{n}/\beta\mu(\bar{\theta})$, and so the result follows from equation (2.15). Of course we already knew this had to be the case because of Walras's law.

2.1.8 The Measured Labor Wedge

Consider an economist who believes that households have preferences given by equation (1.1), with disutility of leisure $\hat{\gamma}$ and Frisch labor supply elasticity $\hat{\varepsilon}$, that the production function is Cobb–Douglas with capital share $\hat{\alpha}$, and that the labor market clears without any search frictions. Then, from equation (1.12), he would measure the labor wedge as

$$\hat{\tau} = 1 - \frac{\hat{\gamma}}{1 - \hat{\alpha}}\frac{c}{y}n^{(1+\hat{\varepsilon})/\hat{\varepsilon}}.$$

But if the model in this section were the true data-generating process, consumption would equal output and employment would be given by equation (2.8). Thus he would measure

$$\hat{\tau} = 1 - \frac{\hat{\gamma}}{1 - \hat{\alpha}}\left(\frac{f(\bar{\theta})}{f(\bar{\theta}) + x}\right)^{(1+\hat{\varepsilon})/\hat{\varepsilon}}.$$

In particular, if the economist correctly understood that production used only labor ($\hat{\alpha} = 0$) and that the Frisch labor supply elasticity was infinite ($\hat{\varepsilon} = \infty$), he would measure

$$\hat{\tau} = 1 - \hat{\gamma}\frac{f(\bar{\theta})}{f(\bar{\theta}) + x}. \tag{2.24}$$

It is not surprising that the labor wedge is constant in steady state. The important point is that it bears little resemblance to the true tax rate τ. The economist would attribute less-than-full employment to taxes or the disutility of work, when in fact it is also a consequence of the search frictions.

A particularly acute example occurs if $\gamma = 0$, so there is no disutility of work. In this case, equation (2.23) implies that the recruiter-unemployment ratio is independent of the tax rate τ, because the pre-tax wage and hence the incentive to create jobs is independent of the tax rate (equation (2.20)). Put differently, suppose that the labor income tax rate differed across countries. This would not cause any difference in employment rates. But an economist viewing the world through the lens of the frictionless model would conclude that there must be some disutility of labor, $\hat{\gamma} > 0$; otherwise, he would expect everyone to work. Using equation (2.24), he would then have difficulty understanding why there is no difference in employment rates across countries despite large differences in taxes.[2]

2.2 Productivity Shocks

I now extend the model to allow for shocks to the production technology. As in chapter 1, denote time by $t = 0, 1, 2, \ldots$ and the state of the economy at time t by s_t. Let $s^t = \{s_0, s_1, \ldots, s_t\}$ denote the history of the economy and let $\Pi(s^t)$ denote the time-0 belief about the probability of observing an arbitrary history s^t through time t. I allow productivity and lump-sum transfers to be history dependent. Each producer in history s^t produces output $z(s^t)$ and each worker, employed or unemployed, receives a lump-sum transfer $T(s^t)$, set at a level to ensure that the government runs a balanced budget in each period. Assume that $z(s^t)$ is strictly positive for all s^t and, to ensure that utility is finite, assume that

$$-\infty < \sum_{t=0}^{\infty} \sum_{s^t} \beta^t \Pi(s^t) \log z(s^t) < \infty. \tag{2.25}$$

[2] Of course, this problem is not present in the data. There are substantial differences in tax rates across countries, but these can only partially explain the differences in employment rates, even if the elasticity of labor supply is large (see, for example, Prescott 2004).

In this section, I prove that consumption $c(s^t)$ and the wage $w(s^t)$ are each proportional to contemporaneous productivity $z(s^t)$, while the recruiter–unemployment ratio $\theta(s^t)$, the employment rate $n(s^t)$, and the fraction of employed workers in recruiting $v(s^t)$ are constant and independent of the stochastic process for productivity. The notion of equilibrium is the same as in the model without productivity shocks and so I proceed somewhat less formally, presenting the model and the key equilibrium relationships together.

2.2.1 Firms

A representative firm employs $n_0 = n(s^0)$ workers at time 0 and subsequently assigns employees to the stochastic production technology and the deterministic recruiting technology. Let $n(s^t, n_0)$ denote the size of the firm in history s^t and let $v(s^t, n_0)$ denote the number of recruiters that the firm uses. Then the present value of its profits is

$$J(s^0, n_0) = \sum_{t=0}^{\infty} \sum_{s^t} q_0(s^t)(z(s^t)(n(s^t, n_0) - v(s^t, n_0)) - w(s^t)n(s^t, n_0)), \tag{2.26}$$

where $q_0(s^t)$ is the price of an Arrow–Debreu security that pays one unit of consumption following history s^t, denominated in units of history-s^0 consumption. Output in history s^t is $z(s^t)$ times the number of employees not devoted to recruiting, $n - v$, while the wage is $w(s^t)$ per employee. In addition, the firm's size evolves according to

$$n(s^{t+1}, n_0) = v(s^t, n_0)\mu(\theta(s^t)) + (1 - x)n(s^t, n_0) \tag{2.27}$$

for all $s^{t+1} = \{s^t, s_{t+1}\}$. Each recruiter attracts $\mu(\theta(s^t))$ new workers, while a fraction x of the existing labor force leaves. The firm chooses history-contingent recruiting $v(s^t, n_0)$ to maximize the value of profits $J(s^0, n_0)$.

A simple argument proves that the firm's value is linear in n_0. Take any two initial sizes, $n_0 > n_0' > 0$. Suppose a firm with initial size n_0' sets recruiting to $(n_0'/n_0)v(s^t, n_0)$ in each history s^t. Then, using induction on equation (2.27), one can verify that the firm's size is $(n_0'/n_0)n(s^t, n_0)$ in each history. From equation (2.26), the firm's profits are $(n_0'/n_0)J(s^0, n_0)$. Since behaving optimally generally yields more profits, $J(s^0, n_0') \geqslant (n_0'/n_0)J(s^0, n_0)$. A symmetric argument—that a firm with n_0 workers can mimic a scaled version of the optimal policy for a firm with n_0' workers—establishes that $J(s^0, n_0) \geqslant (n_0/n_0')J(s^0, n_0')$. Combining these inequalities implies $J(s^0, n_0)/n_0 = J(s^0, n_0')/n_0' = \bar{J}(s^0)$, so the value of the firm per employee is independent of firm size.

The same logic implies that $\nu(s^t) = v(s^t, n_0)/n(s^t, n_0)$, the fraction of workers devoted to recruiting, is independent of n_0.

This allows me to simplify the analysis by focusing on the firm's value per employee. Let $\bar{J}(s^t)$ denote the present value of the firm's profits per employee following history s^t, evaluated in history-s^t units of consumption. This solves the recursive equation

$$\bar{J}(s^t) = \max_{\nu \in [0,1]} \Big(z(s^t)(1-\nu) - w(s^t) + (\nu\mu(\theta(s^t)) + 1 - x) \sum_{s^{t+1}|s^t} q_t(s^{t+1})\bar{J}(s^{t+1}) \Big), \tag{2.28}$$

where $q_t(s^{t+1})$ is the price of a unit of consumption in history $s^{t+1} \equiv \{s^t, s_{t+1}\}$, paid in units of history-s^t consumption. The firm chooses the fraction of its workers who are recruiters, ν. It earns revenue $z(s^t)(1-\nu)$ per worker this period, pays a wage $w(s^t)$, and then, from equation (2.27), grows by a factor $\nu\mu(\theta(s^t)) + 1 - x$. The summation gives the expected discounted value of continuation profits from each employee.

Since both the production and recruiting technologies are linear, an individual firm's choice of whether to produce or recruit is typically indeterminate; however, aggregate production and recruiting is determined in equilibrium. To see this, note from equation (2.28) that an interior solution, $0 < \nu(s^t) < 1$, requires

$$z(s^t) = \mu(\theta(s^t)) \sum_{s^{t+1}|s^t} q_t(s^{t+1})\bar{J}(s^{t+1}), \tag{2.29}$$

so the foregone profits from devoting a worker to recruiting rather than production are exactly offset by the increase in the continuation value of the firm. If this condition holds, the Bellman equation (2.28) can be simplified to read

$$\bar{J}(s^t) = z(s^t)\left(1 + \frac{1-x}{\mu(\theta(s^t))}\right) - w(s^t). \tag{2.30}$$

Part of the revenue from a job comes from the output that the worker can produce, $z(s^t)$. In addition, suppose the firm has a target size next period. An additional employee this period remains at the firm next period with probability $1 - x$. Since each recruiter can attract $\mu(\theta(s^t))$ new workers, the presence of an additional employee frees $(1-x)/\mu(\theta(s^t))$ other employees from recruiting, enabling them to produce $z(s^t)$ units of output each. The value of a job is the sum of these two components, net of the wage $w(s^t)$ that the worker receives.

Finally, compute the value of a job that pays an arbitrary wage w in history s^t and then pays $w(s^T)$ if it survives until a continuation history

$s^{\tau}, \tau > t$. I obtain the following equation in the same way that I obtained equation (2.18):

$$\tilde{J}_n(s^t, w) = w(s^t) - w + \bar{J}(s^t). \tag{2.31}$$

This simply increments the value of a job by the reduction in the wage below the equilibrium, $w(s^t) - w$.

2.2.2 Households

The representative household allocates total consumption following history s^t, $c(s^t)$, in order to maximize the sum of household utility, acting as if it has a utility function

$$\sum_{t=0}^{\infty} \sum_{s^t} \beta^t \Pi(s^t)(\log c(s^t) - \gamma n(s^t)), \tag{2.32}$$

where $n(s^t)$ is the fraction of household members who are employed following history s^t. The household faces a single lifetime budget constraint:

$$a_0 = \sum_{t=0}^{\infty} \sum_{s^t} q_0(s^t)(c(s^t) - (1-\tau)w(s^t)n(s^t) - T(s^t)). \tag{2.33}$$

Here a_0 is the household's initial level of assets in units of consumption at time 0.

The household also faces a constraint on unemployment. The probability of an unemployed worker finding a job depends on the contemporaneous ratio of recruiters to unemployed workers, $f(\theta(s^t))$, while the probability of an employed worker losing her job is a constant x. Thus the household takes n_0 as given and recognizes that

$$n(s^{t+1}) = (1-x)n(s^t) + f(\theta(s^t))(1 - n(s^t)) \tag{2.34}$$

for any $s^{t+1} = \{s^t, s_{t+1}\}$. Note that the household cannot control its employment rate, which depends on parameters and on the endogenous ratio of recruiters to unemployed workers. The household chooses a path for consumption $c(s^t)$ to maximize equation (2.32) subject to the budget constraint in equation (2.33), with the path of its employment rate fixed by equation (2.34).

Define the representative household's assets following any history s^t as the present value of future consumption in excess of labor income and transfers,

$$a(s^t) = \sum_{t'=t}^{\infty} \sum_{s^{t'}|s^t} q_t(s^{t'})(c(s^{t'}) - (1-\tau)w(s^{t'})n(s^{t'}) - T(s^{t'})), \tag{2.35}$$

denominated in units of consumption in history s^t. Here $q_t(s^{t'})$ is the price of one unit of consumption in continuation history $s^{t'}$, paid in units of consumption in history s^t. This implies a standard sequence of intertemporal budget constraints:

$$a(s^t) + (1-\tau)w(s^t)n(s^t) + T(s^t) = c(s^t) + \sum_{s^{t+1}|s^t} q_t(s^{t+1})a(s^{t+1}). \quad (2.36)$$

Following any history, initial assets plus current-period after-tax labor income and transfers must equal consumption plus the purchase of one-period Arrow securities that provide next period's assets.

As in the case of firms, I express the household's problem recursively. Let $V(s^t, a, n)$ denote the household's utility in history s^t, given assets a and employment n. This solves the Bellman equation

$$V(s^t, a, n) = \max_{\{a(s^{t+1})\}} \left(\log c - \gamma n + \beta \sum_{s^{t+1}|s^t} \frac{\Pi(s^{t+1})}{\Pi(s^t)} V(s^{t+1}, a(s^{t+1}), n') \right), \quad (2.37)$$

where $a(s^{t+1})$ is the household's purchase of Arrow securities that pay off in history $s^{t+1} = \{s^t, s_{t+1}\}$; consumption c solves the intertemporal budget constraint (equation (2.36)),

$$c = a + (1-\tau)w(s^t)n + T(s^t) - \sum_{s^{t+1}|s^t} q_t(s^{t+1})a(s^{t+1});$$

and next period's employment solves equation (2.34),

$$n' = (1-x)n + f(\theta(s^t))(1-n).$$

The envelope condition for current assets is

$$V_a(s^t, a, n) = \frac{1}{\tilde{c}(s^t, a, n)},$$

where $\tilde{c}(s^t, a, n)$ is the consumption of a household that starts history s^t with assets a and employment n. The first-order condition for next period's assets is

$$\frac{q_t(s^{t+1})}{\tilde{c}(s^t, a, n)} = \beta \frac{\Pi(s^{t+1})}{\Pi(s^t)} V_a(s^{t+1}, a(s^{t+1}), n').$$

Combining these and looking at a household with initial assets $a(s^t)$ and employment $n(s^t)$ gives the Euler equation that prices an Arrow security:

$$q_t(s^{t+1}) = \beta \frac{\Pi(s^{t+1})c(s^t)}{\Pi(s^t)c(s^{t+1})} \quad (2.38)$$

for any $s^{t+1} = \{s^t, s_{t+1}\}$, where $c(s^t) \equiv \tilde{c}(s^t, a(s^t), n(s^t))$ is the household's equilibrium level of consumption. This is, of course, a completely standard equation for the price of a one-period state-contingent asset.

The envelope condition for current employment for a household with assets $a(s^t)$ and employment $n(s^t)$ in history s^t is

$$\begin{aligned} V_n(s^t, a(s^t), n(s^t)) \\ &= \frac{(1-\tau)w(s^t)}{c(s^t)} - \gamma \\ &\quad + \beta(1 - x - f(\theta(s^t))) \sum_{s^{t+1}|s^t} \frac{\Pi(s^{t+1})}{\Pi(s^t)} V_n(s^{t+1}, a(s^{t+1}), n(s^{t+1})). \end{aligned} \tag{2.39}$$

Finally, compute the marginal value to a household with the equilibrium level of employment and assets of having one employed worker in a job that pays an arbitrary wage w in history s^t and then pays $w(s^T)$ if it survives until a continuation history s^T, $T > t$. Analogous with equation (2.12), this solves

$$\tilde{V}_n(s^t, w) = \frac{(1-\tau)(w - w(s^t))}{c(s^t)} + V_n(s^t, a(s^t), n(s^t)). \tag{2.40}$$

This increments the value of an employed worker by the increase in the after-tax wage, measured in units of marginal utility.

2.2.3 Government

The government runs a balanced budget in each period, rebating tax revenue as a lump sum to households:

$$T(s^t) = \tau w(s^t) n(s^t). \tag{2.41}$$

Continue to assume that there is no government spending.

2.2.4 Wages

Wages are determined at the start of each period by bargaining between households and firms. If they agree on a wage w following history s^t, the household's utility increases by $\tilde{V}_n(s^t, w)$ and the value of the job is $\tilde{J}_n(s^t, w)$. The wage $w(s^t)$ maximizes the weighted geometric average of the gains from trade,

$$w(s^t) = \arg\max_w \tilde{V}_n(s^t, w)^{\phi} \tilde{J}_n(s^t, w)^{1-\phi}, \tag{2.42}$$

where $\phi \in [0, 1]$ represents workers' bargaining power.

Equation (2.31) implies that

$$\frac{\partial \tilde{J}_n(s^t, w)}{\partial w} = -1 \quad \text{and} \quad \tilde{J}_n(s^t, w(s^t)) = \bar{J}(s^t).$$

Equation (2.40) implies that

$$\frac{\partial \tilde{V}_n(s^t, w)}{\partial w} = \frac{1-\tau}{c(s^t)} \quad \text{and} \quad \tilde{V}_n(s^t, w(s^t)) = V_n(s^t, a(s^t), n(s^t)).$$

Maximizing equation (2.42) is therefore equivalent to setting

$$(1-\phi)V_n(s^t, a(s^t), n(s^t))c(s^t) = \phi(1-\tau)\bar{J}(s^t).$$

Use this to eliminate $V_n(s^t, a(s^t), n(s^t))$ and $V_n(s^{t+1}, a(s^{t+1}), n(s^{t+1}))$ from equation (2.39):

$$\begin{aligned}\phi(1-\tau)\bar{J}(s^t) \\ &= (1-\phi)((1-\tau)w(s^t) - \gamma c(s^t)) \\ &\quad + \phi(1-\tau)\beta(1-x-f(\theta(s^t))) \sum_{s^{t+1}|s^t} \frac{\Pi(s^{t+1})c(s^t)}{\Pi(s^t)c(s^{t+1})}\bar{J}(s^{t+1}).\end{aligned}$$

Next eliminate $\bar{J}(s^t)$ using equation (2.30) and $\bar{J}(s^{t+1})$ using equation (2.29), with $q_t(s^{t+1})$ given by equation (2.38). After simplifying I obtain the wage equation

$$(1-\tau)w(s^t) = \phi(1-\tau)z(s^t)(1+\theta(s^t)) + (1-\phi)\gamma c(s^t). \qquad (2.43)$$

This is only a slight generalization of equation (2.20), with the wage depending on contemporaneous values of productivity, the ratio of recruiters to unemployed workers, and consumption, rather than steady-state values. The interpretation of the wage as a weighted average of the MPL and the MRS is similarly unchanged.

2.2.5 Market Clearing

Close the model using two market-clearing conditions. First, consumption is equal to output:

$$c(s^t) = z(s^t)n(s^t)(1-\nu(s^t)). \qquad (2.44)$$

For the representative household, a fraction $n(s^t)$ of workers are employed, and of those, a fraction $1-\nu(s^t)$ produce $z(s^t)$ units of the consumption good each. Second, the ratio of recruiters to unemployed workers is

$$\theta(s^t) = \frac{\nu(s^t)n(s^t)}{1-n(s^t)}. \qquad (2.45)$$

2.2.6 Equilibrium

Let $\bar{\theta}$ solve equation (2.23) and suppose the initial employment level solves equation (2.8), i.e.,

$$n_0 = \bar{n} = \frac{f(\bar{\theta})}{f(\bar{\theta}) + x}.$$

I claim that there is an equilibrium with the desired properties: consumption, wages, and transfers are proportional to contemporaneous productivity, $c(s^t) = \bar{c}z(s^t)$, $w(s^t) = \bar{w}z(s^t)$, and $T(s^t) = \bar{T}z(s^t)$; while the recruiter-unemployment ratio, the share of recruiters in employment, and the employment rate are constant, $\theta(s^t) = \bar{\theta}$, $\nu(s^t) = \bar{\nu}$, and $n(s^t) = \bar{n}$.[3]

To prove this, note that if $\theta(s^t) = \bar{\theta}$ for all s^t, the initial condition $n_0 = \bar{n}$ and the law of motion for employment, equation (2.34), ensure that $n(s^t) = \bar{n}$ for all s^t. Then equation (2.45) implies that

$$\nu(s^t) = x/\mu(\bar{\theta}) \equiv \bar{\nu}$$

for all s^t; equation (2.44) implies that $c(s^t) = \bar{c}z(s^t)$, where

$$\bar{c} = \bar{n}(1 - \bar{\nu}) = \frac{f(\bar{\theta}) - x\bar{\theta}}{f(\bar{\theta}) + x}; \tag{2.46}$$

and equation (2.43) implies that $w(s^t) = \bar{w}z(s^t)$, where

$$\bar{w} = \phi(1 + \bar{\theta}) + (1 - \phi)\gamma\bar{c}/(1 - \tau). \tag{2.47}$$

To confirm that this is an equilibrium, substitute these results into the condition for an interior equilibrium, equation (2.29), with $\bar{J}(s^{t+1})$ given by equation (2.30):

$$z(s^t) = (1 - x + \mu(\bar{\theta})(1 - \bar{w})) \sum_{s^{t+1}|s^t} q_t(s^{t+1})z(s^{t+1}).$$

Equation (2.38) and $c(s^t) = \bar{c}z(s^t)$ imply that

$$q_t(s^{t+1}) = \beta\frac{\Pi(s^{t+1})z(s^t)}{\Pi(s^t)z(s^{t+1})}.$$

Substitute this into the previous equation and eliminate $z(s^t)$ to get

$$1 = \beta(1 - x + \mu(\bar{\theta})(1 - \bar{w})). \tag{2.48}$$

[3] If $n_0 \neq \bar{n}$, the model has some transitional dynamics. I show how to deal with this in chapter 3, in models where productivity shocks necessarily affect the unemployment rate. In practice, I find that the economy converges rapidly to steady state. Also, there may be other equilibria of the model. For example, in a deterministic discrete-time version of Pissarides (1985), a deterministic cycle can arise. In that environment, one can prove uniqueness if the period length is sufficiently short.

Eliminating $\bar{w}$ and then $\bar{c}$ using equations (2.47) and (2.46) delivers equation (2.23). Finally, condition (2.25) ensures that the household's utility is finite. This completes the proof that there is an equilibrium where productivity shocks do not affect employment.

To understand this neutrality result, consider a temporary increase in productivity. Since this does not alter the efficiency of hiring workers, all else being equal, firms would shift workers from recruiting to production, raising consumption and reducing hiring, i.e., future employment and output. But there is an offsetting general equilibrium effect. Since productivity is temporarily high, consumption is temporarily high. For this to be an equilibrium, the interest rate must be low, i.e., the intertemporal price q must be high, which makes future output more valuable, encouraging hiring. With the preferences in equation (2.32), these effects exactly offset each other, regardless of the stochastic process for productivity. Indeed, the stochastic process for productivity does not itself affect the recruiter–unemployment ratio or the unemployment rate.

This finding builds on Blanchard and Galí's (2006) neutrality result in a model with labor adjustment costs. It also recalls some results from frictionless business cycle models. Take a standard framework, as in chapter 1, but assume there are two production technologies: one for producing the consumption good and one for producing the investment good. If there is no government spending and if households have preferences as in equation (1.1), productivity shocks in the consumption-good-producing sector do not affect employment or the allocation of labor across the two sectors. Again, this is because income and substitution effects exactly offset each other. On the other hand, shocks to the investment-good-producing sector, which would be equivalent here to shocks to the matching function μ, cause movements in both employment and investment.

The assumption that the recruiting technology uses labor rather than goods is critical for this neutrality result. If the recruiting technology used goods, a positive productivity shock would effectively reduce the cost of recruiting, inducing an increase in hiring during booms. Many authors assume that recruiting is in fact goods intensive (see Merz (1995) and Andolfatto (1996) for examples). On the other hand, the textbook matching model (Pissarides 1985, 2000) assumes that, while recruiting costs are denominated in goods, a productivity shock raises the recruiting cost proportionately. This is technically equivalent to assuming that the recruiting technology uses labor and is unaffected by the productivity shock. This assumption seems empirically more plausible. Recruiting is, in fact, a time-intensive activity. Moreover, it seems a priori implausible that shocks to the cost of recruiting drive cyclical fluctuations in employment.

The neutrality result is stronger than the finding in Shimer (2005), where I argued that productivity shocks have a quantitatively small effect on employment in a calibrated version of the Pissarides (1985) model. There are several important differences between the frameworks. First, in my earlier paper, I assumed that households have linear preferences over consumption and leisure and so there are no general equilibrium effects on interest rates. When future productivity is anticipated to be low relative to current productivity, firms reduce hiring. Second, in that paper I assumed that recruiting uses goods rather than labor. Moving away from linear preferences and recognizing that recruiting is a labor-intensive activity, both seem like desirable modifications to the model.[4]

2.2.7 The Measured Labor Wedge

Since productivity shocks do not affect employment and the consumption–output ratio is fixed at 1, such shocks do not affect the measured labor wedge. Again consider an economist who believes that households have preferences given by equation (1.1), with disutility of leisure $\hat{\gamma}$ and Frisch labor supply elasticity $\hat{\varepsilon}$, that the production function is Cobb–Douglas with capital share $\hat{\alpha}$, and that the labor market clears without any search frictions. If this model were the data-generating process, he would measure

$$\hat{\tau} = 1 - \frac{\hat{\gamma}}{1-\hat{\alpha}}\left(\frac{f(\bar{\theta})}{f(\bar{\theta})+x}\right)^{(1+\hat{\varepsilon})/\hat{\varepsilon}}. \tag{2.49}$$

The measured labor wedge would be constant. Thus this model fails to generate either fluctuations in employment or fluctuations in the labor wedge.

2.3 The Planner's Problem

The previous section argued that in the benchmark search model, productivity shocks do not affect employment, unemployment, or the labor wedge. This section asks whether they *should* have any effect on these outcomes. I consider a hypothetical social planner who wants to maximize the utility of the representative household. He takes as given an

[4] It is worth stressing that the finding in Shimer (2005) is quantitative while the neutrality result here is exact. Some authors have argued with the calibration in that earlier paper: see especially Hagedorn and Manovskii (2008), in which a different calibration of the value of leisure and the bargaining parameter ϕ is argued for. The neutrality result holds here regardless of bargaining power and regardless of how much workers like leisure, i.e., regardless of the value of γ.

initial level of employment $n_0 = n(s^0)$ and decides how many workers to allocate to production and how many to recruiting in each state. The measure of recruiters determines future employment, while the measure of producers determines current consumption. I examine how the planner responds to productivity shocks.

My main finding is that neutrality is socially optimal, in the sense that the planner keeps consumption proportional to productivity and keeps employment constant. This section can be safely skipped since the material in chapters 3 and 4 do not depend directly on it; however, the planner's problem helps to clarify the neutrality result in the decentralized economy. Indeed, the proof that productivity shocks are neutral is much more straightforward here, as I show in the next two paragraphs.

Formally, it is easiest to assume that the planner chooses the history-contingent share of recruiters in employment $\{v(s^t)\}$ and the history-contingent recruiter-unemployment ratio $\{\theta(s^t)\}$ to maximize the household's utility

$$\sum_{t=0}^{\infty}\sum_{s^t}\beta^t\Pi(s^t)(\log(z(s^t)n(s^t)(1-v(s^t)))-\gamma n(s^t)),$$

where $n(s^t)$ is employment in history s^t and $z(s^t)n(s^t)(1-v(s^t))$ is consumption in that history, subject to the usual constraint on the evolution of employment:

$$n(s^{t+1}) = (1-x)n(s^t) + f(\theta(s^t))(1-n(s^t)),$$

where $s^{t+1} = \{s^t, s_{t+1}\}$ and where $\theta(s^t) = v(s^t)n(s^t)/(1-n(s^t))$ is the recruiter-unemployment ratio.

Taking advantage of the properties of the log function, express the objective function as

$$\sum_{t=0}^{\infty}\sum_{s^t}\beta^t\Pi(s^t)(\log(n(s^t)(1-v(s^t)))-\gamma n(s^t)) + Z(s^0),$$

where

$$Z(s^0) \equiv \sum_{t=0}^{\infty}\sum_{s^t}\beta^t\Pi(s^t)\log z(s^t)$$

is a finite constant. Note that the objective function is additively separable between the exogenous productivity process, summarized through $Z(s^0)$, and the planner's choice variables. Moreover, productivity does not appear in the constraint on the evolution of employment. It is immediate that the solution to the planner's problem is independent of $Z(s^0)$, i.e., $v(s^t)$, $\theta(s^t)$, and $n(s^t)$ do not depend on the path of productivity shocks. This proves the neutrality result for the planner's problem.

To see whether the decentralized equilibrium is socially optimal, let $W(n)$ be the value of the planner's objective function minus $Z(s^t)$, the expected present value of the sum of future $\log z(s^{t'})$:

$$W(n) \equiv \sum_{t=0}^{\infty} \sum_{s^t} \beta^t \Pi(s^t)(\log(n(s^t)(1 - v(s^t))) - \gamma n(s^t)).$$

When $\theta(s^t)$ is chosen optimally, this solves a standard Bellman equation

$$W(n) = \max_{\theta}(\log(n - \theta(1 - n)) - \gamma n + \beta W((1 - x)n + f(\theta)(1 - n))),$$

where $n - \theta(1-n) = n(1-v)$ since $v = \theta(1-n)/n$. The first term is utility from consumption, the second is disutility from work, and the third is the continuation value, which depends on the next period's employment.

The first-order and envelope conditions are

$$\frac{1}{n - \theta(1 - n)} = \beta f'(\theta) W'((1 - x)n + f(\theta)(1 - n))$$

and

$$W'(n) = \frac{1 + \theta}{n - \theta(1 - n)} - \gamma + \beta(1 - x - f(\theta)) W'((1 - x)n + f(\theta)(1 - n)).$$

In steady state, $n = (1-x)n + f(\theta)(1-n)$, and so the previous equations reduce to $\mathcal{T}^*(\bar{\theta}) = 0$, where

$$\mathcal{T}^*(\theta) = \frac{1 - \beta(1 - x - f(\theta))}{\beta f'(\theta)} - (1 + \theta) + \gamma \frac{f(\theta) - \theta x}{f(\theta) + x}.$$

Note that $\mathcal{T}^*$ is continuous in θ with $\mathcal{T}^*(0) = -1$ and that

$$\mathcal{T}^*(\tilde{\theta}) = \frac{1 - \beta}{\beta f'(\tilde{\theta})} + \left(\frac{f(\tilde{\theta})}{\tilde{\theta} f'(\tilde{\theta})} - 1\right)(1 + \tilde{\theta}) > 0,$$

where $f(\tilde{\theta})/\tilde{\theta} = x$.[5] By the intermediate-value theorem, there must exist a $\bar{\theta} \in (0, \tilde{\theta})$ such that $\mathcal{T}^*(\bar{\theta}) = 0$.

In general, the social planner's recruiter-unemployment ratio is not an equilibrium allocation, but it is under one set of conditions. Assume that $\tau = 0$, so there are no distortionary taxes, and that $\phi = 1 - \theta f'(\theta)/f(\theta)$, so workers' bargaining power is equal to the elasticity of the number of meetings with respect to the unemployment rate: the Mortensen-Hosios condition (see Hosios 1990; Mortensen 1982). One can then verify that $\mathcal{T}(\theta) = (\theta f'(\theta)/f(\theta))\mathcal{T}^*(\theta)$ in equation (2.23), so that any solution to $\mathcal{T}^*(\bar{\theta})$ also solves $\mathcal{T}(\bar{\theta}) = 0$. If the Mortensen-Hosios condition is violated (and $\tau = 0$), the equilibrium level of unemployment is inefficient.

[5] Concavity of f ensures that $f(\theta) \geqslant \theta f'(\theta)$ for all $\theta > 0$.

The relationship between the equilibrium and the solution to the social planner's problem is not purely a normative issue. Moen (1997) and Shimer (1996) consider an environment in which firms can post wage contracts in an effort to attract workers. Workers observe all the contracts and decide where to apply, trading off the probability of getting a contract $f(\theta)$ against the terms of the contract. Thus when one firm offers a relatively high wage, its recruiters are more productive. Those papers find that the allocation in a *competitive search equilibrium* without taxes solves a social planner's problem, maximizing the utility of the representative household. Establishing this result in the current environment would require a significant investment in new notation and so I omit the proof. But the point is that there are reasons to believe that a decentralized economy may achieve the planner's allocation.

2.4 Extensions

This section considers some extensions to the benchmark model. I have two objectives. First, the extensions add realism to the model. Second, they should help to clarify which of my assumptions are important for neutrality and which can be relaxed. I first allow for a nontrivial labor force participation decision; next I consider an intensive margin for hours worked; and then I briefly examine other extensions, including unemployment benefits, government spending, and a two-sector model with capital and with productivity shocks in the consumption-goods sector but not in the investment-goods sector. The neutrality result is robust to each of these extensions. Again, this section can be safely skipped without breaking the flow of the book since the material in chapters 3 and 4 does not depend directly on it.

2.4.1 Labor Force Participation

In the benchmark model, a household has no control over its employment rate, which is determined by the balance between the exogenous separation rate x and the endogenous (but exogenous to the household) job-finding rate $f(\theta(s^t))$; see equation (2.34). This section generalizes the model by giving households control over their future employment rate through the allocation of nonemployed workers between two tasks: unemployment, which allows workers to find jobs; and inactivity, which provides more leisure. This extension is interesting for two reasons. First, it shows that the neutrality result does not rely on households being passive actors in the labor market. Second, figure 1.6 shows that the employment-population ratio is somewhat more volatile than the unemployment–population ratio, so some fluctuations in employment induce workers to drop out of the labor force, rather than become unemployed. Thinking about labor force participation potentially allows the model to address this fact.

The representative household allocates total consumption following history s^t, $c(s^t)$, in order to maximize the sum of its individuals' utilities, acting as if it has a utility function

$$\sum_{t=0}^{\infty}\sum_{s^t}\beta^t\Pi(s^t)(\log c(s^t) - \gamma_n n(s^t) - \gamma_u u(s^t)), \qquad (2.50)$$

where $n(s^t)$ is the fraction of household members who are employed following history s^t and $u(s^t)$ is the fraction of household members who are unemployed. The remaining $1 - n(s^t) - u(s^t)$ household members are inactive. Implicit in this formulation, the utility of an employed household member who consumes c is $\log c - \gamma_n$; the utility of an unemployed household member who consumes c is $\log c - \gamma_u$; and the utility of an inactive household member who consumes c is $\log c$. I assume that $\gamma_u > 0$, so workers suffer some disutility from unemployment compared with the omitted third category, inactivity. In addition, it may be natural to assume that $\gamma_n \geqslant \gamma_u$, so unemployed workers enjoy more leisure than do employed workers; however, that restriction is not necessary for what follows.

The household faces a single lifetime budget constraint, identical to equation (2.33) and repeated here for convenience:

$$a_0 = \sum_{t=0}^{\infty}\sum_{s^t} q_0(s^t)(c(s^t) - (1-\tau)w(s^t)n(s^t) - T(s^t)). \qquad (2.51)$$

The household can freely move workers between unemployment and inactivity. However, workers can only find jobs by going through unemployment, which constrains employment. The probability that an unemployed worker finds a job depends only on the contemporaneous ratio of recruiters to unemployed workers, $\theta(s^t)$, while the probability that an employed worker loses her job is a constant x. Inactive workers cannot find jobs. Thus the household takes n_0 as given and recognizes that

$$n(s^{t+1}) = (1-x)n(s^t) + f(\theta(s^t))u(s^t) \qquad (2.52)$$

for any $s^{t+1} = \{s^t, s_{t+1}\}$. The household can raise its future employment rate by increasing its current unemployment rate, at the cost of higher current disutility. The household chooses a path for consumption $c(s^t)$ and unemployment $u(s^t)$ to maximize equation (2.50) subject to the budget constraint in equation (2.51) and the law of motion for employment in equation (2.52).

To express this problem recursively, let $V(s^t, a, n)$ denote the value of a household in history s^t with assets a and n employed members. This solves

$$V(s^t, a, n) = \max_{\{a(s^{t+1})\}, u \in [0, 1-n]} \Big(\log c - \gamma_n n - \gamma_u u + \beta \sum_{s^{t+1}|s^t} \frac{\Pi(s^{t+1})}{\Pi(s^t)} V(s^{t+1}, a(s^{t+1}), n') \Big), \tag{2.53}$$

with c defined by the intertemporal budget constraint,

$$c = a + (1 - \tau)w(s^t)n + T(s^t) - \sum_{s^{t+1}|s^t} q_t(s^{t+1})a(s^{t+1}),$$

and the next period's employment determined from current employment and unemployment as

$$n' = (1 - x)n + f(\theta(s^t))u.$$

As before, the first-order condition for $a(s^{t+1})$,

$$\frac{q_t(s^{t+1})}{c(s^t)} = \beta \frac{\Pi(s^{t+1})}{\Pi(s^t)} V_a(s^{t+1}, a(s^{t+1}), n(s^{t+1})),$$

and the envelope condition for $a(s^t)$,

$$V_a(s^t, a(s^t), n(s^t)) = \frac{1}{c(s^t)},$$

yield the standard Euler equation for the price of an Arrow security, equation (2.38), which is repeated here:

$$q_t(s^{t+1}) = \beta \frac{\Pi(s^{t+1})c(s^t)}{\Pi(s^t)c(s^{t+1})}. \tag{2.54}$$

Assuming an interior solution for next period's employment, so some workers are unemployed and some are inactive, the first-order condition for $u(s^t)$,

$$\gamma_u = \beta f(\theta(s^t)) \sum_{s^{t+1}|s^t} \frac{\Pi(s^{t+1})}{\Pi(s^t)} V_n(s^{t+1}, a(s^{t+1}), n(s^{t+1})),$$

and the envelope condition for $n(s^t)$,

$$V_n(s^t, a(s^t), n(s^t)) = \frac{(1 - \tau)w(s^t)}{c(s^t)} - \gamma_n + \beta(1 - x) \sum_{s^{t+1}|s^t} \frac{\Pi(s^{t+1})}{\Pi(s^t)} V_n(s^{t+1}, a(s^{t+1}), n(s^{t+1})),$$

reduce to

$$\gamma_u = \beta f(\theta(s^t)) \sum_{s^{t+1}|s^t} \frac{\Pi(s^{t+1})}{\Pi(s^t)} \left(\frac{(1-\tau)w(s^{t+1})}{c(s^{t+1})} - \gamma_n + \frac{\gamma_u(1-x)}{f(\theta(s^{t+1}))} \right). \tag{2.55}$$

The left-hand side is the current cost of switching a marginal worker from inactivity to unemployment: foregone leisure. The right-hand side is the benefit: next period, if the worker is hired, with probability $f(\theta(s^t))$, the household will earn more labor income, valued at the marginal utility of wealth $1/c(s^{t+1})$. From this, subtract the disutility of working, γ_n. Moreover, the household can offset the increase in employment at $t+1$ by reducing unemployment and increasing inactivity by enough to return the employment rate to its normal value in period $t+2$. This generates some additional leisure from additional inactivity in period $t+1$; the exact amount is given by the last term in equation (2.55).

The rest of the household's problem is unchanged; in particular, the marginal value to the household of an employed worker in a job that pays an arbitrary wage w in history s^t and then pays $w(s^\tau)$ if it survives until a continuation history s^τ is still given by equation (2.40), rewritten here as

$$\tilde{V}_n(s^t, w) = \frac{(1-\tau)(w - w(s^t))}{c(s^t)} + V_n(s^t, a(s^t), n(s^t)). \tag{2.56}$$

The firm's problem is unchanged and so the wage solves

$$(1-\tau)w(s^t) = \phi(1-\tau)z(s^t)(1+\theta(s^t)) + (1-\phi)\gamma_n c(s^t), \tag{2.57}$$

which is identical to equation (2.43) except in the notation for the marginal rate of substitution between consumption and leisure. For firms to be indifferent between current production and recruiting, it must be the case that

$$z(s^t) = \mu(\theta(s^t)) \sum_{s^{t+1}|s^t} q_t(s^{t+1})\bar{J}(s^{t+1}). \tag{2.58}$$

This ensures that the value of employing a worker is equal to the amount she produces plus the number of recruiters that she frees up times the amount they produce minus the wage:

$$\bar{J}(s^t) = z(s^t)\left(1 + \frac{1-x}{\mu(\theta(s^t))}\right) - w(s^t). \tag{2.59}$$

Finally, market clearing imposes that consumption is equal to output,

$$c(s^t) = z(s^t)n(s^t)(1 - v(s^t)), \tag{2.60}$$

and that the ratio of recruiters to unemployed workers is

$$\theta(s^t) = \frac{v(s^t)n(s^t)}{u(s^t)}. \tag{2.61}$$

As in the benchmark model, I claim that there is an equilibrium with a constant ratio of recruiters to unemployed workers, $\theta(s^t) = \bar{\theta}$, a constant share of workers in recruiting, $v(s^t) = \bar{v}$, constant employment and unemployment, $n(s^t) = \bar{n}$ and $u(s^t) = \bar{u}$, and with the wage and consumption proportional to productivity, $w(s^t) = \bar{w}z(s^t)$ and $c(s^t) = \bar{c}z(s^t)$. To prove this, observe that in such an equilibrium, equation (2.55) reduces to

$$\gamma_u = \frac{\beta f(\bar{\theta})((1-\tau)\bar{w} - \gamma_n\bar{c})}{(1-\beta(1-x))\bar{c}}, \tag{2.62}$$

while the wage equation (2.57) becomes

$$(1-\tau)\bar{w} = \phi(1-\tau)(1+\bar{\theta}) + (1-\phi)\gamma_n\bar{c}.$$

Eliminating $\bar{c}$ between these equations gives

$$\bar{w} = \frac{((1-\beta(1-x))\gamma_u + \beta f(\bar{\theta})\gamma_n)\phi(1+\bar{\theta})}{(1-\beta(1-x))\gamma_u + \beta\phi f(\bar{\theta})\gamma_n}. \tag{2.63}$$

This defines the ratio of the wage to productivity as a function of model parameters and of the ratio of recruiters to unemployed workers. To close the model, proceed as in the case without a labor force participation margin: equations (2.54), (2.58), and (2.59) imply

$$1 = \beta(1 - x + \mu(\bar{\theta})(1-\bar{w})), \tag{2.64}$$

which is identical to equation (2.48), a second relationship between the wage and the ratio of recruiters to unemployed workers. Eliminate $\bar{w}$ between these two equations to get an expression for $\bar{\theta}$ alone, $\mathcal{T}(\bar{\theta}) = 0$, where

$$\mathcal{T}(\theta) \equiv \frac{\theta(1-\beta(1-x))}{\beta f(\theta)} - 1 + \frac{((1-\beta(1-x))\gamma_u + \beta f(\theta)\gamma_n)\phi(1+\theta)}{(1-\beta(1-x))\gamma_u + \beta\phi f(\theta)\gamma_n}, \tag{2.65}$$

which is a modest variant of equation (2.23). Observe that

$$\lim_{\theta\to 0} f(\theta)/\theta = \infty,$$

implies that

$$\mathcal{T}(0) = -1 + \phi < 0.$$

At the other extreme,

$$\lim_{\theta\to\infty} f(\theta)/\theta = 0$$

implies that

$$\lim_{\theta \to \infty} \mathcal{T}(\theta) = \infty.$$

Since $\mathcal{T}$ is continuous on $(0, \infty)$, there is a solution to $\mathcal{T}(\theta) = 0$ on this interval. Moreover, each of the terms in $\mathcal{T}$ is increasing in θ, which ensures that the equilibrium is unique.

Once I have found $\bar{\theta}$, it is straightforward to recover the remaining variables of interest. Obtain $\bar{w}$ from equation (2.63) and $\bar{c}$ from equation (2.62). In the proposed equilibrium, equation (2.52) reduces to $x\bar{n} = f(\bar{\theta})\bar{u}$, while equation (2.61) becomes $\bar{\theta} = \bar{v}\bar{n}/\bar{u}$. Eliminating $\bar{n}/\bar{u}$ from the latter equation using the former gives $\bar{v} = x\bar{\theta}/f(\bar{\theta})$; this ensures that firms' hiring rate $\bar{v}\mu(\bar{\theta})$ just offsets their attrition rate x. Finally, pin down the employment level from equation (2.60), $\bar{n} = \bar{c}/(1 - \bar{v})$, and the unemployment level $\bar{u}$ from $\bar{u} = \bar{v}\bar{n}/\bar{\theta}$.

A curious property of the equilibrium is that $\bar{\theta}$, $\bar{w}$, and $\bar{v}$ are independent of the tax rate τ, while $\bar{c}$, $\bar{n}$, and $\bar{u}$ are proportional to $1 - \tau$. Raising taxes to fund lump-sum transfers discourages participation in the labor force but does not distort activities for workers who are in the labor force. More relevant to the theme of this book, this model has both equilibrium unemployment and inactivity, but neither is affected by productivity shocks.

2.4.2 Variable Hours

I now extend the model to consider an intensive margin for hours. More precisely, I assume that employed workers and firms bargain both over an hourly wage and over the number of hours worked. This ensures that the choice of hours is bilaterally efficient, so workers and firms exploit all the gains from trade. Again, the objective is twofold: to verify the robustness of the neutrality result and to allow the model to address the data along additional dimensions. Figure 1.5 shows that the correlation between detrended employment and detrended hours is 0.97, but the standard deviation of detrended hours is 1.3 times as large as the standard deviation of detrended employment. In other words, during periods when employment is high relative to trend, hours per employee is typically also above trend. For simplicity I abstract from the decision to participate in the labor market, although one could allow for both margins.

The representative household chooses a sequence for $\{c(s^t)\}$ to maximize

$$\sum_{t=0}^{\infty} \sum_{s^t} \beta^t \Pi(s^t) \left(\log c(s^t) - \frac{\gamma \varepsilon}{1 + \varepsilon} n(s^t) h(s^t)^{(1+\varepsilon)/\varepsilon} \right), \tag{2.66}$$

where $n(s^t)$ is the fraction of household members who are employed and $h(s^t)$ is the hours worked by each employed household member following history s^t. I continue to think of this as representing the sum of individual utilities, where the utility of an individual who consumes c and works h hours (possibly $h = 0$) is

$$\log c - \frac{\gamma\varepsilon}{1+\varepsilon} h^{(1+\varepsilon)/\varepsilon}.$$

The household faces a single lifetime budget constraint,

$$a_0 = \sum_{t=0}^{\infty} \sum_{s^t} q_0(s^t)(c(s^t) - (1-\tau)w(s^t)n(s^t)h(s^t) - T(s^t)), \qquad (2.67)$$

where $w(s^t)$ is the hourly wage, while its employment rate evolves exogenously according to

$$n(s^{t+1}) = (1-x)n(s^t) + f(\theta(s^t))(1-n(s^t)). \qquad (2.68)$$

Below I discuss how employed workers and firms bargain over wages and hours.

Let $V(s^t, a, n)$ denote the value of a household with assets a and n employed workers in history s^t. This solves

$$V(s^t, a, n) = \max_{\{a(s^{t+1})\}} \Bigg(\log c - \frac{\gamma\varepsilon}{1+\varepsilon} n h(s^t)^{(1+\varepsilon)/\varepsilon} + \beta \sum_{s^{t+1}|s^t} \frac{\Pi(s^{t+1})}{\Pi(s^t)} V(s^{t+1}, a(s^{t+1}), n') \Bigg), \qquad (2.69)$$

where c satisfies the intertemporal budget constraint,

$$c = a + (1-\tau)w(s^t)nh(s^t) + T(s^t) - \sum_{s^{t+1}|s^t} q_t(s^{t+1})a(s^{t+1}),$$

and next period's employment is determined from current employment and unemployment as

$$n' = (1-x)n + f(\theta(s^t))(1-n).$$

As usual, the first-order condition for next period's assets and the envelope condition for current assets yield the Euler equation:

$$q_t(s^{t+1}) = \beta \frac{\Pi(s^{t+1})c(s^t)}{\Pi(s^t)c(s^{t+1})}. \qquad (2.70)$$

The envelope condition for employment is

$$V_n(s^t, a(s^t), n(s^t)) = \frac{(1-\tau)w(s^t)h(s^t)}{c(s^t)} - \frac{\gamma\varepsilon}{1+\varepsilon}h(s^t)^{(1+\varepsilon)/\varepsilon} + \beta(1 - x - f(\theta(s^t))) \sum_{s^{t+1}|s^t} \frac{\Pi(s^{t+1})}{\Pi(s^t)} V_n(s^{t+1}, a(s^{t+1}), n(s^{t+1})), \tag{2.71}$$

which is a generalization of equation (2.39). Also let $\tilde{V}_n(s^t, w, h)$ denote the marginal value to a household with the equilibrium level of assets and employment of having a worker employed at a wage w and working h hours rather than unemployed in history s^t. If she remains employed in continuation history s^{t+1}, she earns the equilibrium wage $w(s^{t+1})$ and works the equilibrium number of hours $h(s^{t+1})$. This satisfies

$$\tilde{V}_n(s^t, w, h) = \frac{(1-\tau)(wh - w(s^t)h(s^t))}{c(s^t)} - \frac{\gamma\varepsilon}{1+\varepsilon}(h^{(1+\varepsilon)/\varepsilon} - h(s^t)^{(1+\varepsilon)/\varepsilon}) + V_n(s^t, a(s^t), n(s^t)). \tag{2.72}$$

The first term gives the after-tax income generated by a worker employed at (w, h) rather than at the equilibrium wage–hour pair $(w(s^t), h(s^t))$, evaluated in utils by multiplying by marginal utility $1/c(s^t)$. The second term gives the utility cost of the extra hours of work. The third term is the marginal value of having the worker employed at the equilibrium wage and hours rather than unemployed.

The representative firm earns profit $z(s^t)$ from each hour of labor devoted to production and recruits $\mu(\theta(s^t))$ workers with each hour of labor devoted to recruiting, where I now interpret $\theta(s^t)$ as the ratio of the number of recruiting hours to the number of unemployed workers. The firm's value in history s^0 with n_0 workers is

$$J(s^0, n_0) = \sum_{t=0}^{\infty} \sum_{s^t} q_0(s^t)(z(s^t)(n(s^t) - v(s^t)) - w(s^t)n(s^t))h(s^t), \tag{2.73}$$

where $v(s^t)$ is the number of employees devoted to recruiting in history s^t. The firm employs $n(s^t) - v(s^t)$ producers, each of whom works $h(s^t)$ hours and produces $z(s^t)$ per hour in history s^t. In addition, it pays a wage $w(s^t)$ for each hour of work. Firm growth satisfies

$$n(s^{t+1}) = v(s^t)h(s^t)\mu(\theta(s^t)) + (1-x)n(s^t), \tag{2.74}$$

where $s^{t+1} = \{s^t, s_{t+1}\}$. Each of the $v(s^t)$ recruiters works $h(s^t)$ hours and recruits $\mu(\theta(s^t))$ new workers per hour of work. In addition, a fraction $1 - x$ of the old labor force remains for another period.

As usual, the firm's value is linear in its employment rate and so its value per employee solves the recursion

$$\bar{J}(s^t) = \max_{\nu} \Big((z(s^t)(1-\nu) - w(s^t))h(s^t) + (\nu h(s^t)\mu(\theta(s^t)) + 1 - x) \sum_{s^{t+1}|s^t} q_t(s^{t+1})\bar{J}(s^{t+1}) \Big), \quad (2.75)$$

where ν is the fraction of the workforce devoted to recruiting. The condition for an interior equilibrium for recruiting is

$$z(s^t) = \mu(\theta(s^t)) \sum_{s^{t+1}|s^t} q_t(s^{t+1})\bar{J}(s^{t+1}), \quad (2.76)$$

which is unchanged from equation (2.29). If this holds, the Bellman equation (2.75) reduces to

$$\bar{J}(s^t) = z(s^t)\left(h(s^t) + \frac{1-x}{\mu(\theta(s^t))}\right) - w(s^t)h(s^t). \quad (2.77)$$

An additional employee can produce $z(s^t)h(s^t)$ units of output. In addition, with probability $1 - x$ she remains at the firm next period, so the firm can reduce the number of recruiters by $(1 - x)/h(s^t)\mu(\theta(s^t))$ while keeping its size unchanged. The workers released from recruiting instead produce $z(s^t)h(s^t)$ units of output. Finally, the worker is paid an hourly wage $w(s^t)$.

Again let $\tilde{J}_n(s^t, w, h)$ denote the marginal value to the firm of having a worker employed at an arbitrary wage w and working an arbitrary number of hours h in history s^t, and then the equilibrium wage and hours thereafter. This satisfies

$$\tilde{J}_n(s^t, w, h) = (z(s^t) - w)h - (z(s^t) - w(s^t))h(s^t) + \bar{J}(s^t). \quad (2.78)$$

This is the marginal value of an employed worker at the equilibrium wage and hours plus the additional profits from paying the worker w for h hours of work, rather than the equilibrium values $(w(s^t), h(s^t))$.

I assume that the household and firm bargain jointly over both wages and hours, so the equilibrium wage and hours satisfy the Nash bargaining solution

$$(w(s^t), h(s^t)) = \arg\max_{w,h} \tilde{V}_n(s^t, w, h)^{\phi} \tilde{J}_n(s^t, w, h)^{1-\phi}. \quad (2.79)$$

This ensures that the household and the firm agree on a Pareto-optimal division of the gains from trade.[6] Under equation (2.79), the first-order condition for wages is

$$(1-\phi)V_n(s^t,a(s^t),n(s^t))c(s^t) = \phi(1-\tau)\bar{J}(s^t), \tag{2.80}$$

which is unchanged from the model without an hours margin. The first-order condition for the choice of hours is

$$\frac{\phi(\gamma c(s^t)h(s^t)^{1/\varepsilon} - (1-\tau)w(s^t))}{V_n(s^t,a(s^t),n(s^t))c(s^t)} = \frac{(1-\phi)(z(s^t)-w(s^t))}{\bar{J}(s^t)}.$$

Solve these two equations for the choice of hours:

$$h(s^t) = \left(\frac{(1-\tau)z(s^t)}{\gamma c(s^t)}\right)^{\varepsilon}. \tag{2.81}$$

The choice of hours does not directly depend on workers' bargaining power but rather is set at a bilaterally efficient level to maximize the monetary gains from trade between a worker and a firm, $\tilde{V}_n(s^t,w,h)c(s^t) + (1-\tau)\tilde{J}_n(s^t,w,h)$. Instead, the worker and the firm use the wage to divide the gains from trade.

As in the model without hours, it is possible to solve equations (2.70), (2.71), (2.76), (2.77), and (2.80) for the equilibrium wage:

$$(1-\tau)w(s^t) = \phi(1-\tau)z(s^t)\left(1+\frac{\theta(s^t)}{h(s^t)}\right) + (1-\phi)c(s^t)\frac{\gamma\varepsilon}{1+\varepsilon}h(s^t)^{1/\varepsilon},$$

which is a generalization of equation (2.43). The after-tax hourly wage is a weighted average of the marginal product of labor—the increase in output from having an additional worker, both because of the output she produces and because of the recruiters who can be reallocated to production—and the marginal rate of substitution between consumption and leisure. Eliminating $h(s^t)$ from the last term using equation (2.81) simplifies this further:

$$w(s^t) = \left(\phi\left(1+\frac{\theta(s^t)}{h(s^t)}\right) + (1-\phi)\frac{\varepsilon}{1+\varepsilon}\right)z(s^t). \tag{2.82}$$

To close the model, I use the two market-clearing conditions: consumption is equal to output,

$$c(s^t) = z(s^t)n(s^t)h(s^t)(1-v(s^t)); \tag{2.83}$$

---

[6] One can conceive of other assumptions here. For example, the household and the firm may bargain over the wage and then the firm unilaterally sets hours. Typically this will lead to a Pareto-inefficient outcome. This alternative does not affect the main result: neutrality of productivity shocks. I focus on this assumption because it seems implausible that workers and firms who repeatedly interact would get stuck at an inefficient allocation.

and the ratio of hours of recruiters' time to unemployed workers is

$$\theta(s^t) = \frac{v(s^t)n(s^t)h(s^t)}{1 - n(s^t)}. \tag{2.84}$$

I look for an equilibrium with a constant ratio of recruiting hours to unemployed workers, $\theta(s^t) = \bar{\theta}$, a constant share of workers in recruiting, $v(s^t) = \bar{v}$, constant employment, $n(s^t) = \bar{n}$, constant hours, $h(s^t) = \bar{h}$, and with the wage and consumption proportional to productivity: $w(s^t) = \bar{w}z(s^t)$ and $c(s^t) = \bar{c}z(s^t)$. To find the six constants, use equations (2.70), (2.76), and (2.77) to prove that if such an equilibrium exists,

$$1 = \beta(1 - x + \bar{h}\mu(\bar{\theta})(1 - \bar{w})).$$

The algebra is similar to that behind equation (2.48). Then eliminate $\bar{w}$ using this expression and equation (2.82). Solving for hours gives

$$\bar{h} = \frac{1+\varepsilon}{1-\phi}\left(\frac{1-\beta(1-x)}{\beta\mu(\bar{\theta})} + \phi\bar{\theta}\right). \tag{2.85}$$

Similarly, in an equilibrium with this characterization, eliminate $\bar{c}$, $\bar{n}$, and $\bar{v}$ between the employment equation (2.68), the hours equation (2.81), the market-clearing condition in equation (2.83), and the definition of θ in equation (2.84). This gives

$$\bar{h} = \left(\frac{(1-\tau)(x + f(\bar{\theta}))}{\gamma(\mu(\bar{\theta})\bar{h} - x)\bar{\theta}}\right)^{\varepsilon}. \tag{2.86}$$

Eliminate $\bar{h}$ between equations (2.85) and (2.86) to obtain an equation for $\bar{\theta}$ alone. Write this as $\mathcal{T}(\bar{\theta}) = 0$, where

$$\mathcal{T}(\theta) = \frac{1+\varepsilon}{1-\phi}\left(\frac{1-\beta(1-x)}{\beta\mu(\theta)} + \phi\theta\right) - \left(\frac{\beta(1-\phi)(1-\tau)(x+f(\theta))}{\gamma\theta((1+\varepsilon)(1-\beta(1-x)+\beta\phi f(\theta)) - \beta(1-\phi)x)}\right)^{\varepsilon}.$$

The first term is increasing in θ, rising from 0 at $\theta = 0$ (since $\mu(0) = \infty$) to ∞ at $\theta = \infty$. The second term is decreasing in θ, since $(x + f(\theta))/\theta$ is decreasing while the rest of the denominator is nondecreasing in θ. It evaluates to ∞ at $\theta = 0$ and then drops to 0 at $\theta = \infty$. Since both terms are continuous in θ, $\mathcal{T}$ is continuous, increasing, and maps the positive real line into the real line. The equation $\mathcal{T}(\bar{\theta}) = 0$ therefore has a unique solution.

Using this solution it is straightforward to recover $\bar{h}$, $\bar{c}$, $\bar{n}$, $\bar{v}$, and $\bar{w}$ from the expressions used to construct equations (2.85)–(2.86). Since productivity shocks affect neither employment nor hours worked, I again conclude that they do not affect the measured labor wedge.

2.4.3 Other Extensions

Many other extensions fail to alter the neutrality result. I mention three here but omit the proofs, since they simply repeat the structure of the previous arguments.

First, I have assumed that unemployed workers get leisure but no monetary transfer. In reality, however, many also receive unemployment benefits. Suppose that each unemployed worker gets a benefit that is proportional to the average wage, say $\bar{b}w(s^t)$ in history s^t for some $\bar{b} \in (0,1)$. Assuming that benefits are taxed, the household budget constraint reads

$$a_0 = \sum_{t=0}^{\infty} \sum_{s^t} q_0(s^t)(c(s^t) - (1-\tau)w(s^t)(n(s^t) + \bar{b}(1-n(s^t))) - T(s^t)).$$

The government uses tax revenue to pay both benefits and transfers, with the constraint that

$$T(s^t) + (1-\tau)\bar{b}w(s^t)(1-n(s^t)) = \tau w(s^t)n(s^t).$$

I find that unemployment benefits put upward pressure on wages and so reduce recruiting and hence employment; however, the neutrality result stands.[7]

Second, I have assumed that the government rebates all of its tax revenue to households. In reality, government spending also represents a significant part of the budget. Suppose that the representative household has preferences over consumption, labor supply, and government spending $g(s^t)$,

$$\sum_{t=0}^{\infty} \sum_{s^t} \beta^t \Pi(s^t)(\log c(s^t) - \gamma n(s^t) + \psi(g(s^t))),$$

and faces the usual budget constraint, equation (2.33). The government uses tax revenue to fund both spending and lump-sum rebates:

$$T(s^t) + g(s^t) = \tau w(s^t)n(s^t).$$

The resource constraint, equation (2.44), must be modified to account for the additional use of output:

$$c(s^t) + g(s^t) = z(s^t)n(s^t)(1-\nu(s^t)).$$

If government spending is proportional to productivity, that is, if $g(s^t) = \bar{g}z(s^t)$ for all histories s^t, then the neutrality result carries over to this environment. Consumption, spending, and wages are all proportional to productivity, while employment is constant.

[7] In reality, unemployment benefits are usually indexed to past, not current, wages. This would create some nonneutrality in response to productivity shocks.

Is the assumed proportionality of government spending and productivity reasonable? It is optimal if $\psi(g) \propto \log g$, in which case the government should keep public and private spending proportional. Moreover, $g(s^t) = \bar{g}z(s^t)$ is a plausible description of how governments in fact behave. The assumption implies that government spending is also proportional to tax revenue, i.e., $g(s^t) = \tilde{g}\tau w(s^t)n(s^t)$, where $\bar{g} \equiv \tilde{g}\tau\bar{w}\bar{n}$. While this ignores the possibility of government spending shocks, it is consistent with procyclical spending induced by a balanced-budget requirement. Again, the neutrality result seems like a reasonable benchmark.

Third, I have assumed that production uses only labor. Suppose there are two types of firms or, equivalently, two production technologies that are available to all firms.[8] A capital-good producer converts $\ell_k(s^t)$ units of labor and $k_k(s^t)$ units of capital into $z_k k_k(s^t)^{\alpha_k} \ell_k(s^t)^{1-\alpha_k}$ units of capital, which it sells at a price $p(s^t)$, denominated in units of the consumption good. A consumption-good producer converts $\ell_c(s^t)$ units of labor and $k_c(s^t)$ units of capital into $z_c(s^t) k_c(s^t)^{\alpha_c} \ell_c(s^t)^{1-\alpha_c}$ units of the consumption good, with relative price 1. Both types of firms also recruit new workers, with each recruiter attracting $\mu(\theta(s^t))$ workers in the following period. Capital partially depreciates in production and capital used in history $s^{t+1} = \{s^t, s_{t+1}\}$ is purchased in history s^t.

In this environment, I find that shocks to the technology for producing the consumption good, $z_c(s^t)$, affect neither the amount of capital used nor the number of producers or recruiters in either sector. Instead, consumption, the wage, and the price of the capital good are all proportional to the productivity shock. Effectively, capital and labor are now both acquired through investment technologies—the capital production technology and the recruiting technology—that are not subject to shocks. Given the symmetry between the two technologies, it is not surprising that the neutrality result in the model with only a recruiting technology carries over to this more general model.

2.5 Discussion

Search-and-matching models help explain why there is unemployment. In the absence of unemployment, recruiting would be unproductive and wages would be high. Both forces would deter firms from putting

[8] In chapter 3 I consider a one-sector model with capital, where a single technology is used to produce both the consumption and the capital good, and find that this breaks the neutrality result. The key difference is that in the one-sector model, a temporary increase in productivity makes investment more productive and so encourages capital accumulation. This effect is absent from the two-sector model.

resources into recruiting new workers, which would push up the unemployment rate. The models that I have developed in this chapter show exactly how the equilibrium unemployment rate is determined.

But it does not follow that search-and-matching models can explain why there are fluctuations in unemployment. In the models in this chapter, the stochastic process for productivity and the realization of productivity shocks have no impact on the unemployment rate. This finding is useful for two reasons. First, it makes solving the models relatively straightforward, and in particular ensures that a closed-form solution is available. This is convenient for understanding how the model works. Second, the neutrality result provides a convenient benchmark. In the remainder of the book, I look at extensions to this model that break the neutrality result, but it will always be useful to refer back to this benchmark to understand the behavior of those more complicated models.

3
Real Effects of Productivity Shocks

I now extend the benchmark search model to study environments in which productivity shocks affect employment. The assumptions that drive the exact neutrality result in chapter 2 are special, in the sense that many modifications of the model imply that unemployment fluctuates cyclically. The modifications I consider here are based on two criteria: tractability and empirical relevance.

I start, in section 3.1, with the easiest modification of the benchmark model: an alternative formulation of preferences. More precisely, I maintain the assumption that preferences are consistent with balanced growth, but I relax the assumption that the intertemporal elasticity of substitution in consumption is equal to one, or equivalently that preferences are additively separable in consumption and leisure. If households are less willing to substitute intertemporally, then interest rates need to rise less in response to a temporary increase in productivity. This raises the profitability of recruiting new workers, so firms shift employees from production to recruiting. This behavioral response both moderates the initial consumption response and induces a prolonged rise in employment. But in a calibrated version of the model, I find that this change in preferences causes only tiny movements in employment and the labor wedge. This example is particularly easy to analyze because there is only one endogenous state variable: the level of employment. I exploit this simplicity to illustrate a method for approximating the comovements of equilibrium outcomes. Although this approach is standard, it has not been used extensively in the search-and-matching literature and may therefore be new to some readers.

In section 3.2, I reintroduce physical capital into a one-sector version of the model. This is not only a realistic assumption, it is a qualitatively important one because it gives households a savings technology. Even with the preferences in chapter 2, a temporary increase in productivity causes a smaller reduction in interest rates when households can save some of their additional income. This again raises the profitability of recruiting new workers, pulling down the unemployment rate. But in a calibrated version of the model, the response of employment and the labor wedge to productivity shocks remains very small. Moreover, I confirm the intuition that search frictions create a positive correlation between employment and the labor wedge, in contrast to the data in table 1.1. Effectively, search frictions moderate the response of employment to the shock. An economist who looked at data generated by the model, but who did not recognize the existence of the frictions, would incorrectly conclude that the labor wedge rises in booms, dampening what would otherwise be a larger increase in employment.

In section 3.3, I introduce a shock to the employment-exit probability x, which is imperfectly correlated with the productivity shock. I do this mainly for realism. Since the seminal book by Davis et al. (1996), a number of authors have stressed that the job-destruction rate rises sharply in downturns. Building on this, Mortensen and Pissarides (1994) extend the Pissarides (1985) search-and-matching model to allow for an endogenous increase in the employment-exit probability during downturns. Although I maintain the simpler assumption that the employment-exit probability is exogenous, I can still examine whether fluctuations in x significantly affect the behavior of the model. My conclusion is negative. Fluctuations in employment and the labor wedge are modest and the correlation between the two outcomes is positive, not negative as in the data. Intuitively, an increase in the employment-exit probability has little effect on the desired employment rate, but instead leads to an increase in recruiting effort as households and firms work to restore the usual level of employment. This change in the balance between recruiting and production has only a small impact on the outcomes that I study in this book.

3.1 General Preferences

I start by relaxing the assumption that the marginal utility of consumption is independent of work effort, allowing for more general balanced-growth preferences. I find that, unless the stochastic process for productivity satisfies a particular condition, productivity shocks have real effects on employment because income and substitution effects no longer cancel. To evaluate the size of these effects, I calibrate the model and linearize it around a stochastic steady state. Since I will build on this calibration and on the numerical approach throughout the remainder of the book, I describe them carefully here. I conclude that the impact of productivity shocks is quantitatively minuscule.

3.1.1 Households

Assume that the period utility function of household member i is

$$\frac{c^{1-\sigma}(1+(\sigma-1)\gamma)^{\sigma}-1}{1-\sigma}$$

if she consumes c and is employed, and

$$\frac{c^{1-\sigma}-1}{1-\sigma}$$

if she consumes c and is not employed, where $\sigma > 0$ describes the substitutability of consumption and leisure and $\gamma > 0$ describes the disutility of work. The utility function for an employed household member recalls equation (1.13), specialized to the case with indivisible labor.

A representative household maximizes the sum of utilities of its members, acting as if it has utility function

$$\sum_{t=0}^{\infty}\sum_{s^t}\beta^t \Pi(s^t)\biggl(\frac{c_{\mathrm{e}}(s^t)^{1-\sigma}(1+(\sigma-1)\gamma)^{\sigma}-1}{1-\sigma}n(s^t) + \frac{c_{\mathrm{u}}(s^t)^{1-\sigma}-1}{1-\sigma}(1-n(s^t))\biggr), \tag{3.1}$$

where $c_{\mathrm{e}}(s^t)$ is the consumption of each employed household member, $c_{\mathrm{u}}(s^t)$ is the consumption of each unemployed household member, and $n(s^t)$ is the household employment rate in history s^t.

The household faces a single lifetime budget constraint: that initial assets must be equal to the difference between the present value of consumption and the present value of after-tax labor income plus transfers,

$$a_0 = \sum_{t=0}^{\infty}\sum_{s^t} q_0(s^t)(c_{\mathrm{e}}(s^t)n(s^t) + c_{\mathrm{u}}(s^t)(1-n(s^t)) - (1-\tau)w(s^t)n(s^t) - T(s^t)). \tag{3.2}$$

The budget constraint is unchanged from that in the previous chapter, i.e., (2.33), except that a distinction is made between the consumption of the employed and the consumption of the unemployed. As before, the evolution of employment is exogenous to the household and is determined by the law of motion

$$n(s^{t+1}) = (1-x)n(s^t) + f(\theta(s^t))(1-n(s^t)) \tag{3.3}$$

for any $s^{t+1} = \{s^t, s_{t+1}\}$. This too is unchanged from equation (2.34). The household maximizes equation (3.1) subject to equation (3.2) and equation (3.3).

The new piece of this problem is the choice of the relative consumption of employed and unemployed household members. Place a multiplier λ on the lifetime budget constraint and take the first-order condition for the choice of c_e and c_u to get

$$\beta^t \Pi(s^t) c_e(s^t)^{-\sigma}(1+(\sigma-1)\gamma)^{\sigma} = \beta^t \Pi(s^t) c_u(s^t)^{-\sigma} = \lambda q_0(s^t),$$

proving that the consumption of employed workers is always proportional to the consumption of unemployed workers: $c_e(s^t)/c_u(s^t) = 1+(\sigma-1)\gamma$. Let $c(s^t) \equiv c_e(s^t)n(s^t) + c_u(s^t)(1-n(s^t))$ denote average consumption. Then

$$c_u(s^t) = \frac{c(s^t)}{1+(\sigma-1)\gamma n(s^t)} \quad \text{and} \quad c_e(s^t) = \frac{c(s^t)(1+(\sigma-1)\gamma)}{1+(\sigma-1)\gamma n(s^t)}.$$

Substituting these results into equations (3.1) and (3.2) implies that the household acts as if it has a utility function defined over average consumption $c(s^t)$ and labor supply $n(s^t)$,

$$\sum_{t=0}^{\infty}\sum_{s^t} \beta^t \Pi(s^t) \frac{c(s^t)^{1-\sigma}(1+(\sigma-1)\gamma n(s^t))^{\sigma}-1}{1-\sigma}, \tag{3.4}$$

as if it faces the same budget constraint as in the previous chapter,

$$a_0 = \sum_{t=0}^{\infty}\sum_{s^t} q_0(s^t)(c(s^t)-(1-\tau)w(s^t)n(s^t)-T(s^t)), \tag{3.5}$$

and as if it faces the same law of motion for employment, equation (3.3). Notably, household preferences over consumption and the fraction of the household that works are identical to the balanced-growth, constant-Frisch-elasticity case I studied in equation (1.13), with an infinite Frisch elasticity of labor supply.

To proceed further, write the household's problem recursively:

$$V(s^t,a,n) = \max_{\{a(s^{t+1})\}} \left(\frac{c^{1-\sigma}(1+(\sigma-1)\gamma n)^{\sigma}-1}{1-\sigma} + \beta \sum_{s^{t+1}|s^t} \frac{\Pi(s^{t+1})}{\Pi(s^t)} V(s^{t+1},a(s^{t+1}),n') \right), \tag{3.6}$$

where consumption solves the intertemporal budget constraint

$$c = a + (1-\tau)w(s^t)n + T(s^t) - \sum_{s^{t+1}|s^t} q_t(s^{t+1})a(s^{t+1}),$$

and next period's employment solves

$$n' = (1-x)n + f(\theta(s^t))(1-n).$$

Using the envelope condition for assets and the first-order condition for $a(s^{t+1})$, I obtain an expression for the price of an Arrow security:

$$q_t(s^{t+1}) = \beta \frac{\Pi(s^{t+1})}{\Pi(s^t)} \left(\frac{c(s^t)(1 + (\sigma - 1)\gamma n(s^{t+1}))}{c(s^{t+1})(1 + (\sigma - 1)\gamma n(s^t))} \right)^{\sigma}. \tag{3.7}$$

This modification of equation (2.38) recognizes that the marginal utility of consumption depends on the household's employment rate when $\sigma \neq 1$.

Next write the envelope condition for employment for a household with the equilibrium level of assets and employment:

$$\begin{aligned} V_n(s^t, a(s^t), n(s^t)) \\ = \left(\frac{c(s^t)}{1 + (\sigma - 1)\gamma n(s^t)} \right)^{-\sigma} (1 - \tau) w(s^t) - \left(\frac{c(s^t)}{1 + (\sigma - 1)\gamma n(s^t)} \right)^{1-\sigma} \sigma\gamma \\ + \beta(1 - x - f(\theta(s^t))) \sum_{s^{t+1}|s^t} \frac{\Pi(s^{t+1})}{\Pi(s^t)} V_n(s^{t+1}, a(s^{t+1}), n(s^{t+1})). \end{aligned} \tag{3.8}$$

The first term gives the increase in utility from the additional consumption afforded by having one more working household member. The second term gives the decrease in utility from the lower leisure. The third term is the continuation utility. Finally, the marginal value of having a worker employed at an arbitrary wage w this period and at the equilibrium wage thereafter satisfies

$$\begin{aligned} \tilde{V}_n(s^t, w) \\ = \left(\frac{c(s^t)}{1 + (\sigma - 1)\gamma n(s^t)} \right)^{-\sigma} (1 - \tau)(w - w(s^t)) + V_n(s^t, a(s^t), n(s^t)), \end{aligned} \tag{3.9}$$

since the marginal utility of consumption is

$$\left(\frac{c(s^t)}{1 + (\sigma - 1)\gamma n(s^t)} \right)^{-\sigma}.$$

The proof of this result follows the same logic as is behind equation (2.12).

3.1.2 Firms

The change in household preferences does not affect the firm's problem. I repeat the key equations here for convenience. First, there is an interior solution for recruiting effort if productivity is equal to the expected value of the jobs created by a recruiter:

$$z(s^t) = \mu(\theta(s^t)) \sum_{s^{t+1}|s^t} q_t(s^{t+1}) \bar{J}(s^{t+1}). \tag{3.10}$$

Second, the value of a job is equal to the worker's productivity plus the productivity of the other workers released from recruiting minus the wage:

$$\bar{J}(s^t) = z(s^t)\left(1 + \frac{1-x}{\mu(\theta(s^t))}\right) - w(s^t). \tag{3.11}$$

Finally, the marginal value of a job paying an arbitrary wage w this period and the equilibrium wage thereafter is equal to the marginal value of a job paying the equilibrium wage minus the increase in the wage $w - w(s^t)$:

$$\tilde{J}_n(s^t, w) = w(s^t) - w + \bar{J}(s^t). \tag{3.12}$$

3.1.3 Wages

As in the benchmark model, I assume that wages are determined at the start of each period by bargaining between households and firms. If they agree on a wage w following history s^t, household utility increases by $\tilde{V}_n(s^t, w)$ and the value of the job is $\tilde{J}_n(s^t, w)$. The wage $w(s^t)$ maximizes the weighted geometric average of the gains from trade:

$$w(s^t) = \arg\max_w \tilde{V}_n(s^t, w)^{\phi} \tilde{J}_n(s^t, w)^{1-\phi}, \tag{3.13}$$

where $\phi \in [0, 1]$ represents workers' bargaining power.

Take the first-order condition for w. Using equations (3.9) and (3.12) to compute $\tilde{V}_n(s^t, w)$, $\tilde{J}_n(s^t, w)$, and their derivatives with respect to w, I obtain

$$(1-\phi)V_n(s^t, a(s^t), n(s^t))\left(\frac{c(s^t)}{1 + (\sigma - 1)\gamma n(s^t)}\right)^{\sigma} = \phi(1-\tau)\bar{J}(s^t).$$

Use this to eliminate V_n from equation (3.8). Simplifying with the Euler equation (3.7) gives

$$\begin{aligned}\phi(1-\tau)\bar{J}(s^t) = (1-\phi)(1-\tau)w(s^t) - \frac{(1-\phi)\sigma\gamma c(s^t)}{1 + (\sigma-1)\gamma n(s^t)} \\ + \phi(1-\tau)(1 - x - f(\theta(s^t))) \sum_{s^{t+1}|s^t} q_t(s^{t+1})\bar{J}(s^{t+1}).\end{aligned}$$

Eliminate $\bar{J}(s^{t+1})$ using equation (3.10) and $\bar{J}(s^t)$ using equation (3.11):

$$(1-\tau)w(s^t) = \phi(1-\tau)z(s^t)(1 + \theta(s^t)) + \frac{(1-\phi)\gamma\sigma c(s^t)}{1 + (\sigma-1)\gamma n(s^t)}. \tag{3.14}$$

This is a modest generalization of equation (2.43), recognizing the more complicated expression for the marginal rate of substitution between consumption and leisure.

3.1.4 Equilibrium

The remainder of the model is unchanged. Consumption is equal to the output created by the $n(s^t)(1 - \nu(s^t))$ producers,

$$c(s^t) = z(s^t)n(s^t)(1 - \nu(s^t)), \tag{3.15}$$

and θ is the recruiter-unemployment ratio:

$$\theta(s^t) = \frac{\nu(s^t)n(s^t)}{1 - n(s^t)}. \tag{3.16}$$

In addition, the government budget constraint pins down the transfer:

$$T(s^t) = \tau w(s^t)n(s^t). \tag{3.17}$$

The notion of equilibrium is also unchanged.

3.1.5 A Special Case

Under some conditions there is an equilibrium in which productivity shocks do not affect employment. To prove this, I again look for an equilibrium with a constant ratio of recruiters to unemployed workers, $\theta(s^t) = \bar{\theta}$, a constant share of workers in recruiting, $\nu(s^t) = \bar{\nu}$, and constant employment, $n(s^t) = \bar{n}$, with the wage and aggregate consumption proportional to productivity, $w(s^t) = \bar{w}z(s^t)$ and $c(s^t) = \bar{c}z(s^t)$.

In such an equilibrium, the wage equation (3.14) reduces to

$$(1 - \tau)\bar{w} = \phi(1 - \tau)(1 + \bar{\theta}) + \frac{(1 - \phi)\gamma\sigma\bar{c}}{1 + (\sigma - 1)\gamma\bar{n}}.$$

Eliminate $\bar{c}$, $\bar{\nu}$, and $\bar{n}$ using steady-state versions of equations (3.3), (3.15), and (3.16):

$$\bar{w} = \phi(1 + \bar{\theta}) + \frac{(1 - \phi)\gamma\sigma(f(\bar{\theta}) - x\bar{\theta})}{(1 - \tau)(x + f(\bar{\theta})(1 + (\sigma - 1)\gamma))}. \tag{3.18}$$

Then substitute equation (3.11) into equation (3.10), eliminating $q_t(s^{t+1})$ using equation (3.7):

$$z(s^t)^{1-\sigma} = \beta\mu(\bar{\theta}) \sum_{s^{t+1}|s^t} \frac{\Pi(s^{t+1})}{\Pi(s^t)} z(s^{t+1})^{1-\sigma}\left(\frac{1 - x + \mu(\bar{\theta})}{\mu(\bar{\theta})} - \bar{w}\right). \tag{3.19}$$

There is an equilibrium of this form if and only if this equation is satisfied in any history s^t. That in turn requires that there exists a number $\bar{s}$ satisfying

$$e^{\bar{s}} = \left(\sum_{s^{t+1}|s^t} \frac{\Pi(s^{t+1})z(s^{t+1})^{1-\sigma}}{\Pi(s^t)z(s^t)^{1-\sigma}}\right)^{1/(1-\sigma)} \tag{3.20}$$

for all histories s^t. That is, the expected growth rate of $z^{1-\sigma}$ must be history independent. This restriction is trivially satisfied when $\sigma = 1$, the case I studied in chapter 2. It also holds whenever productivity growth is independently and identically distributed over time, so $z(s^{t+1}) = z(s^t)e^{s_{t+1}}$, where s_{t+1} is independently and identically distributed. In that case, equation (3.20) defines $\bar{s}$ so that the expected value of $e^{(1-\sigma)s_{t+1}}$ is $e^{(1-\sigma)\bar{s}}$. Otherwise the restriction is violated.

If equation (3.20) holds, eliminate $\bar{w}$ from equation (3.19) using equation (3.18). This proves that an equilibrium is characterized by $\mathcal{T}(\bar{\theta}) = 0$, where

$$\mathcal{T}(\theta) \equiv \frac{e^{-\bar{s}(1-\sigma)} - \beta(1-x)}{\beta\mu(\theta)} - 1 + \phi(1+\theta) + \frac{(1-\phi)\gamma\sigma(f(\theta) - x\theta)}{(1-\tau)(x + f(\theta)(1 + (\sigma - 1)\gamma))}. \tag{3.21}$$

This generalizes equation (2.23) to the case where preferences are not separable between consumption and leisure. However, the generalization only works under a particular joint restriction on preferences and on the stochastic process for productivity.

3.1.6 Productivity and Unemployment

Even when equation (3.20) holds, the productivity growth rate affects the employment rate. For example, suppose $\sigma = 0$, so workers are risk neutral. Also assume that productivity follows a geometric random walk, so the growth rate of productivity is independently and identically distributed over time, with expectation $\bar{s}$. An equilibrium is then characterized by a zero of $\mathcal{T}$, which reduces to

$$\mathcal{T}(\theta) = \frac{e^{-\bar{s}} - \beta(1-x)}{\beta\mu(\theta)} - 1 + \phi(1+\theta).$$

In this case $\mathcal{T}$ is increasing in θ, ensuring that there is a unique equilibrium. Moreover, it is decreasing in $\bar{s}$. It follows that higher productivity growth raises the ratio of recruiting effort to unemployment and hence lowers unemployment. To understand this result, think of the related social planner's problem, where the planner's objective is maximizing workers' utility. Since the intertemporal elasticity of substitution in consumption is infinite when $\sigma = 0$, the planner does not much mind delaying consumption to take advantage of future productivity growth. He does this by putting more workers into recruiting. In the decentralized economy, the intertemporal price $q_t(s^{t+1})$ does not depend on consumption growth when $\sigma = 0$ (equation (3.7)). Then faster productivity growth raises the value of a job next period and encourages firms to recruit more workers today (equation (3.10)).

To proceed further, I calibrate the parameters of the model. I spend some time here discussing the choice of parameters because I use them throughout the remainder of the book. First it is necessary to set the length of a time period. Unemployment duration in the United States is typically quite short, with most unemployed workers managing to find a job within one quarter. To avoid a corner solution for workers' matching probability $f(\theta)$, I think of a time period as being one month. I set the discount factor at $\beta = 0.996$, just under five percent annually. The Bureau of Labor Statistics measures multifactor productivity growth annually. I fix the productivity growth rate at $\bar{s} = 0.0012$, about 1.4 percent per year, consistent with the annual measures of multifactor productivity growth in the private business sector constructed by the Bureau of Labor Statistics.[1] I fix the tax rate at $\tau = 0.4$, which is the average marginal rate constructed by Prescott (2004).

I turn next to the parameters that determine flows between employment and unemployment. In Shimer (2005), I measure the average exit probability from employment to unemployment in the United States at $x = 0.034$ per month and I stick with that number here for comparability. Although there are many estimates of the matching function f in the literature (see the survey by Petrongolo and Pissarides (2001)), most papers assume that firms create job vacancies in order to attract workers and so estimate matching functions using data on unemployment and vacancies. The technology in this paper is slightly different, with firms using workers to recruit workers. Unfortunately, there is no good time series showing the number of workers (or hours of work) devoted to recruiting, and so the choice of f is somewhat arbitrary. Still, following much of the search-and-matching literature, I focus on an isoelastic function, $f(\theta) = \bar{\mu}\theta^{\eta}$, and look at the symmetric case, $\eta = 0.5$.[2]

To pin down the efficiency parameter in the matching function $\bar{\mu}$, I build on evidence in Hagedorn and Manovskii (2008) and Silva and Toledo (2009). Those papers argue that recruiting a worker uses approximately four percent of one worker's quarterly wage, i.e., a recruiter can attract approximately twenty-five new workers in a quarter, or 8.33 in a month. Using this and the fact that the unemployment rate in the United

[1] See ftp://ftp.bls.gov/pub/special.requests/opt/mp/prod3.mfptablehis.zip, table 4. Between 1948 and 2007, productivity grew by 0.818 log points, or approximately 0.014 log points per year.

[2] Formally, I assume that $f(\theta) = \min\{\bar{\mu}\theta^{\eta}, 1\}$ to ensure that it is a proper probability. In steady state $f(\theta) < 1$ and so when I linearize around the steady state, the constraint $f(\theta) \leqslant 1$ is not binding.

States was five percent on average during the postwar period, I determine $\bar{\mu}$. I proceed in several steps. First, from equation (3.3), the steady-state employment rate satisfies

$$n = \frac{f(\theta)}{x + f(\theta)}.$$

Setting $n = 0.95$ and $x = 0.034$ implies that $f(\theta) = 0.646$ in steady state. Second, the functional form $f(\theta) = \bar{\mu}\theta^{\eta}$ implies that

$$\bar{\mu} = \frac{f(\theta)}{\theta^{\eta}} = f(\theta)^{1-\eta}\mu(\theta)^{\eta},$$

where the second equation follows because $\mu(\theta) \equiv f(\theta)/\theta$. From this equation, I set $\bar{\mu} = 2.32$, consistent with $f(\theta) = 0.646$, $\mu(\theta) = 8.33$, and $\eta = \frac{1}{2}$. Note that this implies that the recruiter-unemployment ratio is $\theta = f(\theta)/\mu(\theta) \approx 0.078$. Using equation (3.16), the share of recruiters in employment is $v = \theta(1-n)/n \approx 0.004$, with 99.6 percent of employees devoted to production. Thus in this calibration, the implicit hiring costs are small, at least on average.

Finally, I turn to bargaining and preference parameters. I impose symmetry in the bargaining problem, $\phi = 0.5$. This assumption is important, and so I discuss the implications of other choices for ϕ in various places throughout the book. I set the preference parameter governing consumption-labor complementarities at $\sigma = 2$, consistent with a moderate difference between the consumption of the employed and nonemployed (see section 1.4). Finally, I set the parameter governing the taste for leisure to match a five percent unemployment rate along the balanced-growth path; this imposes $\gamma \approx 0.399$. This last parameter is obviously sensitive to the extent of consumption-labor complementarity. Table 3.1 summarizes these parameter choices. Note that the last two rows are irrelevant with deterministic productivity growth.

I use the calibrated model to examine how responsive the unemployment rate is to steady-state growth. Consider an economy with the same parameters but $\bar{s} = 0.01$, i.e., twelve percent annual growth, a rate normally associated with a growth miracle. Because the income effect outweighs the substitution effect when $\sigma > 1$, expectations of higher future growth raises interest rates by enough to discourage firms from recruiting, raising current production and the unemployment rate. Quantitatively, however, this effect is trivial. In steady state, the unemployment rate rises from 5 to 5.05 percent as a result of this enormous change in productivity growth. Changes in other parameters do not much alter this conclusion. For example, set the complementarity parameter at $\sigma = 4$

Table 3.1. Calibrated parameter values with consumption–labor complementarities.

Parameter	Value
Discount factor β	0.996
Mean productivity growth $\bar{s}$	0.0012
Tax rate τ	0.4
Employment-exit probability x	0.034
Matching function $f(\theta)$	$2.32\theta^{0.5}$
Workers' bargaining power ϕ	0.5
Consumption–labor complementarity σ	2
Disutility of work γ	0.399
Autocorrelation of productivity growth ρ	0.4
Standard deviation of productivity growth ς	0.00325

and recalibrate the disutility of work to have a five percent unemployment rate. One percent monthly productivity growth raises the unemployment rate to 5.16 percent. At the other extreme, with $\sigma \to 0$ and γ again recalibrated, the unemployment rate remains at five percent when growth increases to one percent per month.

3.1.7 Productivity Shocks

In general, comparative statics need not be informative about how the economy responds to shocks. I therefore next examine the behavior of the model when productivity growth is stochastic. To be concrete, I assume that productivity has a stochastic trend,

$$\log z(s^{t+1}) = \log z(s^t) + s_{t+1},$$

where $s^{t+1} = \{s^t, s_{t+1}\}$ and productivity growth s_t follows a first-order Markov process: $\Pi(s^{t+1})/\Pi(s^t) = \pi(s_{t+1}|s_t)$ is the probability of state s_{t+1} next period conditional on state s_t this period. If productivity growth is serially correlated, so that the distribution of s_{t+1} in fact depends on s_t, then the restriction in equation (3.20) fails. In this case, the recruiter–unemployment ratio and employment vary with the state of the economy. I establish how by solving the model numerically in a neighborhood of a balanced-growth path.

One might alternatively assume that productivity has a deterministic trend, $\log z(s^t) = \bar{s}t + s_t$, where s_t follows a stationary first-order Markov process with mean 0 and where $\bar{s}$ is trend productivity growth. This structure is common to much of the RBC literature since Kydland and Prescott (1982). The results are similar and so I omit them for the sake of brevity; however, in the remainder of the book I compare the behavior of economies with deterministic and stochastic trends.

To describe the equilibrium, I find a pair of stationary equations that implicitly define how employment and the recruiter-unemployment ratio depend on productivity growth. Substitute equation (3.15) for $c(s^t)$ into equation (3.14) and write the wage relative to productivity as

$$\frac{w(s^t)}{z(s^t)} = \phi(1 + \theta(s^t)) + \frac{(1-\phi)\gamma\sigma n(s^t)(1-\nu(s^t))}{(1-\tau)(1+(\sigma-1)\gamma n(s^t))}. \tag{3.22}$$

Then substitute equation (3.11) into equation (3.10), eliminating $q_t(s^{t+1})$ using equation (3.7) and $c(s^t)$ and $c(s^{t+1})$ using equation (3.15). Since, by assumption, $z(s^{t+1})/z(s^t) = \mathrm{e}^{s_{t+1}}$,

$$\begin{aligned} 1 = \beta\mu(\theta(s^t)) \sum_{s^{t+1}|s^t} &\pi(s_{t+1}|s_t)\mathrm{e}^{s_{t+1}(1-\sigma)} \\ &\times \left(\frac{n(s^t)(1-\nu(s^t))(1+(\sigma-1)\gamma n(s^{t+1}))}{n(s^{t+1})(1-\nu(s^{t+1}))(1+(\sigma-1)\gamma n(s^t))}\right)^{\sigma} \\ &\times \left(1 + \frac{1-x}{\mu(\theta(s^{t+1}))} - \frac{w(s^{t+1})}{z(s^{t+1})}\right). \end{aligned} \tag{3.23}$$

Eliminate $w(s^{t+1})/z(s^{t+1})$ using equation (3.22). Finally, both $\nu(s^t)$ and $\nu(s^{t+1})$ are determined from equation (3.16) as

$$\nu(s^t) = \frac{\theta(s^t)(1-n(s^t))}{n(s^t)} \quad \text{and} \quad \nu(s^{t+1}) = \frac{\theta(s^{t+1})(1-n(s^{t+1}))}{n(s^{t+1})}, \tag{3.24}$$

while $n(s^{t+1})$ satisfies equation (3.3). After making the various substitutions, I obtain an equation relating current and future values of θ and n to current and future values of productivity growth:

$$\begin{aligned} 1 = \beta\mu(\theta(s^t)) \sum_{s^{t+1}|s^t} &\pi(s_{t+1}|s_t)\mathrm{e}^{s_{t+1}(1-\sigma)} \\ &\times \left(\frac{(n(s^t)-\theta(s^t)(1-n(s^t)))(1+(\sigma-1)\gamma n(s^{t+1}))}{(n(s^{t+1})-\theta(s^{t+1})(1-n(s^{t+1})))(1+(\sigma-1)\gamma n(s^t))}\right)^{\sigma} \\ &\times \left(1 + \frac{1-x}{\mu(\theta(s^{t+1}))} - \phi(1+\theta(s^{t+1})) \right. \\ &\left. \quad - \frac{(1-\phi)\gamma\sigma(n(s^{t+1})-\theta(s^{t+1})(1-n(s^{t+1})))}{(1-\tau)(1+(\sigma-1)\gamma n(s^{t+1}))}\right). \end{aligned} \tag{3.25}$$

I close the model using the law of motion for employment in equation (3.3), which also relates current θ and n to future n.

Equations (3.3) and (3.25) define the recruiter-unemployment ratio and employment as functions of the history of shocks. However, past shocks directly enter the equations only through the current level of productivity growth s_t, which in turn affects the distribution of next period's productivity growth s_{t+1}. This motivates me to look for a solution to these equations in which the recruiter–unemployment ratio depends only on the current productivity growth rate and current employment: $\theta(s^t) = \Theta(s_t, n(s^t))$, say. Substitute this conjecture and equation (3.3) into equation (3.25) to obtain an equation of the form

$$\mathcal{T}(\theta(s^t), s_t, n(s^t)) = 0. \tag{3.26}$$

The functional form of $\mathcal{T}$ is messy, so I do not write it out explicitly. The point is that a solution to this functional equation describes an equilibrium. Note that in such an equilibrium, employment depends only on lagged productivity growth and lagged employment, $n(s^{t+1}) = N(s_t, n(s^t))$.

Unfortunately, I cannot solve equation (3.26) exactly. Instead, I approximate the dynamics of the model in a neighborhood of the stochastic steady state. I assume that

$$s_{t+1} = \bar{s} + \rho(s_t - \bar{s}) + \varsigma v_{t+1}, \tag{3.27}$$

where v is a white-noise innovation with mean 0 and standard deviation 1 and ς is therefore the standard deviation of the productivity shock, while $\rho \in (0, 1)$ is its autocorrelation. I then look for a log-linear approximation to the policy function $\Theta(s, n)$:

$$\log \theta = \log \bar{\theta} + \theta_s(s - \bar{s}) + \theta_n(\log n - \log \bar{n}). \tag{3.28}$$

The parameter $\bar{\theta}$ is the recruiter–unemployment ratio in the stochastic steady state, while θ_s represents the elasticity of the recruiter–unemployment ratio with respect to productivity growth and θ_n represents the corresponding elasticity with respect to current employment. To find these elasticities, eliminate $\theta(s^t)$ from equation (3.26) using equation (3.28):

$$\mathcal{T}(\bar{\theta} \exp(\theta_s(s - \bar{s}) + \theta_n(\log n - \log \bar{n})), s, n) = 0. \tag{3.29}$$

I impose that $\mathcal{T}(\bar{\theta}, \bar{s}, \bar{n}) = 0$ and that the derivatives of $\mathcal{T}$ with respect to s and n are zero at the steady state as well. Together with the equation for the steady-state employment rate, $\bar{n} = f(\bar{\theta})/(x + f(\bar{\theta}))$, this pins down the four unknowns $\bar{n}$, $\bar{\theta}$, θ_s, and θ_n.[3]

[3]More precisely, I fix $\bar{n} = 0.95$ and treat the disutility of work γ as an unknown parameter.

Calibration

Compared with the deterministic model, there are two new parameters: the autocorrelation and standard deviation of shocks to the productivity growth rate. I again pin these down using annual measures of multifactor productivity growth in the private business sector. The unconditional standard deviation of annual productivity growth is 0.0180, while the annual autocorrelation is 0.043, barely positive. Because of time aggregation, determining these as functions of the monthly productivity growth process takes a bit of algebra.[4]

To start, let s_{+t} denote the t-periods-ahead value of productivity growth when current productivity growth is s. We first use equation (3.27) to compute the unconditional variance of productivity growth s:

$$\mathbb{E}(s_{+1}-\bar{s})^2 = \mathbb{E}(\rho(s-\bar{s})+\varsigma \upsilon_{+1})^2 = \rho^2\mathbb{E}(s-\bar{s})^2+2\rho\varsigma\mathbb{E}(s-\bar{s})\upsilon_{+1}+\varsigma^2\mathbb{E}\upsilon_{+1}^2.$$

Because productivity shocks are independent over time, $\mathbb{E}(s-\bar{s})\upsilon_{+1} = 0$. They have a unit variance, so $\mathbb{E}\upsilon_{+1}^2 = 1$. The unconditional expectation of the variance of productivity growth then satisfies

$$\mathbb{E}(s_{+1}-\bar{s})^2 = \mathbb{E}(s-\bar{s})^2 = \frac{\varsigma^2}{1-\rho^2}.$$

This is a standard formula for the variance of a linear first-order autoregressive process, but the construction of the more complicated expressions that follow use a similar logic.[5]

Repeated substitution for s_{+t} using equation (3.27) gives

$$s_{+t} = \bar{s} + \rho^t(s-\bar{s}) + \varsigma \sum_{t'=1}^{t} \rho^{t-t'}\upsilon_{+t'},$$

where s is the current value of productivity growth. The unconditional variance of annual productivity growth is then

$$\mathbb{E}\Bigg(\sum_{t=0}^{11}(s_{+t}-\bar{s})\Bigg)^2 = \mathbb{E}\Bigg(\sum_{t=0}^{11}\Bigg(\rho^t(s-\bar{s}) + \varsigma\sum_{t'=1}^{t}\rho^{t-t'}\upsilon_{+t'}\Bigg)\Bigg)^2.$$

Expand all the terms in the summation. Most are zero because productivity shocks are independent over time: $\mathbb{E}\upsilon_{+t}\upsilon_{+t'} = \mathbb{E}(s-\bar{s})\upsilon_{+t} = 0$ for all $t' \neq t > 0$. Moreover, the shock has unit variance, $\mathbb{E}(\upsilon_{+t}\upsilon_{+t}) = 1$,

[4] A naive calculation might suggest a correlation of ρ^{12} between productivity growth in consecutive years, since ρ is the monthly autocorrelation. This is incorrect because it ignores the comparatively high correlation between growth rates in December of one year and January of the next year. The formulas that follow explicitly account for this.

[5] For a thorough treatment of stochastic linear difference equations, see Ljungqvist and Sargent (2004, section 2.4).

while the previous paragraph gives an expression for the unconditional variance of the productivity growth s. After some algebra, I find

$$\mathbb{E}\left(\sum_{t=0}^{11}(s_{+t}-\bar{s})\right)^2 = \left(12+\sum_{t=1}^{11}2(12-t)\rho^t\right)\frac{\varsigma^2}{1-\rho^2}.$$

A similar logic implies that the unconditional covariance of productivity growth in consecutive years is

$$\mathbb{E}\left(\sum_{t=0}^{11}(s_{+t}-\bar{s})\right)\left(\sum_{t=12}^{23}(s_{+t}-\bar{s})\right) = \rho\left(\sum_{t=0}^{11}\rho^t\right)^2\frac{\varsigma^2}{1-\rho^2}.$$

Finally, the ratio of the covariance to the variance gives the unconditional correlation between productivity growth in consecutive years:

$$\frac{\mathbb{E}(\sum_{t=0}^{11}(s_{+t}-\bar{s}))(\sum_{t=12}^{23}(s_{+t}-\bar{s}))}{\mathbb{E}(\sum_{t=0}^{11}(s_{+t}-\bar{s}))^2} = \frac{\rho(\sum_{t=0}^{11}\rho^t)^2}{12+\sum_{t=1}^{11}2(12-t)\rho^t}.$$

One can verify that this is always larger than the naive value of ρ^{12}, and in practice the difference can be substantial.

Using this expression and the target annual autocorrelation of 0.043, I pin down $\rho = 0.4$. I then use the expression for the unconditional variance and the target for the standard deviation of annual productivity growth, 0.0180, to pin down $\varsigma = 0.00325$. I leave the remaining parameters unchanged at their values in table 3.1.

Solution

With these parameter values I solve the log-linearized system and find that

$$\log\theta = -2.557 - 0.779(s-0.0012) + 0.228(\log n - \log 0.95),$$

which describes how the current recruiter-unemployment ratio depends on current productivity and employment. Since consumption and leisure are substitutes, higher productivity encourages firms to produce rather than recruit, reducing future employment. Note that for these parameters, higher employment also raises the recruiter-unemployment ratio; this happens only with sufficiently high values of the substitutability parameter σ. When more workers are employed, firms put more workers into recruiting, which mitigates the rise in current production and hence consumption but raises future employment and consumption. This takes advantage of the substitutability between consumption and leisure in preferences.

Using the expression for θ, I then log-linearize equation (3.3) to characterize employment next period as a function of current productivity and employment:

$$\log n_{+1} = \log 0.95 - 0.013(s - 0.0012) + 0.324(\log n - \log 0.95).$$

Finally, I use equation (3.27) to write next period's productivity as

$$s_{+1} = 0.0012 + 0.4(s - 0.0012) + 0.00325 \upsilon_{+1}.$$

These last two equations are a linear dynamic system. A key issue is their stability. That is, if productivity and employment start away from their steady-state values, do they tend to return to them? To answer this, let $m \equiv \{s - \bar{s}, \log n - \log \bar{n}\}$ denote the state of the economy. Represent the transitional dynamics as $m_{+1} = Am + D\upsilon_{+1}$, where A is a 2×2 transition matrix. Am is the expected value of m_{+1} conditional on m and D determines how the shock υ_{+1} affects the state of the system. For this choice of parameters,

$$A = \begin{pmatrix} 0.4 & 0 \\ -0.013 & 0.324 \end{pmatrix} \quad \text{and} \quad D = \begin{pmatrix} \varsigma \\ 0 \end{pmatrix},$$

where ς is the standard deviation of the innovation to the productivity process and the 0 in the second entry for D indicates that productivity shocks have no direct effect on employment.

The dynamic system is locally stable, converging toward the steady state from any nearby value of $m = \{s - \bar{s}, \log n - \log \bar{n}\}$, if and only if the eigenvalues of A all lie between -1 and 1. Given the triangular structure of the transition matrix, the eigenvalues are just the diagonal elements, 0.4 and 0.324, and so the system is in fact locally stable. Moreover, the size of the eigenvalues tells us about the speed of convergence. The larger eigenvalue, 0.4, is associated with the adjustment of productivity growth back to its normal level. The smaller eigenvalue, 0.324, is associated with the slightly faster adjustment of employment. This indicates that if productivity is at its normal value but employment is not, sixty-eight percent of the deviation of employment from steady state is wiped out within a month. This finding of fast employment adjustment dynamics is endemic in the search-and-matching literature. A number of authors have modified the model in an effort to explain why the unemployment rate is in fact quite persistent (see Cole and Rogerson 1999; Hall 1995; Pries 2004), but I do not pursue that route in this book.

Next I compute the unconditional variance and covariance of the state variables, $\Sigma \equiv \mathbb{E}(mm')$. Since this is an unconditional variance-covariance matrix, the expected value of $m_{+1}m'_{+1}$ is also Σ. Then, using

$m_{+1} = Am + Dv_{+1}$, I obtain

$$\Sigma = \mathbb{E}(m_{+1}m'_{+1}) = \mathbb{E}((Am + Dv_{+1})(m'A' + v'_{+1}D')) = A\Sigma A' + DD',$$

where the last equality uses the fact that v_{+1} is a shock and is hence orthogonal to m, $\mathbb{E}(mv'_{+1}) = \mathbb{E}(vm'_{+1}) = 0$, and has unit variance, $\mathbb{E}(v_{+1}v'_{+1}) = 1$. This equation is easily solved numerically for Σ:

$$\Sigma = \begin{pmatrix} 1.1905 & -0.0072 \\ -0.0072 & 0.0003 \end{pmatrix} \varsigma^2.$$

In particular, the unconditional standard deviation of employment is $\sqrt{0.0003}\varsigma = 0.00006$, a tiny number.

With a larger value of the complementarity parameter, $\sigma = 4$, the response of employment is bigger but still quantitatively unimpressive. The policy function becomes

$$\log\theta = -2.557 - 2.297(s - 0.0012) + 1.884(\log n - \log 0.95),$$

and the state equation is

$$\log n_{+1} = \log 0.95 - 0.039(s - 0.0012) + 0.352(\log n - \log 0.95).$$

The unconditional standard deviation of employment is now 4.8 percent of the unconditional standard deviation of monthly productivity growth. While this is about three times larger than before, it is still a tiny number and it relies on an implausibly strong complementarity between consumption and leisure.

Finally, I can compute the labor wedge. Imagine an economist who ignores the existence of labor market frictions and so measures the wedge between the marginal rate of substitution of consumption for leisure and the marginal product of labor using equation (1.14). He fixes the average labor wedge at $\hat{\tau} = 0.4$, sets the capital share of income at $\alpha = 0$, and recognizes that the Frisch elasticity of labor supply is $\varepsilon = \infty$ and that the parameter governing the substitutability of consumption and leisure is $\sigma = 2$. Then, using employment data, with the employment rate averaging $\bar{n} = 0.95$, he measures the labor wedge in period t as

$$\hat{\tau}(s^t) = 1 - \frac{\hat{\gamma}\sigma n(s^t)}{1 + (\sigma - 1)\hat{\gamma}n(s^t)}, \tag{3.30}$$

so, ignoring Jensen's inequality, the average labor wedge satisfies

$$\hat{\tau} = 1 - \frac{\hat{\gamma}\sigma\bar{n}}{1 + (\sigma - 1)\hat{\gamma}\bar{n}}.$$

He would solve this equation for the disutility of work and conclude that $\hat{\gamma} = 0.451$, which is higher than the true value of $\gamma = 0.399$. This is because he fails to realize that workers are unemployed not only because they have a taste for leisure but also because of search frictions.

The economist would also uncover movements in the labor wedge that are negatively correlated with the employment rate, as in the data. However, the size of these movements would be small. To see this, log-linearize $\hat{\tau}$ around the stochastic steady state. From equation (3.30),

$$\log \hat{\tau} = \log 0.4 - 1.050(\log n - \log 0.95).$$

The economist would conclude that whenever employment is above its normal level, the labor wedge is roughly the same proportion below its normal level. This is broadly consistent with the evidence in table 1.1 when the elasticity of labor supply is infinite. Still, the fact that the model yields only very small movements in the employment rate implies that it yields equally small movements in the labor wedge. Both of these findings are inconsistent with the data. The search model with substitutability between consumption and leisure is a quantitative failure at explaining the behavior of the employment rate and the labor wedge.

3.2 Capital

I now reintroduce productive capital—and shocks to the production technology of the capital good—into the model. In the benchmark search model in chapter 2, the economy can smooth shocks to the production technology only by changing the allocation of workers between recruiting and production. Since the productivity of the recruiting technology is constant, a temporary improvement in the efficiency of the production technology induces offsetting effects: on the one hand, it is a good time to produce rather than recruit; on the other hand, the marginal utility of consumption is low, encouraging firms to defer production. With the preferences in equation (2.32), these effects cancel and recruiting is therefore acyclic. With the more general preferences in equation (3.1), they do not quite cancel, but the previous section showed that recruiting was still nearly constant.

Capital accumulation, like recruiting, is an investment. The key difference between the two types of investment is that it is reasonable to assume that shocks to the technology for producing the consumption good do not affect the efficiency of the recruiting technology; however, many shocks that improve the efficiency of producing the consumption good are likely to also improve the efficiency of producing the investment good. This implies that when the productivity is high, it is a good time to produce investment goods. This endogenous propagation mechanism has been well understood since the advent of the RBC model (Kydland and Prescott 1982), but is neglected in any business cycle model without capital.[6]

3.2.1 Households

The household's problem is unchanged from section 2.2, i.e., it is still the model with logarithmic utility over consumption and separability between consumption and leisure. To keep the analysis as brief as possible, I only mention the three main results: the Euler equation,

$$q_t(s^{t+1}) = \beta \frac{\Pi(s^{t+1})c(s^t)}{\Pi(s^t)c(s^{t+1})}; \tag{3.31}$$

the marginal value of an employed household member,

$$\begin{aligned} V_n(s^t, a(s^t), n(s^t)) &= \frac{(1-\tau)w(s^t)}{c(s^t)} - \gamma \\ &\quad + \beta(1 - x - f(\theta(s^t))) \sum_{s^{t+1}|s^t} \frac{\Pi(s^{t+1})}{\Pi(s^t)} V_n(s^{t+1}, a(s^{t+1}), n(s^{t+1})); \end{aligned} \tag{3.32}$$

and the marginal value of having a worker employed in a job that pays an arbitrary wage w in history s^t and the equilibrium wage thereafter,

$$\tilde{V}_n(s^t, w) = \frac{(1-\tau)(w - w(s^t))}{c(s^t)} + V_n(s^t, a(s^t), n(s^t)). \tag{3.33}$$

I omit the derivation of these results because they do not depend on whether there is capital in the economy; see section 2.2.2 for details.

3.2.2 Firms

I start by describing the firm's problem verbally. A representative firm employs $n_0 = n(s^0)$ workers and owns capital $k_0 = k(s^0)$ at time 0. In history s^t, it assigns a fraction $\nu(s^t)$ of its $n(s^t)$ workers to recruiting and the remaining $n(s^t)(1-\nu(s^t))$ workers to production. The producers use the capital $k(s^t)$ to generate $z(s^t)k(s^t)^\alpha(n(s^t)(1-\nu(s^t)))^{1-\alpha}$ units of a single good that is used both for consumption and for investment. A fraction δ of the capital depreciates during production. The recruiters each attract $\mu(\theta(s^t))$ workers to the firm, while a fraction x of the workers leave the firm, thus determining $n(s^{t+1})$. Finally, the firm can freely

[6] It is also ignored in a model with a separate technology for producing the consumption good and the investment good, as in section 2.4.3.

buy or sell capital in history s^t, determining $k(s^{t+1})$. Because there is a single technology for producing the capital and consumption goods, the relative price of the capital good is always equal to 1.

More formally, the present value of the firm's profits is given by

$$J(s^0, n_0, k_0) = \sum_{t=0}^{\infty} \sum_{s^t} q_0(s^t)(z(s^t)k(s^t)^{\alpha}(n(s^t)(1 - v(s^t)))^{1-\alpha} + (1-\delta)k(s^t) - k(s^{t+1}) - w(s^t)n(s^t)), \quad (3.34)$$

where firm growth satisfies

$$n(s^{t+1}) = n(s^t)(v(s^t)\mu(\theta(s^t)) + 1 - x). \quad (3.35)$$

This extends equation (1.4) to recognize that in the search-and-matching model, the level of employment is a state variable in the firm's problem. Note that $k(s^{t+1})$ and $n(s^{t+1})$, the capital stock and the total workforce in history s^{t+1}, are determined in the prior history s^t. This implies that $k(\{s^t, s_{t+1}\}) = k(\{s^t, s'_{t+1}\})$ and $n(\{s^t, s_{t+1}\}) = n(\{s^t, s'_{t+1}\})$ for all s^t, s_{t+1}, and s'_{t+1}.

To characterize the firm's behavior, let $J(s^t, n, k)$ denote the value of a firm that starts history s^t with n workers and k units of capital. This solves the recursive equation

$$J(s^t, n, k) = \max_{v,k'} \Big(z(s^t)k^{\alpha}(n(1-v))^{1-\alpha} + (1-\delta)k - k' - nw(s^t) + \sum_{s^{t+1}|s^t} q_t(s^{t+1})J(s^{t+1}, n(v\mu(\theta(s^t)) + 1 - x), k') \Big). \quad (3.36)$$

In each period, the firm chooses the fraction of its workforce that is assigned to be recruiters and its capital stock next period in order to maximize current revenue net of investment costs and labor costs plus the expected continuation value of the firm.

Assuming an interior solution for the share of recruiters v, I obtain the first-order condition

$$(1-\alpha)z(s^t)\left(\frac{k(s^t)}{n(s^t)(1-v(s^t))}\right)^{\alpha} = \mu(\theta(s^t)) \sum_{s^{t+1}|s^t} q_t(s^{t+1})J_n(s^{t+1}, n(s^{t+1}), k(s^{t+1})). \quad (3.37)$$

The left-hand side is the marginal product of a producer. The right-hand side is the expected value of the additional workers attracted by a recruiter. Additionally, we can write the envelope condition for employment as

$$J_n(s^t, n(s^t), k(s^t))$$
$$= (1-\alpha)z(s^t)\left(\frac{k(s^t)}{n(s^t)(1-v(s^t))}\right)^{\alpha}(1-v(s^t)) - w(s^t)$$
$$+ (v(s^t)\mu(\theta(s^t)) + 1 - x) \sum_{s^{t+1}|s^t} q_t(s^{t+1}) J_n(s^{t+1}, n(s^{t+1}), k(s^{t+1})).$$

Eliminate the continuation value using equation (3.37) to obtain

$$J_n(s^t, n(s^t), k(s^t))$$
$$= (1-\alpha)z(s^t)\left(\frac{k(s^t)}{n(s^t)(1-v(s^t))}\right)^{\alpha}\left(1 + \frac{1-x}{\mu(\theta(s^t))}\right) - w(s^t). \quad (3.38)$$

This extends equation (2.30) to an environment where the marginal product of labor depends on the capital-producer ratio. As before, the term $1 + (1-x)/\mu(\theta(s^t))$ recognizes that when a firm employs an additional worker, this raises current output directly and also raises output because the firm can afford to move workers from recruiting to production this period, while keeping the same size next period.

Next turn to the first-order condition for next period's capital stock. From equation (3.36),

$$1 = \sum_{s^{t+1}|s^t} q_t(s^{t+1}) J_k(s^{t+1}, n(s^{t+1}), k(s^{t+1})).$$

Purchasing a unit of capital reduces current profit by 1. This must equal the increase in the continuation value of the firm. The envelope condition for capital is

$$J_k(s^t, n(s^t), k(s^t)) = \alpha z(s^t)\left(\frac{k(s^t)}{n(s^t)(1-v(s^t))}\right)^{\alpha-1} + 1 - \delta.$$

Evaluate this in history s^{t+1} and substitute into the first-order condition for next period's capital to get

$$1 = \sum_{s^{t+1}|s^t} q_t(s^{t+1})\left(\alpha z(s^{t+1})\left(\frac{k(s^{t+1})}{n(s^{t+1})(1-v(s^{t+1}))}\right)^{\alpha-1} + 1 - \delta\right). \quad (3.39)$$

Firms are willing to invest in capital if the cost of capital this period is equal to the expected net marginal product of capital next period, including the value of reselling the undepreciated portion of the capital.

Finally, compute the marginal profit of employing a worker at an arbitrary wage w in history s^t and at the equilibrium wage thereafter, rather than losing the worker. For a firm with the equilibrium level of employment $n(s^t)$ and capital $k(s^t)$, this is

$$\tilde{J}_n(s^t, w) = w(s^t) - w + J_n(s^t, n(s^t), k(s^t)). \tag{3.40}$$

This is essentially unchanged from equation (2.31).

3.2.3 Wages

The Nash bargaining solution states that the wage maximizes the Nash product

$$\tilde{V}_n(s^t, w)^{\phi} \tilde{J}_n(s^t, w)^{1-\phi}. \tag{3.41}$$

Replace $\tilde{J}_n(s^t, w)$ using equation (3.40) and $\tilde{V}_n(s^t, w)$ using equation (3.33). The first-order necessary and sufficient condition for a maximum of the Nash product is

$$(1-\phi)V_n(s^t, a(s^t), n(s^t))c(s^t) = \phi(1-\tau)J_n(s^t, n(s^t), k(s^t)). \tag{3.42}$$

Use this to eliminate $V_n(s^t, a(s^t), n(s^t))$ and $V_n(s^{t+1}, a(s^{t+1}), n(s^{t+1}))$ from equation (3.32):

$$\begin{aligned}
&\phi(1-\tau)J_n(s^t, n(s^t), k(s^t)) \\
&\quad = (1-\phi)(1-\tau)w(s^t) - (1-\phi)\gamma c(s^t) \\
&\qquad + \phi(1-\tau)(1-x-f(\theta(s^t))) \sum_{s^{t+1}|s^t} q_t(s^{t+1}) J_n(s^{t+1}, n(s^t), k(s^{t+1})).
\end{aligned}$$

If we replace $J_n(s^t, n(s^t), k(s^t))$ using equation (3.38) and

$$\sum_{s^{t+1}|s^t} q_t(s^{t+1}) J_n(s^{t+1}, n(s^{t+1}), k(s^{t+1}))$$

using equation (3.37), we obtain the wage equation

$$\begin{aligned}
(1-\tau)w(s^t) = \phi(1-\tau)(1-\alpha)z(s^t)&\left(\frac{k(s^t)}{n(s^t)(1-v(s^t))}\right)^{\alpha} \\
&\times (1+\theta(s^t)) + (1-\phi)\gamma c(s^t), \quad (3.43)
\end{aligned}$$

which is a natural generalization of equation (2.43). The after-tax wage is a weighted average of two terms: the after-tax marginal product of labor both of this worker and of the workers released from recruiting by her employment; and the marginal rate of substitution between consumption and leisure.

3.2.4 Equilibrium

I assume that the government levies labor taxes and rebates the proceeds as a lump sum transfer to households in every period. For notational simplicity, I impose a balanced budget:

$$T(s^t) = \tau w(s^t) n(s^t). \tag{3.44}$$

Ricardian equivalence holds in this environment, so alternative assumptions on government debt would not affect the equilibrium allocations.

I then close the model with a set of market-clearing conditions. The economy's resource constraint implies that next period's capital stock is

$$k(s^{t+1}) = z(s^t)k(s^t)^\alpha (n(s^t)(1-\nu(s^t)))^{1-\alpha} + (1-\delta)k(s^t) - c(s^t), \tag{3.45}$$

which is the sum of output and undepreciated capital minus consumption. Next period's employment is determined from current employment and current recruiting in the usual way:

$$n(s^{t+1}) = (1-x)n(s^t) + f(\theta(s^t))(1-n(s^t)). \tag{3.46}$$

And the recruiter–unemployment ratio θ satisfies

$$\theta(s^t) = \frac{\nu(s^t)n(s^t)}{1-n(s^t)}. \tag{3.47}$$

The definition of equilibrium is now standard, so I omit it.

3.2.5 Balanced Growth

Suppose there is deterministic Hicks-neutral productivity growth at rate $\bar{s}$, $\log z(s^{t+1}) = \log z(s^t) + \bar{s}$. I claim that there is an equilibrium where consumption, capital, and wages grow at rate $\bar{s}/(1-\alpha)$, while employment, the ratio of recruiters to unemployed, and the share of recruiters in employment are constant. That is, $c(s^t) = \bar{c}z(s^t)^{1/(1-\alpha)}$, $k(s^t) = \bar{k}z(s^t)^{1/(1-\alpha)}$, $w(s^t) = \bar{w}z(s^t)^{1/(1-\alpha)}$, $n(s^t) = \bar{n}$, $\theta(s^t) = \bar{\theta}$, and $\nu(s^t) = \bar{\nu}$. This result is useful both for understanding how the economy works and also later for characterizing stochastic deviations from the balanced-growth path due to technology shocks.

To prove this claim, I assume that there is such an equilibrium and show how to solve for the unknown constants. Eliminate the intertemporal price $q_t(s^{t+1})$ from equation (3.39) using equation (3.31) and eliminate the share of recruiters $\nu(s^t)$ and $\nu(s^{t+1})$ using equation (3.47). This gives

$$1 = \beta e^{-\bar{s}/(1-\alpha)}\left(\alpha\left(\frac{\bar{k}}{\bar{n}-\bar{\theta}(1-\bar{n})}\right)^{\alpha-1} + 1 - \delta\right). \tag{3.48}$$

Then eliminate $J_n(s^{t+1}, n(s^{t+1}), k(s^{t+1}))$ from equation (3.37) using equation (3.38) evaluated in history s^{t+1}. Again eliminate q and v using equations (3.31) and (3.47):

$$\bar{w} = (1-\alpha)\left(\frac{\bar{k}}{\bar{n} - \bar{\theta}(1-\bar{n})}\right)^{\alpha}\left(1 - \frac{1-\beta(1-x)}{\beta\mu(\bar{\theta})}\right). \tag{3.49}$$

The wage equation (3.43) and equation (3.47) imply

$$(1-\tau)\bar{w} = \phi(1-\tau)(1-\alpha)\left(\frac{\bar{k}}{\bar{n} - \bar{\theta}(1-\bar{n})}\right)^{\alpha}(1+\bar{\theta}) + (1-\phi)\gamma\bar{c}. \tag{3.50}$$

Finally, the resource constraint equation (3.45) and the law of motion for employment in equation (3.46) each simplify slightly:

$$e^{\bar{s}/(1-\alpha)}\bar{k} = \bar{k}^{\alpha}(\bar{n} - \bar{\theta}(1-\bar{n}))^{1-\alpha} + (1-\delta)\bar{k} - \bar{c} \tag{3.51}$$

and

$$\bar{n} = \frac{f(\bar{\theta})}{x + f(\bar{\theta})}. \tag{3.52}$$

The preceding five equations (3.48)–(3.52) have five unknowns: the wage constant $\bar{w}$, the capital constant $\bar{k}$, the consumption constant $\bar{c}$, employment $\bar{n}$, and the recruiter–unemployment ratio $\bar{\theta}$. It is possible to reduce them to an implicit equation for $\bar{\theta}$. Eliminate $\bar{w}$ between equations (3.49) and (3.50), then eliminate $\bar{k}$ using equation (3.48), next $\bar{c}$ using equation (3.51), and finally eliminate $\bar{n}$ using equation (3.52). This algebra yields $\mathcal{T}(\bar{\theta}) = 0$, where

$$\mathcal{T}(\theta) \equiv (1-\tau)(1-\alpha)\left(1 - \frac{1-\beta(1-x)}{\beta\mu(\theta)} - \phi(1+\theta)\right) - (1-\phi)\gamma\left(\frac{(1-\alpha\beta)e^{\bar{s}/(1-\alpha)} - (1-\alpha)\beta(1-\delta)}{e^{\bar{s}/(1-\alpha)} - \beta(1-\delta)}\right)\left(\frac{f(\theta)-\theta x}{f(\theta)+x}\right).$$

Clearly $\mathcal{T}$ is continuous. When $\theta = 0$, $\mathcal{T}(0) = (1-\tau)(1-\alpha)(1-\phi) > 0$. Also let $\tilde{\theta} > 0$ solve $f(\tilde{\theta}) = \tilde{\theta}x$, so $\mu(\tilde{\theta}) = x$. Simplifying the definition of $\mathcal{T}$ gives

$$\mathcal{T}(\tilde{\theta}) = -(1-\tau)(1-\alpha)\left(\frac{1-\beta}{\beta x} + \phi(1+\tilde{\theta})\right) < 0.$$

By the intermediate-value theorem, there is a solution to $\mathcal{T}(\theta) = 0$, an equilibrium, in between these two points.

Using $\bar{\theta}$, it is straightforward to compute the value of the other variables of interest along a balanced-growth path. Note that since both capital and employment are state variables, the economy is on a balanced-growth path only for particular initial conditions for the capital stock and employment. I defer an analysis of the stability of the system, i.e., whether it converges to the balanced-growth path from nearby initial conditions, until after I discuss the full model with a productivity shock.

3.2.6 Productivity Shocks: Deterministic Trend

Suppose that $\log z(s^t) = \bar{s}t + s_t$, where s_t follows a stationary first-order Markov process with mean 0. Thus $\bar{s}$ is the deterministic-growth rate while s_t represents a transitory deviation from trend. Let $\pi(s_{t+1}|s_t) \equiv \Pi(s^{t+1})/\Pi(s^t)$ denote the probability of state s_{t+1} next period conditional on state s_t this period. This nests the balanced-growth path as a special case with $s_t = 0$ for all t.

Stationary Equilibrium

Inspired by the balanced-growth path, I define consumption, capital, and wages relative to trend productivity as $\tilde{c}(s^t) \equiv c(s^t)e^{-\bar{s}t/(1-\alpha)}$, $\tilde{k}(s^t) \equiv k(s^t)e^{-\bar{s}t/(1-\alpha)}$, and $\tilde{w}(s^t) \equiv w(s^t)e^{-\bar{s}t/(1-\alpha)}$. Along a balanced-growth path, I found that $\tilde{c}(s^t)$, $\tilde{k}(s^t)$, and $\tilde{w}(s^t)$ are constant. I look for an equilibrium of the stochastic-growth model where they are stationary. Similarly, since employment, the share of recruiters in employment, and the recruiter-unemployment ratio are all constant along a balanced-growth path, I look for an equilibrium of the stochastic-growth model where these variables are stationary.

To proceed, I construct a stationary system of equations in these new variables. Use equation (3.31) to eliminate the intertemporal price q from the condition for an interior solution for capital, equation (3.39), and then use equation (3.47) to eliminate the share of recruiters in employment ν:

$$e^{\bar{s}/(1-\alpha)} = \beta \sum_{s^{t+1}|s^t} \pi(s_{t+1}|s_t)\frac{\tilde{c}(s^t)}{\tilde{c}(s^{t+1})} \times \left(\alpha e^{s_{t+1}}\left(\frac{\tilde{k}(s^{t+1})}{n(s^{t+1}) - \theta(s^{t+1})(1-n(s^{t+1}))}\right)^{\alpha-1} + 1 - \delta\right). \tag{3.53}$$

Similarly, eliminate $J_n(s^{t+1}, n(s^{t+1}), k(s^{t+1}))$ from the condition for an interior solution for recruiting, equation (3.37), using the envelope condition for employment, equation (3.38), evaluated in history s^{t+1}. Then eliminate q and ν using equations (3.31) and (3.47):

$$\begin{aligned}(1-\alpha)e^{s_t}&\left(\frac{\tilde{k}(s^t)}{n(s^t) - \theta(s^t)(1-n(s^t))}\right)^{\alpha} \\ &= \beta\mu(\theta(s^t)) \sum_{s^{t+1}|s^t} \pi(s_{t+1}|s_t)\frac{\tilde{c}(s^t)}{\tilde{c}(s^{t+1})} \\ &\quad\times \left((1-\alpha)e^{s_{t+1}}\left(\frac{\tilde{k}(s^{t+1})}{n(s^{t+1}) - \theta(s^{t+1})(1-n(s^{t+1}))}\right)^{\alpha}\right. \\ &\quad\left.\times\left(1 + \frac{1-x}{\mu(\theta(s^{t+1}))}\right) - \tilde{w}(s^{t+1})\right).\end{aligned} \tag{3.54}$$

Next use equation (3.47) to rewrite the wage equation (3.43), evaluated in history s^{t+1}, as

$$
\begin{aligned}
&(1-\tau)\tilde{w}(s^{t+1}) \\
&\quad = (1-\phi)\gamma\tilde{c}(s^{t+1}) \\
&\qquad + \phi(1-\tau)(1-\alpha)e^{s_{t+1}}\left(\frac{\tilde{k}(s^{t+1})}{n(s^{t+1})-\theta(s^{t+1})(1-n(s^{t+1}))}\right)^{\alpha}(1+\theta(s^{t+1})).
\end{aligned} \tag{3.55}
$$

Again using equation (3.47), the resource constraint equation (3.45) becomes

$$
\begin{aligned}
&\tilde{k}(s^{t+1})e^{\bar{s}/(1-\alpha)} \\
&\quad = e^{s_t}\tilde{k}(s^t)^{\alpha}(n(s^t)-\theta(s^t)(1-n(s^t)))^{1-\alpha}+(1-\delta)\tilde{k}(s^t)-\tilde{c}(s^t).
\end{aligned} \tag{3.56}
$$

Equation (3.46) is unaffected by this notation.

Equations (3.46) and (3.53)–(3.56) describe a stationary set of relationships between the variables of interest and so may in fact admit a stationary solution. I look for a solution with the property that the policy variables $\theta(s^t)$ and $\tilde{c}(s^t)$ depend on the exogenous state s_t, on employment n, and on the capital stock relative to trend $\tilde{k}$. Using the Markov property of the state variable and equations (3.46) and (3.56), this implies that s_{t+1}, $n(s^{t+1})$, and $\tilde{k}(s^{t+1})$ depend on the same objects. To characterize such a solution, eliminate $\tilde{w}(s^{t+1})$ between equations (3.54) and (3.55):

$$
\begin{aligned}
&(1-\alpha)e^{s_t}\left(\frac{\tilde{k}(s^t)}{n(s^t)-\theta(s^t)(1-n(s^t))}\right)^{\alpha} \\
&\quad = \beta\mu(\theta(s^t))\sum_{s^{t+1}|s^t}\pi(s_{t+1}|s_t)\frac{\tilde{c}(s^t)}{\tilde{c}(s^{t+1})} \\
&\qquad \times\Bigg(-\frac{(1-\phi)\gamma\tilde{c}(s^{t+1})}{1-\tau} \\
&\qquad\qquad + (1-\alpha)e^{s_{t+1}}\left(\frac{\tilde{k}(s^{t+1})}{n(s^{t+1})-\theta(s^{t+1})(1-n(s^{t+1}))}\right)^{\alpha} \\
&\qquad\qquad\qquad \times\left(\frac{1-x}{\mu(\theta(s^{t+1}))}+1-\phi-\phi\theta(s^{t+1})\right)\Bigg).
\end{aligned} \tag{3.57}
$$

Now let the functions Θ and C denote the equilibrium recruiter–unemployment ratio and the equilibrium level of consumption as functions of the current state $(s,n,\tilde{k})$, so $\theta(s^t) = \Theta(s_t,n(s^t),\tilde{k}(s^t))$ and $\tilde{c}(s^t) = C(s_t,n(s^t),\tilde{k}(s^t))$. After substituting these functions into equations (3.53) and (3.57), eliminate $\tilde{k}(s^{t+1})$ using equation (3.56) and $n(s^{t+1})$ using equation (3.46) to obtain a pair of nonlinear equations that implicitly define Θ and C.

Table 3.2. Calibrated parameter values in the model with capital, deterministic trend.

Parameter	Value
Discount factor β	0.996
Mean productivity growth $\bar{s}$	0.0012
Tax rate τ	0.4
Employment-exit probability x	0.034
Matching function $f(\theta)$	$2.32\theta^{1/2}$
Workers' bargaining power ϕ	0.5
Disutility of work γ	0.471
Capital share α	0.33
Depreciation rate δ	0.0028
Autocorrelation of detrended productivity ρ	0.98
Standard deviation of detrended productivity ς	0.005

Calibration

As in section 3.1, I solve the model by log-linearizing around a stochastic steady state. I assume that the deviation of productivity from trend follows a linear process,

$$s_{t+1} = \rho s_t + \varsigma \upsilon_{t+1}, \tag{3.58}$$

where υ is a white-noise innovation with mean 0 and standard deviation 1 and ς is therefore the standard deviation of the productivity shock, while $\rho \in (0, 1)$ is its autocorrelation. I then look for a log-linear approximation to the policy functions

$$\log \theta = \log \bar{\theta} + \theta_s s + \theta_n(\log n - \log \bar{n}) + \theta_k(\log \tilde{k} - \log \bar{k}), \tag{3.59}$$

$$\log \tilde{c} = \log \bar{c} + c_s s + c_n(\log n - \log \bar{n}) + c_k(\log \tilde{k} - \log \bar{k}). \tag{3.60}$$

In these equations, $\bar{\theta}$ is the recruiter–unemployment ratio, $\bar{c}$ is consumption relative to productivity, $\bar{n}$ is employment, and $\bar{k}$ is capital relative to productivity in the stochastic steady state. The remaining six parameters represent the elasticity of the two policy functions with respect to the three state variables.

The introduction of capital changes neither the strategy for calibrating most of the parameters nor the results, and so I keep their values fixed at those I used in the model with consumption–labor complementarity. Of course, moving from a stochastic to a deterministic trend changes the productivity process. I continue to assume that mean productivity growth is $\bar{s} = 0.0012$ and I set the autocorrelation of productivity growth to $\rho = 0.98$ and the standard deviation to $\varsigma = 0.005$. These values are similar to standard calibrations of total factor productivity (Cooley and

Prescott 1995), with an adjustment to account for the fact that time periods are one month long.

Since the model now assumes that consumption and leisure are additively separable, I change the disutility of work so as to keep the average employment rate fixed at 0.95. This requires setting $\gamma = 0.471$.

The model with capital has two new parameters: the capital share α and the monthly depreciation rate δ. I fix $\alpha = 0.33$ to match the capital share of income in the National Income and Product Accounts. I set $\delta = 0.0028$ per month, which pins down the capital-output ratio in the stochastic steady state. To see how, rewrite equation (3.48) along a balanced-growth path as

$$1 = \beta e^{-\bar{s}/(1-\alpha)}\left(\alpha\frac{\bar{y}}{\bar{k}} + 1 - \delta\right),$$

where $y(s^t) \equiv z(s^t)k(s^t)^\alpha(n(s^t) - \theta(s^t)(1 - n(s^t)))^{1-\alpha}$ is gross output and $\bar{y} \equiv y(s^t)z(s^t)^{-1/(1-\alpha)}$ is output relative to trend. This choice of parameter values then implies that the ratio of capital to monthly output, $\bar{k}/\bar{y}$, is 38.3. Equivalently, the ratio of capital to annual output is 3.2, which is the average capital-output ratio in the United States since 1948.[7] The remaining parameters are unchanged; I show their values in table 3.2 for convenience.

This leaves nine unknowns in equations (3.59) and (3.60): the recruiter-unemployment ratio $\bar{\theta}$, consumption relative to productivity $\bar{c}$, and capital relative to productivity $\bar{k}$, all in the stochastic steady state; and the six elasticities of the policy functions with respect to the state variables. In addition, I effectively treat the value of leisure γ as a residual, a tenth unknown variable. I pin these down using ten equations. As described above, I substitute the log-linear approximations $\theta(s^t) = \Theta(s_t, n(s^t), \tilde{k}(s^t))$ and $c(s^t) = C(s_t, n(s^t), \tilde{k}(s^t))$ into equations (3.53) and (3.57) and then eliminate $\tilde{k}(s^{t+1})$ using equation (3.56) and $n(s^{t+1})$ using equation (3.46). This gives two equations, which I log-linearize around the steady state $\{s, n, k\} = \{0, \bar{n}, \bar{k}\}$. The resulting system yields eight equations. The two remaining equations come from steady-state versions of the state equations (3.46) and (3.56):

$$\bar{n} = (1 - x)\bar{n} + f(\bar{\theta})(1 - \bar{n}),$$
$$\bar{k}e^{\bar{s}/(1-\alpha)} = \bar{k}^\alpha(\bar{n} - \bar{\theta}(1 - \bar{n}))^{1-\alpha} + (1 - \delta)\bar{k} - \bar{c}.$$

I solve these ten equations numerically.

---

[7] More precisely, I use the Bureau of Economic Analysis's Fixed Asset Table 1.1, line 1 to measure the current-cost net stock of fixed assets and consumer durable goods. I use National Income and Product Accounts Table 1.1.5, line 1 to measure nominal gross domestic product.

Solution

I find that the policy functions are

$$\left.\begin{aligned}\log\theta &= \log 0.078 + 7.387s - 0.480(\log n - \log 0.95)\\ &\qquad - 2.779(\log\tilde{k} - \log 218.2),\\ \log\tilde{c} &= \log 4.696 + 0.250s + 0.014(\log n - \log 0.95)\\ &\qquad + 0.603(\log\tilde{k} - \log 218.2),\end{aligned}\right\} \tag{3.61}$$

where 0.078 is the recruiter-unemployment ratio, 0.95 is the employment rate, 218.2 is capital relative to trend, and 4.696 is consumption relative to trend, all in the stochastic steady state.

When productivity is above trend, the recruiter-unemployment ratio and consumption both increase. The increase in the recruiter-unemployment ratio raises next period's employment rate. Since the elasticity of consumption with respect to current productivity is less than 1, physical capital investment also rises with productivity. Thus both endogenous state variables increase with current productivity. I confirm this by looking at the implied log-linear approximation to the state equations (3.46) and (3.56):

$$\left.\begin{aligned}\log n_{+1} &= \log 0.95 + 0.126s + 0.312(\log n - \log 0.95)\\ &\qquad - 0.047(\log\tilde{k} - \log 218.2),\\ \log\tilde{k}_{+1} &= \log 218.2 + 0.020s + 0.019(\log n - \log 0.95)\\ &\qquad + 0.991(\log\tilde{k} - \log 218.2).\end{aligned}\right\} \tag{3.62}$$

To understand these dynamics, focus on households' desire to maintain smooth consumption. Following a positive productivity shock, households would like to save more. This pushes down the interest rate (raises $q_t(s^{t+1})$), which encourages firms to invest both in capital and in recruiting workers. The increase in employment raises the marginal product of capital, which encourages more investment, and also enables firms to devote more resources to recruiting. Eventually, however, the wealth effect from the increase in the capital stock raises wages, which puts downward pressure on recruiting. This reduces employment and returns the economy to steady state.

To examine these dynamics more systematically, express the log-linear approximation to the model's dynamics as $m_{+1} = Am + Dv_{+1}$ where $m = \{s, \log n - \log\bar{n}, \log\tilde{k} - \log\bar{k}\}$ is the state of the system, A is the transition matrix,

$$A = \begin{pmatrix} 0.980 & 0 & 0\\ 0.126 & 0.312 & -0.047\\ 0.020 & 0.019 & 0.991\end{pmatrix},$$

and D translates the univariate white-noise shock υ into next period's state,

$$D = \begin{pmatrix} \varsigma \\ 0 \\ 0 \end{pmatrix}.$$

The eigenvalues of A are 0.99, 0.98, and 0.31, and so the system is locally stable. The largest eigenvalue, 0.99, reflects the slow adjustment of the capital stock to steady state due to the low depreciation rate. The second eigenvalue is equal to the persistence of the productivity shock. The smallest is associated with the rapid adjustment of employment to steady state.

Next I compute the unconditional variance and covariance of the state variables. As I discussed in section 3.1, this is determined by Σ solving $\Sigma = A\Sigma A' + DD'$. I obtain

$$\Sigma = \begin{pmatrix} 25.253 & 3.175 & 19.505 \\ 3.175 & 0.560 & 0.469 \\ 19.505 & 0.469 & 46.550 \end{pmatrix} \varsigma^2.$$

This confirms that deviations of productivity from trend are positively correlated with deviations of both employment and capital from trend. However, the volatility of employment is still small, with an unconditional standard deviation equal to $\sqrt{0.560}\varsigma = 0.004$. Put differently, suppose that productivity suddenly increases to $s_t = 0.01$, approximately four standard deviations above trend, and gets stuck there. In one month, the unemployment rate will decline modestly from its steady-state value of 5.00 percent to 4.88 percent. Moreover, the capital stock will start to increase and this wealth effect will partially reverse the change in unemployment. Asymptotically, the unemployment rate will rise back to 4.98 percent, scarcely different from where it started.

Labor Wedge

A useful way to understand the behavior of employment is to look at the labor wedge. Once again, suppose an economist ignores the existence of labor market frictions and so measures the wedge between the marginal rate of substitution and the marginal product of labor using equation (1.12). He recognizes that the capital share of income is $\alpha = 0.33$ and the Frisch labor supply elasticity is infinite since labor is indivisible. He would then measure

$$\hat{\tau}(s^t) = 1 - \frac{\hat{y}}{1-\alpha}\frac{c(s^t)}{y(s^t)}n(s^t).$$

Using evidence from the stochastic steady state, he would conclude that if the true tax factor is 0.4, the disutility of work is $\hat{\gamma} = 0.513$. Again, this is slightly higher than the true value $\gamma = 0.471$, since our economist does not understand that unemployment is due in part to search frictions.

He could also measure the cyclical dynamics of the labor wedge $\hat{\tau}$. To see how this would be done using model-generated data, note that both $n(s^t)$ and $c(s^t)/y(s^t)$ are stationary, the latter because $c(s^t)/y(s^t) = \tilde{c}(s^t)/\tilde{y}(s^t)$, where

$$\tilde{y}(s^t) \equiv y(s^t)e^{-\bar{s}t/(1-\alpha)} = e^{s_t}\tilde{k}(s^t)^{\alpha}(n(s^t)(1-v(s^t)))^{1-\alpha}$$

is detrended output. I can therefore log-linearize the labor wedge around its steady-state value to obtain

$$\log\hat{\tau} = \log 0.4 + 1.095s - 0.431(\log n - \log 0.95) - 0.398(\log\tilde{k} - \log 218.2).$$

The measured labor wedge is low when productivity is below trend, employment is above trend, or the capital stock is above trend. When productivity is below trend, the desire to maintain smooth consumption keeps the consumption–output ratio high, which lowers the measured labor wedge. High capital also raises the consumption–output ratio due to its wealth effect, and so has the same implication. High employment directly reduces the measured labor wedge.

Finally, the economist might look at the comovement between the labor wedge and the state variables in the economy. In general, consider any set of variables $\tilde{m}$ that are linear functions of the state variables m, say $\tilde{m} = \tilde{A}m$ for some matrix $\tilde{A}$. Then the variance–covariance matrix of these variables satisfies $\mathbb{E}(\tilde{m}\tilde{m}') = \mathbb{E}(\tilde{A}mm'\tilde{A}') = \tilde{A}\Sigma\tilde{A}'$, where I simplify this using the definition of the variance–covariance matrix $\Sigma = \mathbb{E}(mm')$. Critically, he would find that the correlation between the detrended measured labor wedge $\hat{\tau}$ and detrended employment is 0.96. In the data, the correlation is sharply negative: see, for example, table 1.1, which shows that the correlation is always larger in magnitude than -0.6. He would also find a strong negative correlation between the labor wedge and the consumption–output ratio, while in the data the correlation is much weaker and sometimes even switches sign.[8]

It is easy to understand why the model generates a positive correlation between the measured labor wedge and employment. Search frictions act

[8] Throughout this book, I focus on the infinite-sample properties of model-generated data. One has to be cautious in comparing these results with a finite sample of real-world data. An alternative approach would be to simulate the model to generate a finite number of observations. Using Monte Carlo methods, one can create multiple samples and ask whether the observed real-world data are likely to have been generated by the model. Although I do not follow this approach here, I do not expect that this would have a significant impact on my findings.

like an adjustment cost on labor. Our economist ignores the existence of that adjustment cost and so expects to see relatively large movements in employment in response to the observed shocks. When he does not, he interprets this, through the lens of the competitive model from chapter 1, as evidence that the labor wedge rises during expansions, discouraging households from supplying much more labor, and falls during recessions, encouraging households not to contract their labor supply too much. But the failure of the frictionless model occurred because in the data employment fluctuates too much, not too little. An adjustment cost is unlikely to explain this observation.

Comovements: Detrended Variables

Although I focus on the comovement of employment and the labor wedge, the model has many other predictions. Table 3.3 shows the comovement of some key economic outcomes. Table A.1 in appendix A shows comparable numbers constructed from historical U.S. data. The first row shows the ratio of the standard deviation of a detrended variable to the standard deviation of detrended output, $\tilde{y}(s^t)$. I look at consumption, the recruiter-unemployment ratio, capital, employment, the labor share (wn/y), the consumption-output ratio, and the measured labor wedge. For example, the standard deviation of log consumption relative to trend is 0.72 times the standard deviation of log output relative to trend, so consumption is less volatile than output. This reflects the desire to smooth consumption. The lower part of the table shows the contemporaneous correlation between different variables; the correlation between consumption and output is strongly positive, 0.87. These two numbers together imply that when output is above trend, the consumption-output ratio is low, which I verify in the seventh column of the table.

Comovements: Growth Rates

One possible explanation for the gap between the model and the data is that I do not measure the same objects in the two environments. In the model I measure the level of stationary variables including employment, the recruiter-unemployment ratio, the consumption-output ratio, and the labor wedge; and I measure the ratio-to-trend of trending variables including output, consumption, capital, and wages. In contrast, I cannot observe the trend in real-world data. Instead, I estimate the trend using a Hodrick-Prescott filter.

To understand whether this difference in measurement is an issue, I compute annual growth rates for the various variables of interest in the

Table 3.3. Model with capital, deterministic trend; comovements of variables in an infinite sample.

		$\tilde{y}$	$\tilde{c}$	θ	$\tilde{k}$	n	wn/y	c/y	$\hat{\tau}$	s
Relative standard deviation		1	0.717	4.391	0.990	0.109	0.012	0.515	0.614	0.729
Correlations	$\tilde{y}$	1	0.871	0.714	0.748	0.713	−0.886	−0.729	0.728	0.971
	$\tilde{c}$	—	1	0.279	0.978	0.293	−0.563	−0.299	0.298	0.729
	θ	—	—	1	0.070	0.966	−0.938	−0.999	1.000	0.860
	$\tilde{k}$	—	—	—	1	0.092	−0.379	−0.091	0.090	0.569
	n	—	—	—	—	1	−0.877	−0.976	0.962	0.844
	wn/y	—	—	—	—	—	1	0.938	−0.947	−0.967
	c/y	—	—	—	—	—	—	1	−0.998	−0.870
	$\hat{\tau}$	—	—	—	—	—	—	—	1	0.870
	s	—	—	—	—	—	—	—	—	1

model and compare these with the data in the lower part of table 1.1. This has the added advantage that the annual growth rate of trending variables—consumption, capital, output, and wages—is equal to the annual growth rate of their detrended counterparts plus a constant, and so is easy to compute.

I start with some algebraic preliminaries. Again let $\tilde{m} = \tilde{A}m$ and now let $\tilde{m}_{+t} - \tilde{m}$ denote the t-period growth rate of $\tilde{m}$. This then solves

$$\tilde{m}_{+t} - \tilde{m} = \tilde{A}(m_{+t} - m).$$

Moveover, since $m_{+1} = Am + Dv_{+1}$, a simple induction argument implies that

$$m_{+t} = A^t m + \sum_{t'=0}^{t-1} A^{t'} D v_{+(t-t')}.$$

Combining these, I get

$$\mathbb{E}(\tilde{m}_{+t} - \tilde{m})(\tilde{m}_{+t} - \tilde{m})'$$
$$= \mathbb{E}\tilde{A}\Big((A^t - I)m + \sum_{t'=0}^{t-1} A^{t'} D v_{+(t-t')}\Big)\Big((A^t - I)m + \sum_{t'=0}^{t-1} A^{t'} D v_{+(t-t')}\Big)'\tilde{A}',$$

where I is the identity matrix. Since v is serially uncorrelated and $v_{+(t-t')}$ is uncorrelated with m for all $t > t'$, this reduces to

$$\mathbb{E}(\tilde{m}_{+t} - \tilde{m})(\tilde{m}_{+t} - \tilde{m})' = \tilde{A}\Big((A^t - I)\Sigma(A^t - I)' + \sum_{t'=0}^{t'-1} A^{t'} D D' (A^{t'})'\Big)\tilde{A}',$$

where as usual $\Sigma = \mathbb{E}(mm')$. This covariance matrix is straightforward to calculate.

Using this approach, I compute the annual growth rates of the variables of interest and show comovements in table 3.4; table A.2 in appendix A shows comparable numbers constructed from historical U.S. data. The results that I emphasized in table 3.3 are unchanged. The correlation between the annual growth rate of the labor wedge and employment is 0.88, while the correlation with the consumption output ratio is −0.99. This is inconsistent with the data, as shown in the bottom part of table 1.1. Moreover, none of the other numbers change to an economically significant extent when moving from deviations from trend to annual growth rates. For example, among the correlations, only the correlation of the capital stock with four other variables changes sign. In three of those cases, the correlation is economically insignificant: smaller than 0.1 in absolute value under either measure.

Table 3.4. Model with capital, deterministic trend; comovements of annual growth rates in an infinite sample.

		$\tilde{y}$	$\tilde{c}$	θ	$\tilde{k}$	n	wn/y	c/y	$\hat{\tau}$	s
Relative standard deviation		1	0.303	6.552	0.300	0.158	0.019	0.756	0.921	0.900
Correlations	$\tilde{y}$	1	0.858	0.973	0.192	0.912	−0.931	−0.979	0.971	0.994
	$\tilde{c}$	—	1	0.722	0.668	0.712	−0.706	−0.734	0.720	0.804
	θ	—	—	1	−0.033	0.889	−0.968	−0.997	1.000	0.992
	$\tilde{k}$	—	—	—	1	0.067	0.019	0.014	−0.034	0.094
	n	—	—	—	—	1	−0.751	−0.920	0.876	0.897
	wn/y	—	—	—	—	—	1	0.948	−0.975	−0.961
	c/y	—	—	—	—	—	—	1	−0.995	−0.992
	$\hat{\tau}$	—	—	—	—	—	—	—	1	0.991
	s	—	—	—	—	—	—	—	—	1

Impulse Response Functions

Another way to summarize the results is through impulse responses. Suppose that productivity, employment, and capital are all at their stochastic steady-state values in period -1. In period 0, productivity jumps up by one standard deviation, or $\varsigma/\sqrt{1-\rho^2} = 2.5$ percent, before reverting slowly back to steady state, with an autocorrelation of 0.98. The thick dots in figure 3.1 (which look like a thick line in most places) show how the economy responds. Consumption jumps up upon the impact of the shock but soon starts to fall. Since workers would otherwise like to maintain smooth consumption, the decline in consumption must be induced by a decline in the interest rate (a rise in $q_t(s^{t+1})$). This encourages firms both to recruit workers and to invest in capital, leading to the increase in employment n and capital $\tilde{k}$. But with higher consumption and a higher marginal product of labor, the wage increases (equation (3.43)). This moderates the incentive for firms to recruit more workers and eventually returns the economy to steady state.

The figure also confirms that employment (and hence unemployment) is less volatile than output. Following the shock, the unemployment rate falls rapidly from 5.0 percent to 4.6 percent before reversing course, eventually rising slightly above its initial value. While this is an improvement on the earlier search models in this book, the volatility of employment is still modest.

One might expect that breaking the link between wages and the marginal product of labor would help to generate fluctuations in employment, but in practice the labor share wn/y is nearly constant. In the frictionless economy, the labor share is constant at $1 - \alpha = 0.6700$. Search frictions reduce it very slightly, to 0.6697 in the stochastic steady state. Figure 3.1 shows that, upon the impact of a positive productivity shock, the labor share falls by 0.08 percent, to 0.6692, and then recovers rapidly. In this sense, wages are almost exactly equal to the marginal product of labor even in the presence of search frictions.

Sensitivity

I consider the sensitivity of these results along two dimensions. First, one might be concerned that I have taken too small a departure from the frictionless model. In steady state, only 0.4 percent of employed workers are engaged in recruiting, while the remainder are producers. In fact, intuition suggests that more severe search frictions will only dampen fluctuations in employment, and simulations bear that out. I recalibrate the model with more severe search frictions, $\bar{\mu} = 1$, so recruiters can only contact 1.5 new workers per period in the stochastic steady state.

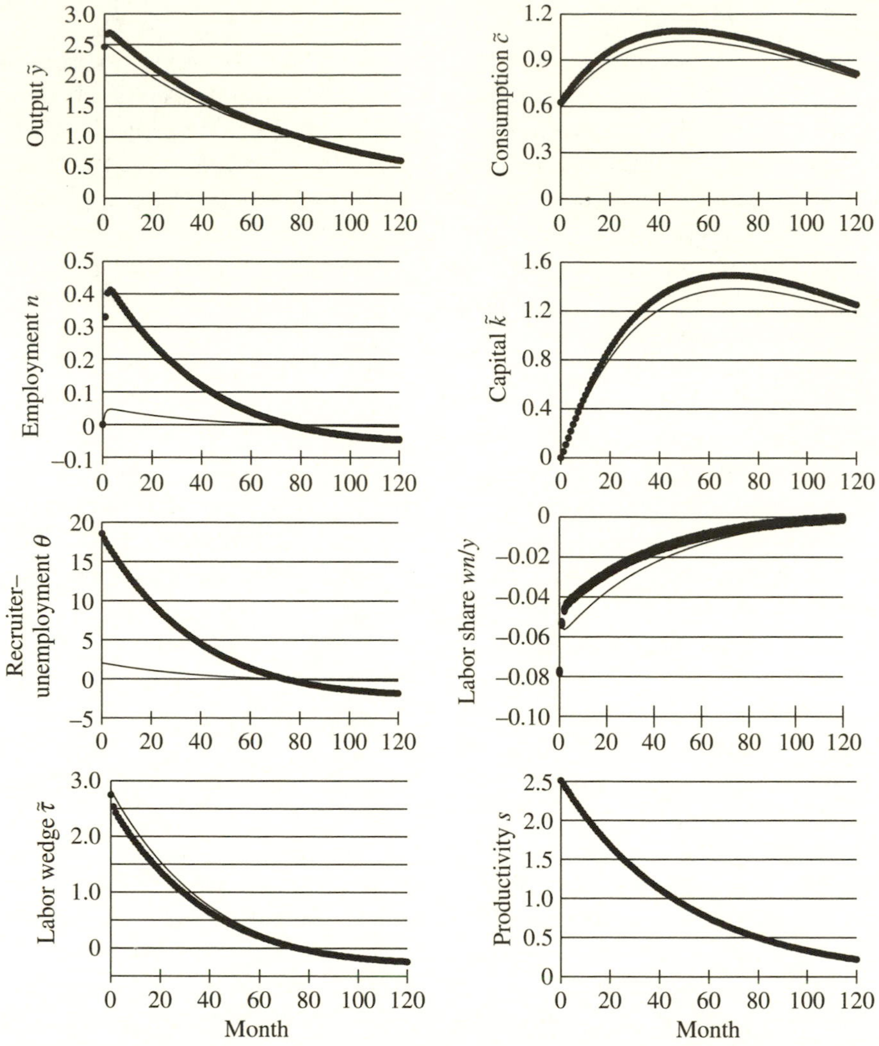

Figure 3.1. Model with capital, deterministic trend. Response to a 2.5 percent increase in productivity at $t = 0$. All variables are expressed as deviations from trend in log points. The thick dots show $\bar{\mu} = 2.32$ and the thin lines show more frictions, $\bar{\mu} = 1$.

I also change the value of leisure so as to leave the steady-state employment rate unchanged. This modification raises the steady-state share of employed workers in recruiting to 2.2 percent, increasing the role of search frictions in labor market outcomes.

The thin lines in figure 3.1 show the resulting impulse response. More severe search frictions moderate fluctuations in employment and the recruiter–unemployment ratio, but otherwise have little effect on outcomes. Notably, the critical pattern, that high productivity raises employment and the measured labor wedge, is unchanged. Conversely, I find that when recruiting is more effective, and the model therefore approaches the frictionless benchmark, employment is more volatile.[9] Search frictions alone do not help to explain the behavior of the measured labor wedge.

Second, my choice of workers' bargaining power, $\phi = 0.5$, was arbitrary. Notably, in a version of this model with linear utility and no capital, Hagedorn and Manovskii (2008) argue for a lower level of bargaining power and a higher value of leisure. They find that these changes significantly amplify employment fluctuations. I confirm that their results carry over to this setting. At one extreme, suppose we insist that the value of leisure is zero, $\gamma = 0$, so unemployment is truly involuntary, caused only by the search frictions. Fixing all the other parameters, the economy has five percent unemployment if workers' bargaining power is very high, $\phi = 0.924$. With these parameters, the unconditional standard deviation of employment falls from 0.004 to 0.00002, so the model generates virtually no unemployment fluctuations.

At the other extreme, we could reduce workers' bargaining power to $\phi = 0.05$ and raise the value of leisure to $\gamma = 0.511$, so as to maintain a five percent unemployment rate in the stochastic steady state. For comparison, recall that in a frictionless economy, a value of leisure of $\hat{\gamma} = 0.513$ results in the same nonemployment rate, while still higher values of leisure are inconsistent with five percent unemployment. Thus this is nearly the highest possible value for γ and the lowest possible value for ϕ. These changes raise the unconditional standard deviation of employment by a factor of five, to 0.020. Moreover, they raise the relative volatility of employment from eleven percent of output to forty-five percent. The model finally generates interesting fluctuations in employment.

But while these findings are promising, the behavior of the labor wedge remains counterfactual. The correlation between the labor wedge and employment is only slightly reduced, to 0.87 in levels (i.e., the correlation between detrended variables) and 0.68 in growth rates (i.e., the correlation between annual growth rates of variables), far from the negative correlations that we observe in the data. Similarly, the theoretical correlation between the labor wedge and the consumption–output ratio remains strongly negative, −0.92 in levels and −0.81 in growth rates. It

[9] The search model does not quite converge to the frictionless benchmark when $\bar{\mu} \to \infty$ because employment is set a period in advance.

thus seems that the choice of workers' bargaining power does not drive my main finding: the counterfactual behavior of the comovement of the labor wedge with employment and the consumption–output ratio.

3.2.7 Productivity Shocks: Stochastic Trend

I turn next to the possibility that there are shocks to the trend of productivity, rather than transitory fluctuations around the trend. Assume that $\log z(s^{t+1}) = \log z(s^t) + s_{t+1}$, where $s^{t+1} = \{s^t, s_{t+1}\}$ and where s_t follows a stationary first-order Markov process. Let $\pi(s_{t+1} | s_t)$ again denote the probability of state s_{t+1} next period conditional on state s_t this period. While this change in the nature of the productivity shock alters many properties of the model, I show in this section that it does not substantially affect the comovement of the labor wedge with employment and the consumption–output ratio.

Again inspired by the balanced-growth path, I look for an equilibrium where appropriately scaled versions of consumption, capital, and wages are stationary. Define relative consumption, capital, and wages as

$$\begin{aligned}\tilde{c}(s^t) &\equiv c(s^t) z(s^t)^{-1/(1-\alpha)},\\ \tilde{k}(s^t) &\equiv k(s^t) z(s^t)^{-1/(1-\alpha)},\\ \tilde{w}(s^t) &\equiv w(s^t) z(s^t)^{-1/(1-\alpha)}.\end{aligned}$$

Similarly, since employment, the share of recruiters in employment, and the recruiter–unemployment ratio are all constant along a balanced-growth path, I look for an equilibrium in which these variables are stationary.

To find a set of equilibrium conditions relating stationary variables, I eliminate the intertemporal price q using equation (3.31) and the share of recruiters ν using equation (3.47) from the remaining equilibrium conditions. The condition for an interior solution for capital, equation (3.39), then reduces to

$$\begin{aligned}1 = \beta \sum_{s^{t+1}|s^t} \pi(s_{t+1}|s_t) \frac{\tilde{c}(s^t)}{\tilde{c}(s^{t+1})} \mathrm{e}^{-s_{t+1}/(1-\alpha)} \\ \times \left(\alpha \left(\frac{\tilde{k}(s^{t+1})}{n(s^{t+1}) - \theta(s^{t+1})(1 - n(s^{t+1}))} \right)^{\alpha-1} + 1 - \delta \right). \quad (3.63)\end{aligned}$$

Eliminating $J_n(s^{t+1}, n(s^{t+1}), k(s^{t+1}))$ from the condition for an interior solution for recruiting, equation (3.37), using the envelope equation

(3.38) for employment, evaluated in history s^{t+1}, yields

$$\begin{aligned}(1-\alpha)&\left(\frac{\tilde{k}(s^t)}{n(s^t)-\theta(s^t)(1-n(s^t))}\right)^{\alpha}\\&=\beta\mu(\theta(s^t))\sum_{s^{t+1}|s^t}\pi(s_{t+1}|s_t)\frac{\tilde{c}(s^t)}{\tilde{c}(s^{t+1})}\\&\quad\times\left((1-\alpha)\left(\frac{\tilde{k}(s^{t+1})}{n(s^{t+1})-\theta(s^{t+1})(1-n(s^{t+1}))}\right)^{\alpha}\right.\\&\quad\quad\left.\times\left(1+\frac{1-x}{\mu(\theta(s^{t+1}))}\right)-\tilde{w}(s^{t+1})\right).\end{aligned}$$

The wage equation (3.43) evaluated in history s^{t+1} reduces to

$$\begin{aligned}(1-\tau)&\tilde{w}(s^{t+1})\\&=(1-\phi)\gamma\tilde{c}(s^{t+1})\\&\quad+\phi(1-\tau)(1-\alpha)\left(\frac{\tilde{k}(s^{t+1})}{n(s^{t+1})-\theta(s^{t+1})(1-n(s^{t+1}))}\right)^{\alpha}(1+\theta(s^{t+1})).\end{aligned}$$

Eliminating $\tilde{w}(s^{t+1})$ between the last two equations gives

$$\begin{aligned}(1-\alpha)&\left(\frac{\tilde{k}(s^t)}{n(s^t)-\theta(s^t)(1-n(s^t))}\right)^{\alpha}\\&=\beta\mu(\theta(s^t))\sum_{s^{t+1}|s^t}\pi(s_{t+1}|s_t)\frac{\tilde{c}(s^t)}{\tilde{c}(s^{t+1})}\\&\quad\times\left(-\frac{(1-\phi)\gamma\tilde{c}(s^{t+1})}{1-\tau}\right.\\&\quad\quad+(1-\alpha)\left(\frac{\tilde{k}(s^{t+1})}{n(s^{t+1})-\theta(s^{t+1})(1-n(s^{t+1}))}\right)^{\alpha}\\&\quad\quad\left.\times\left(\frac{1-x}{\mu(\theta(s^{t+1}))}+1-\phi-\phi\theta(s^{t+1})\right)\right).\end{aligned}\tag{3.64}$$

Finally, the resource constraint equation (3.45) becomes

$$\begin{aligned}\tilde{k}&(s^{t+1})e^{s_{t+1}/(1-\alpha)}\\&=\tilde{k}(s^t)^{\alpha}(n(s^t)-\theta(s^t)(1-n(s^t)))^{1-\alpha}+(1-\delta)\tilde{k}(s^t)-\tilde{c}(s^t).\end{aligned}\tag{3.65}$$

Once again, equation (3.46) is unchanged.

As in the model with a deterministic trend, I look for a solution to equations (3.46) and (3.63)–(3.65) with the property that the policy variables $\theta(s^t)$ and $\tilde{c}(s^t)$ depend on the exogenous state s_t, on employment n, and on the capital stock relative to trend $\tilde{k}$. Using the Markov property of the state variable and the state equations (3.46) and (3.65), this implies that s_{t+1}, $n(s^{t+1})$, and $\tilde{k}(s^{t+1})$ depend on the same objects.

Again let the functions Θ and C denote the equilibrium recruiter-unemployment ratio and the equilibrium consumption relative to trend as functions of the current state $(s, n, \tilde{k})$, so $\theta(s^t) = \Theta(s_t, n(s^t), \tilde{k}(s^t))$ and $\tilde{c}(s^t) = C(s_t, n(s^t), \tilde{k}(s^t))$. After substituting these functions into equations (3.63) and (3.64), eliminate $\tilde{k}(s^{t+1})$ using equation (3.65) and $n(s^{t+1})$ using equation (3.46) to obtain a pair of nonlinear equations that implicitly define Θ and C.

I solve the model by calibrating it and log-linearizing around a stochastic steady state. I leave most of the calibration unchanged from the model with a deterministic trend (table 3.2), except the stochastic process for productivity, which I borrow from my earlier analysis of a stochastic trend in the economy where consumption and leisure are substitutes. Thus I assume that productivity growth follows a linear process: $s_{t+1} = \bar{s} + \rho(s_t - \bar{s}) + \varsigma v_{t+1}$. I set the average monthly productivity growth rate to $\bar{s} = 0.0012$, the autocorrelation of monthly productivity growth to $\rho = 0.4$, and the standard deviation of monthly productivity growth to $\varsigma = 0.00325$. These values are consistent with the observed annual behavior of multifactor productivity in the private business sector in the United States between 1948 and 2007.

I then solve for a log-linear approximation to the equilibrium policy functions, finding

$$\log\theta = \log 0.078 + 1.548(s - 0.0012) - 0.480(\log n - \log 0.95) - 2.779(\log\tilde{k} - \log 218.2),$$

$$\log\tilde{c} = \log 4.696 + 0.381(s - 0.0012) + 0.014(\log n - \log 0.95) + 0.603(\log\tilde{k} - \log 218.2).$$

An increase in the productivity growth raises the recruiter-unemployment ratio θ and increases consumption $\tilde{c}$. Future productivity is expected to be much higher than current productivity and households take advantage of that by increasing consumption immediately. This puts upward pressure on interest rates (downward pressure on q), discouraging investment in both capital and recruiting. Still, because the shock is sufficiently transitory, the interest rate response is modest and recruiting actually rises.[10]

[10] Note that the responses of the recruiter-unemployment ratio and consumption to employment and to detrended capital are identical in the model with stochastic and deterministic trends, at least to the sixth decimal point.

Using the equilibrium policy functions, I then find the log-linear approximation to the state equations:

$$\log n_{+1} = \log 0.95 + 0.026(s - 0.0012) + 0.312(\log n - \log 0.95) - 0.047(\log \tilde{k} - \log 218.2),$$

$$\log \tilde{k}_{+1} = \log 218.2 - 0.605(s - 0.0012) + 0.019(\log n - \log 0.95) + 0.991(\log \tilde{k} - \log 218.2).$$

This confirms that higher productivity growth raises employment but reduces the detrended capital stock by encouraging current consumption.

I next stack the state variables as $m \equiv \{s - \bar{s}, \log n - \log \bar{n}, \log \tilde{k} - \log \bar{k}\}$. I write the transition equation as $m_{+1} = Am + Dv_{+1}$ and compute the eigenvalues of the transition matrix A. The smallest and largest are unchanged at 0.99 and 0.31, corresponding to the slow adjustment of capital and the fast adjustment of employment. The intermediate eigenvalue, 0.4, reflects the modest autocorrelation of shocks.

Finally, I construct other detrended variables as linear combinations of state variables, $\tilde{m} = \tilde{A}m$, and compute the variance-covariance matrix $\mathbb{E}(\tilde{m}\tilde{m}') = \tilde{A}\Sigma\tilde{A}'$, where $\Sigma = \mathbb{E}(mm')$ solves $\Sigma = A\Sigma A' + DD'$. Table 3.5 shows the relative standard deviations and the correlation matrix for the same set of variables as in table 3.3.

Some results appear to be quite different and superficially encouraging. For example, the volatility of employment, $n(s^t)$, relative to detrended output, $\tilde{y}(s^t) = y(s^t)z(s^t)^{-1/(1-\alpha)} = \tilde{k}(s^t)^{\alpha}(n(s^t) - \theta(s^t)(1 - n(s^t)))^{1-\alpha}$, more than doubles from 0.11 to 0.24. On the other hand, the stochastic trend reverses the correlation between these variables, so employment is counterfactually high when output is low relative to productivity. This is because an increase in productivity growth leads to a jump up in consumption, which is partially accommodated by moving workers from recruiting to production. In addition, recall that I measure output relative to the level of productivity, i.e., $\tilde{y}$, not y. I find that when productivity growth increases, output rises but by less than productivity growth. Similar forces drive the negative correlation between employment and capital relative to productivity.

Other results are more robust across models, especially the comovement of the variables I am most interested in: employment, the consumption–output ratio, and the measured labor wedge. The correlation between the labor wedge and employment rises from 0.96 to 0.97, while the correlation between the labor wedge and the consumption–output ratio remains at -1.00. As I have noted before, both predictions are counterfactual. Still, from the perspective of understanding the predictions

Table 3.5. Model with capital, stochastic trend; comovements of variables in an infinite sample.

		$\tilde{y}$	$\tilde{c}$	θ	$\tilde{k}$	n	wn/y	c/y	$\hat{\tau}$	s
Relative standard deviation		1	2.092	9.636	3.478	0.240	0.128	1.102	1.298	0.534
Correlations	$\tilde{y}$	1	0.995	−0.997	1.000	−0.999	0.013	0.981	−0.971	−0.067
	$\tilde{c}$	—	1	−0.983	0.995	−0.996	0.115	0.996	−0.990	0.036
	θ	—	—	1	−0.996	0.994	0.068	−0.962	0.948	0.147
	$\tilde{k}$	—	—	—	1	−0.999	0.018	0.982	−0.972	−0.062
	n	—	—	—	—	1	−0.034	−0.984	0.975	0.046
	wn/y	—	—	—	—	—	1	0.207	−0.253	0.997
	c/y	—	—	—	—	—	—	1	−0.999	0.128
	$\hat{\tau}$	—	—	—	—	—	—	—	1	−0.175
	s	—	—	—	—	—	—	—	—	1

of the model, it is reassuring that this finding does not appear to depend on the specification of the stochastic process for productivity.

Table 3.6 computes the same statistics for the annual growth rates of various variables. Computing growth rates rather than levels has a quantitatively significant impact on many of the results. Still, the correlation of the labor wedge with employment remains strongly positive, 0.85, and the correlation of the labor wedge with the consumption–output ratio is still strongly negative, −1.00. Again these are inconsistent with the data in the bottom part of table 1.1.

Figure 3.2 shows the impulse response to a one standard-deviation increase in the productivity growth rate s from $\bar{s} = 0.0012$ to $\bar{s} + (\varsigma/(\sqrt{1-\rho^2})) = 0.0047$ at $t = 0$. The cumulative impact of this shock is to raise the level of productivity by about 0.6 percent. Since the capital share is $\alpha = 0.33$, this eventually raises output, consumption, and the capital stock by about $1/(1-\alpha)$ times as much: 0.9 percent.

One advantage to looking at the impulse responses is that I can easily plot the behavior of nonstationary variables. Indeed, figure 3.2 shows the behavior of output y, rather than detrended output $\tilde{y}$, and does the same for the other nonstationary variables: consumption and capital. I find that consumption jumps up upon the impact of the shock, but by less than the increase in output. During the subsequent adjustment, the consumption–output ratio falls to an unusually low level before returning to trend. During this intervening period, firms invest heavily in physical capital, propagating the initial shock.

Following the shock, employment rises modestly for five months, peaking at about 0.06 percent above the initial level. It then gradually reverts to trend. This mirrors the pattern of the consumption–output ratio, driving the strong negative correlation between these two variables. Although the labor share responds slightly more in this model than it does with a deterministic trend, the changes are still tiny. Upon the impact of the shock, it jumps up from 0.6697 to 0.6702 before returning gradually to its original value.

The bottom left panel in figure 3.2 shows the behavior of the labor wedge and confirms that it follows virtually the same pattern as employment. While the magnitude of fluctuations in the labor wedge is significantly greater than the magnitude of the fluctuations in employment, the comovement of the two variables is the opposite of what we find in the data.

Once again, the intuition that search frictions act like a labor adjustment cost but otherwise have little effect on the model is borne out. The solid lines in figure 3.2 show what happens when search frictions are more severe, $\bar{\mu} = 1$. This mainly muffles the response of employment

Table 3.6. Model with capital, stochastic trend; comovements of annual growth rates in an infinite sample.

		$\tilde{y}$	$\tilde{c}$	θ	$\tilde{k}$	n	wn/y	c/y	$\hat{\tau}$	s
Relative standard deviation		1	2.243	9.577	3.465	0.235	0.394	1.319	1.668	1.638
Correlations	$\tilde{y}$	1	0.956	−0.969	1.000	−0.988	0.120	0.867	−0.819	0.093
	$\tilde{c}$	—	1	−0.854	0.961	−0.968	0.405	0.975	−0.951	0.380
	θ	—	—	1	−0.965	0.942	0.130	−0.718	0.651	0.157
	$\tilde{k}$	—	—	—	1	−0.992	0.136	0.876	−0.828	0.109
	n	—	—	—	—	1	−0.189	−0.897	0.851	−0.163
	wn/y	—	—	—	—	—	1	0.597	−0.668	1.000
	c/y	—	—	—	—	—	—	1	−0.996	0.575
	$\hat{\tau}$	—	—	—	—	—	—	—	1	−0.647
	s	—	—	—	—	—	—	—	—	1

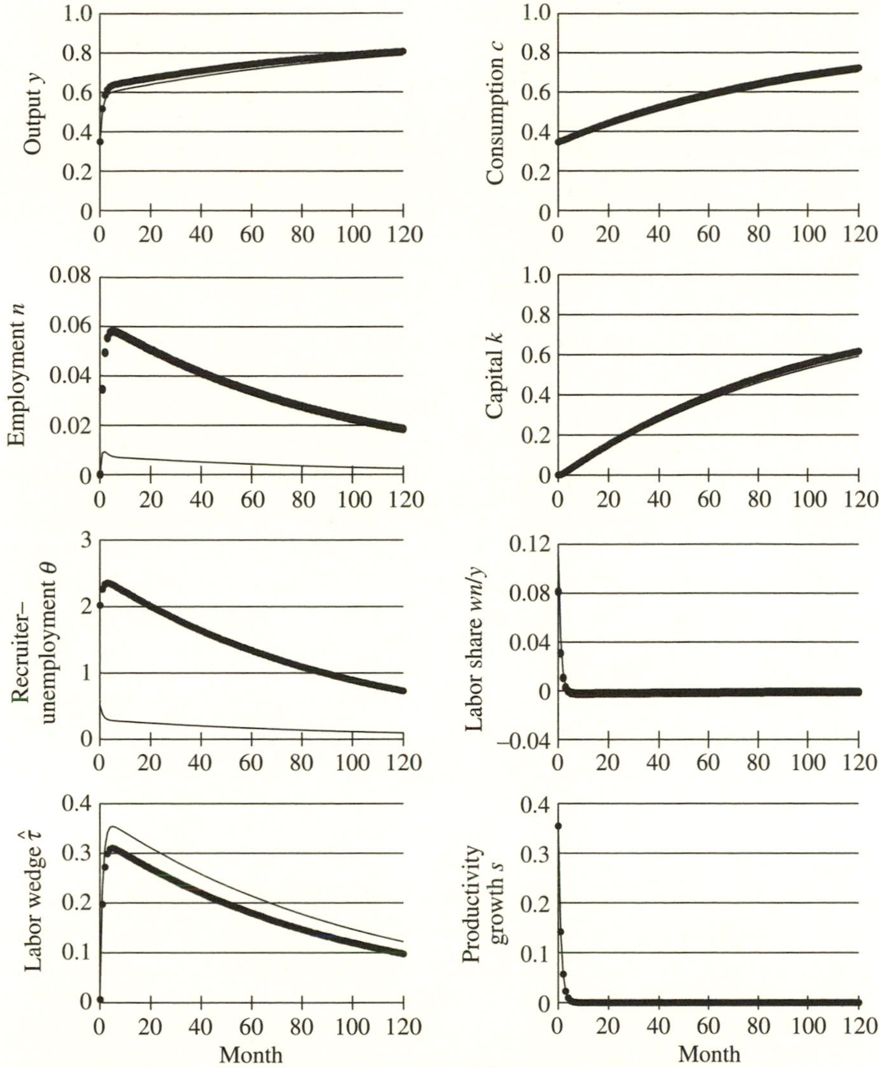

Figure 3.2. Model with capital, stochastic trend. Response to an increase in the productivity growth rate at $t = 0$. All variables are expressed as deviations from initial trend in log points, except the productivity growth rate, which is measured in percentage points. The thick dots show $\bar{\mu} = 2.32$ and the thin lines show more frictions, $\bar{\mu} = 1$.

and the recruiter-unemployment ratio and slightly amplifies the impact on the labor wedge.

As in the model with a deterministic trend, other calibrations of the model, e.g., with workers' bargaining power at $\phi = 0.05$ and the value of leisure at $\gamma = 0.511$, also have little impact on the key result.

While this substantially increases the volatility of employment, until it is 3.6 times as volatile as output (3.5 times in growth rate terms), it does not reverse the positive correlation between the labor wedge and employment (0.68 in levels, 0.45 in growth rates), nor the negative correlation between the labor wedge and the consumption-output ratio (−0.80 in levels, −0.78 in growth rates). Extreme calibrations of the model do not seem to overturn this relationship.

3.2.8 Summary

In a search model with capital, productivity shocks affect employment, much as they do in the frictionless RBC model. But while search frictions provide a notion of unemployment that is absent from the frictionless model, they moderate rather than amplify fluctuations in employment by acting as a labor adjustment cost. The positive comovement between employment and the labor wedge appears to be a robust measure of the model's failure along this dimension. Since the frictionless model already has trouble explaining why hours worked are so volatile and predicts no movement in the labor wedge, this approach to introducing search frictions would seem to be a step in the wrong direction.

3.3 Shocks to the Employment Exit Probability

3.3.1 Model

This section extends the search model with capital to consider the impact of fluctuations in the employment-exit probability x. Such shocks have a direct impact on the employment and unemployment rates by affecting the flow of workers from employment to unemployment. These shocks do not play any role in a model without labor market frictions since they can be costlessly reversed, but they can be an important contributor to aggregate employment fluctuations in an environment where finding a job is time-consuming. For example, research by Davis et al. (1996) showed that the job-destruction rate, measured as the net decline in employment at plants where employment is contracting, is more volatile than the job-creation rate, the net increase in employment at plants where employment is expanding, at least in the U.S. manufacturing sector.

Given the close theoretical link between the job-destruction rate and the employment-exit probability—the fraction of workers who are employed one month but not the next—many economists have presumed that shocks to x, or endogenous fluctuations in x, must be critical in a search model of the business cycle. More recent research using worker flow data has confirmed that variation in the employment-exit probability accounts for one-quarter to one-half of the overall fluctuations in unemployment, while fluctuations in the job-finding rate $f(\theta(s^t))$ account for the remaining portion.[11]

Using the Job Openings and Labor Turnover Survey,[12] I reach a similar conclusion based on quite different data. For example, the hires rate—the annual number of new hires divided by total employment—fell from 46.1 percent to 41.2 percent between the period of expansion in 2007 and the recession in 2008, while the separation rate—the annual number of separations divided by total employment—also fell slightly, from 45.1 percent to 43.3 percent. The fact that hires initially exceeded separations and then fell lower implies that employment was growing in 2007 and shrinking in 2008. But the surprising finding is that total separations actually fell during the downturn. Still, this masks an important divergence between layoffs, which rose from 16.4 percent to 17.8 percent of employment, and quits, which fell from 25.5 percent to 22.6 percent. The behavior of the layoff rate suggests that it may be worth modeling an increase in the employment-exit probability during downturns.

There are two basic approaches to introducing fluctuations in the employment-exit probability into this model. The first is to generate the fluctuations endogenously. In Mortensen and Pissarides (1994), employed workers are subject to idiosyncratic productivity shocks and quit their job when the idiosyncratic shock is too bad. Shocks to aggregate productivity change the endogenous threshold for exiting employment, a potentially important amplification mechanism. The second, simpler, approach treats the employment-exit probability as an exogenous shock, possibly correlated with productivity: say $x = x(s^t)$.

I follow the simpler approach here, allowing for correlated shocks to the deviation of productivity from trend and the deviation of the employment-exit probability from its normal value.[13] Formally, it is useful to think of the state s_t as a vector, $s_t = \{s_{z,t}, s_{x,t}\}$, where $s_{z,t}$ determines the current deviation of productivity from trend, $\log z(s^t) = \bar{s}t + s_{z,t}$, and $s_{x,t}$ determines the deviation of the employment-exit probability from its normal value, $\log x(s^t) = \log \bar{x} + s_{x,t}$. The innovations to the two state variables and their subsequent evolution may be correlated.

[11] The lower bound on the role of the employment-exit probability comes from Shimer (2007b). The upper bound is from Fujita and Ramey (2009), while Elsby et al. (2007) provide an intermediate estimate.

[12] The survey data are available at www.bls.gov/jlt/.

[13] One can also solve the model with a stochastic trend in productivity.

This modification has little effect on the notion of equilibrium or the equations describing it. Again define consumption relative to trend, $\tilde{c}(s^t) \equiv c(s^t)e^{-\bar{s}t/(1-\alpha)}$, capital relative to trend, $\tilde{k}(s^t) \equiv k(s^t)e^{-\bar{s}t/(1-\alpha)}$, and wages relative to trend, $\tilde{w}(s^t) \equiv w(s^t)e^{-\bar{s}t/(1-\alpha)}$. I look for an equilibrium where $\tilde{c}(s^t)$, $\tilde{k}(s^t)$, and $\tilde{w}(s^t)$ are stationary, as are employment $n(s^t)$, the share of recruiters in employment $\nu(s^t)$, and the recruiter–unemployment ratio $\theta(s^t)$.

Following the same logic as in section 3.2, an equilibrium is described by equations (3.53) and (3.56) and a suitably modified version of equations (3.46) and (3.57). First, the employment rate evolves as

$$n(s^{t+1}) = (1 - x(s^t))n(s^t) + f(\theta(s^t))(1 - n(s^t)). \tag{3.66}$$

Second, the combination of the firm's first-order and envelope conditions and the wage equation reduces to

$$\begin{aligned}(1-\alpha)e^{s_{z,t}}&\left(\frac{\tilde{k}(s^t)}{n(s^t)-\theta(s^t)(1-n(s^t))}\right)^{\alpha}\\ &= \beta\mu(\theta(s^t))\sum_{s^{t+1}|s^t}\pi(s_{t+1}|s_t)\frac{\tilde{c}(s^t)}{\tilde{c}(s^{t+1})}\\ &\quad\times\Bigg(-\frac{(1-\phi)\gamma\tilde{c}(s^{t+1})}{1-\tau}\\ &\qquad + (1-\alpha)e^{s_{z,t+1}}\left(\frac{\tilde{k}(s^{t+1})}{n(s^{t+1})-\theta(s^{t+1})(1-n(s^{t+1}))}\right)^{\alpha}\\ &\qquad\quad\times\left(\frac{1-x(s^{t+1})}{\mu(\theta(s^{t+1}))}+1-\phi-\phi\theta(s^{t+1})\right)\Bigg).\end{aligned} \tag{3.67}$$

These last two equations replace the previously constant employment-exit probability with its history-dependent counterpart.

3.3.2 No Productivity Shocks

As usual, I solve the model by log-linearizing around a stochastic steady state. To illustrate the effect of shocks to the employment-exit probability $x(s^t)$, I first calibrate the model with only that shock. That is, I assume that productivity grows deterministically, $\log z(s^t) = \bar{s}t$, and so $s_{z,t} = 0$ for all t. On the other hand, the deviation of the logarithm of the employment-exit probability from its average value, $s_{x,t} = \log x(s^t) - \log \bar{x}$, follows a linear process:

$$s_{x,t+1} = \rho_x s_{x,t} + \varsigma_x v_{x,t+1}, \tag{3.68}$$

where $v_{x,t+1}$ is a white-noise innovation with mean 0 and standard deviation 1. I look for a log-linear approximation to the policy functions

$$\log\theta = \log\bar{\theta} + \theta_x s_x + \theta_n(\log n - \log\bar{n}) + \theta_k(\log\tilde{k} - \log\bar{k}),$$
$$\log\tilde{c} = \log\bar{c} + c_x s_x + c_n(\log n - \log\bar{n}) + c_k(\log\tilde{k} - \log\bar{k}).$$

Here θ_x is the elasticity of the recruiter-unemployment ratio with respect to the deviation of the employment-exit probability from trend and c_x is the analogous elasticity of consumption.

Most of the calibration of the model is unchanged, but I need values for two new parameters: the autocorrelation and standard deviation of the shock to the employment-exit probability, ρ_x and ς_x. I calibrate these using data on the monthly employment-exit probability; see Shimer (2007b) for details on the construction of this time series and the associated series for the monthly job-finding probability.[14] After detrending using a Hodrick–Prescott filter with smoothing parameter 1,600, I find that the quarterly autocorrelation of the employment-exit probability is 0.56, and so I calibrate the monthly autocorrelation to $\rho_x = 0.83 \approx 0.56^{1/3}$. I set the standard deviation to $\varsigma_x = 0.034$ so as to match the unconditional standard deviation of the detrended employment-exit probability:

$$\frac{\varsigma_x}{\sqrt{1-\rho_x^2}} = 0.061.$$

The remaining parameters are fixed at their levels in table 3.2, except that I shut down the productivity shocks.

When I simulate the model, I find that

$$\log\theta = \log 0.078 + 0.098 s_x - 0.480(\log n - \log 0.95) - 2.779(\log\tilde{k} - \log 218.2),$$
$$\log\tilde{c} = \log 4.696 - 0.001 s_x + 0.014(\log n - \log 0.95) + 0.603(\log\tilde{k} - \log 218.2).$$

Notably, an increase in the employment-exit probability raises the recruiter–unemployment ratio. One might have intuitively expected the opposite response. When the employment-exit probability increases, firms do not expect jobs to last as long. This reduces the value of jobs and encourages firms to use their current workers for production rather than recruiting. On the other hand, if firms do not increase their recruiting effort, employment and hence production will be unusually low in

[14] The data are available from my Web site. I use quarterly averages of the underlying monthly data because the monthly data are contaminated by measurement error.

subsequent periods. This reduces the interest rate and gives firms an incentive to recruit more workers. Moreover, wages fall in response to workers' worsening situation, which raises the value of a job and further encourages recruiting. In equilibrium, these last two forces dominate the first.

This has two important implications. First, part of an increase in the employment-exit probability is offset by an endogenous increase in the job-finding probability $f(\theta(s^t))$, reducing the impact on employment. However, this effect is small in practice. I find that the standard deviation of the log job-finding probability is only 0.07 times the standard deviation of the log employment-exit probability. In the data, the job-finding probability is 1.4 times as volatile. Second, the employment-exit probability is positively correlated with the job-finding probability. In the model, the correlation of the logarithm of two variables is 0.91 and the correlation of the annual growth rate of the two variables is 0.98. In the data, the correlation between the two series is −0.43 when detrended and −0.46 when measured as annual growth rates. The model with only a shock to the employment-exit probability fails along both dimensions.

3.3.3 The Two-Shock Model

Next I extend the model to analyze the interaction between shocks to the employment-exit probability and shocks to productivity. More precisely, I allow the shock to the employment-exit probability to also affect productivity; and I introduce a second shock that affects only productivity. I leave the stochastic process for the deviation of the employment-exit probability from its average value (equation (3.68)) unchanged. In addition, I assume that the deviation of log productivity from trend, $s_{z,t} = \log z(s^t) - \bar{s}t$, follows a linear process:

$$s_{z,t+1} = \rho_z s_{z,t} + \varsigma_z \upsilon_{z,t+1} - \varsigma_{zx} \upsilon_{x,t+1}, \tag{3.69}$$

where $\upsilon_{z,t+1}$ is a second white-noise innovation with mean 0 and standard deviation 1, independent from $\upsilon_{x,t+1}$ as well as from all leads and lags of that shock.

It may be useful to think of υ_x as a reallocation shock that affects both the employment-exit probability and productivity, in opposite directions, while υ_z is an aggregate shock that only has an impact on productivity. This approach seems broadly consistent with the idea that some shocks reduce the productivity in all firms, while others reduce average productivity but hurt some firms more than others, leading to an increase in the exit rate from employment (Blanchard and Diamond 1989). Still, labeling one shock "reallocation" and the other "aggregate" is arbitrary, as is introducing the correlation between s_x and s_z through the direct impact of the reallocation shock on productivity.

I leave the stochastic process for the employment-exit probability unchanged, $\rho_x = 0.83$ and $\varsigma_x = 0.034$. I also keep the autocorrelation of productivity fixed at its value in section 3.2.6, $\rho_z = 0.98$. I then use two targets to set the remaining parameters: the weights on the innovations ς_z and ς_{zx}. First, the monthly standard deviation of the deviation of productivity from trend is now equal to $\sqrt{\varsigma_z^2 + \varsigma_{zx}^2}$; I keep that fixed at approximately 0.005. Second, I find that these two parameters are critical for the correlation between the job-finding and employment-exit probabilities: -0.43 in the detrended data.[15] If ς_z is large relative to ς_{zx}, the job-finding and employment-exit probabilities may be positively correlated. When ς_{zx} is relatively large, the two probabilities are too strongly negatively correlated. I set $\varsigma_z = 0.0037$ and $\varsigma_{zx} = 0.0034$ to hit these two targets.

With this calibration, the policy functions become

$$\log \theta = \log 0.078 + 7.387 s_z + 0.098 s_x - 0.480(\log n - \log 0.95) \\ - 2.779(\log \tilde{k} - \log 218.2),$$

$$\log \tilde{c} = \log 4.696 + 0.250 s_z - 0.001 s_x + 0.014(\log n - \log 0.95) \\ + 0.603(\log \tilde{k} - \log 218.2).$$

An increase in reallocation ($\upsilon_{x,t} > 0$) raises s_x and reduces s_z. In this calibration, the latter effect dominates and so the recruiter-unemployment ratio and consumption both fall. An adverse aggregate shock reduces s_z and so has the same effect on the two policy variables.

Turning to the state equations, I find

$$\log n_{+1} = \log 0.95 + 0.126 s_z - 0.032 s_x + 0.312(\log n - \log 0.95) \\ - 0.047(\log \tilde{k} - \log 218.2),$$

$$\log \tilde{k}_{+1} = \log 218.2 + 0.020 s_z + 0.000 s_x + 0.019(\log n - \log 0.95) \\ + 0.991(\log \tilde{k} - \log 218.2).$$

An increase in reallocation reduces next period's employment and slightly increases next period's capital stock.[16] An adverse aggregate shock has the same effect.

As usual, I can express the state of the economy as $m \equiv \{s_z, s_x, \log n - \log \bar{n}, \log \tilde{k} - \log \bar{k}\}$ and represent the transitional dynamics as $m_{+1} =$

[15] In the model, I continue to assume that $f(\theta) = \bar{\mu}\theta^{\eta}$ and so $\log f$ and $\log \theta$ are perfectly correlated. Thus the correlation between the employment-exit probability and the recruiter-unemployment ratio is also -0.43.

[16] The coefficient on s_x is a negligible 0.00002.

$Am + D\upsilon_{+1}$, where A is a 4×4 transition matrix. Am is therefore the expected value of m_{+1} conditional on m and D determines how the shock $\upsilon_{+1} = \{\upsilon_{z,+1}, \upsilon_{x,+1}\}$ affects the state of the system. For this choice of parameters,

$$A = \begin{pmatrix} 0.980 & 0 & 0 & 0 \\ 0 & 0.830 & 0 & 0 \\ 0.126 & -0.032 & 0.312 & -0.047 \\ 0.020 & 0.000 & 0.019 & 0.991 \end{pmatrix} \quad \text{and} \quad D = \begin{pmatrix} \varsigma_z & -\varsigma_{zx} \\ 0 & \varsigma_x \\ 0 & 0 \\ 0 & 0 \end{pmatrix}.$$

The eigenvalues of A are effectively unchanged and remain between 0 and 1. Two of them represent the persistence of the shocks: 0.98 for productivity and 0.83 for the employment-exit probability. The other two eigenvalues represent the slow adjustment of the capital stock to steady state, 0.99, and the comparatively fast adjustment of employment to steady state, 0.31.

The next step is to compute the unconditional variance-covariance matrix of the state variables, $\Sigma \equiv A\Sigma A' + DD'$, and of any associated variables $\tilde{m} \equiv \tilde{A}m$. I confirm that the unconditional standard deviation of the employment-exit probability is 0.061 and that the correlation between the employment-exit probability and the job-finding probability is -0.43. Both numbers are consistent with the detrended data. Moreover, the model predicts that the job-finding probability is slightly more volatile than the employment-exit probability, with a standard deviation of 0.074. In the detrended data, the standard deviation of the job-finding probability is 0.083. Since I did not target this parameter, this may be viewed as a success of the model.

I turn next to the usual matrix of relative standard deviations and correlations in table 3.7. The results are similar to those in the model without the shock to the employment-exit probability: table 3.3. Shocks to the employment-exit probability raise the relative standard deviation of employment from eleven percent of the standard deviation of output to sixteen percent. They also slightly reduce the correlation between employment and all other variables. None of the other numbers in the table change appreciably. In particular, the correlation between the labor wedge and employment remains strongly positive (0.86 instead of 0.96) and the correlation between the labor wedge and the consumption-output ratio weakens slightly, from -1.00 to -0.99. Although I do not include a table with the behavior of annual growth rates, the changes from table 3.4 are similarly modest.

The bottom line is that, although fluctuations in the employment-exit probability may explain some of the movements in employment, they do

Table 3.7. Model with shocks to productivity and to the employment-exit probability, deterministic trend; comovements of variables in an infinite sample.

		$\tilde{y}$	$\tilde{c}$	θ	$\tilde{k}$	n	wn/y	c/y	$\hat{\tau}$	s_z	s_x
Relative standard deviation		1	0.711	4.152	0.984	0.156	0.013	0.525	0.578	0.710	1.713
Correlations	$\tilde{y}$	1	0.865	0.714	0.742	0.674	−0.826	−0.733	0.726	0.974	−0.365
	$\tilde{c}$	—	1	0.272	0.978	0.266	−0.519	−0.293	0.292	0.734	−0.136
	θ	—	—	1	0.066	0.869	−0.877	−0.991	0.999	0.853	−0.432
	$\tilde{k}$	—	—	—	1	0.084	−0.347	−0.089	0.087	0.576	−0.036
	n	—	—	—	—	1	−0.718	−0.925	0.855	0.767	−0.644
	wn/y	—	—	—	—	—	1	0.871	−0.895	−0.905	0.591
	c/y	—	—	—	—	—	—	1	−0.988	−0.861	0.512
	$\hat{\tau}$	—	—	—	—	—	—	—	1	0.863	−0.437
	s_z	—	—	—	—	—	—	—	—	1	−0.402
	s_x	—	—	—	—	—	—	—	—	—	1

not explain the cyclical behavior of the labor wedge. To understand this finding, think back again to a frictionless model. Suppose, for some reason, that there was a shock that forced some household members out of their jobs. The household would immediately respond by sending other members to work, leaving employment and the labor wedge unchanged. With search frictions, the household cannot do this instantaneously, but shocks to the employment-exit probability still act mainly to increase labor turnover and have little effect on the behavior of the labor wedge. The conclusion that search frictions act like a procyclical tax on labor when wages are set by Nash bargaining is unchanged.

3.4 Other Shocks

This model can easily be extended to allow for other shocks, many of which are important in practice. For example, in reality, there are shocks both to the growth rate and to the level of productivity. In reality, the government consumes real resources and the amount of that spending fluctuates over time.[17] Moreover, government spending may vary in a systematic attempt to moderate the impact of shocks. In reality, the technology for producing capital goods has improved more rapidly than the technology for producing consumption goods since World War II, resulting in a systematic decline in the price of capital equipment (Krusell et al. 2000), but there are fluctuations in the relative improvements in these two technologies, i.e., investment-specific technology shocks (Fisher 2006).

Since the methodology for introducing these additional shocks should by now be straightforward, I do not formally develop the models in this book. Still, the effects of these types of shocks are predictable. Without search frictions, each would generate some fluctuations in hours worked and in the consumption–output ratio, but none would break the equivalence between the marginal product of labor in the consumption-goods sector and the tax-adjusted marginal rate of substitution between consumption and leisure. In other words, the labor wedge would be constant. Search frictions then dampen fluctuations in employment or hours worked and so counterfactually cause a positive correlation between the labor wedge and employment and a negative correlation between the labor wedge and the consumption–output ratio. I need to look beyond this model for an explanation of the behavior of the labor wedge.

[17] For a recent attempt to identify government spending shocks, see Blanchard and Perotti (2002).

4
Rigid Wages

The search models in chapters 2 and 3 make two significant departures from the frictionless model in chapter 1. The first is of course the introduction of search frictions. In the search model, firms use some of their employees to recruit new workers, and the difficulty of recruiting depends on the ratio of recruiters to unemployed workers. The second departure is the determination of wages. Although perhaps more subtle, this assumption is no less important. In the presence of search frictions, matched workers and firms are in a bilateral monopoly situation. Standard arguments that competitive forces equate the wage both to the marginal rate of substitution between consumption and leisure and to the marginal product of labor are inapplicable. I have instead assumed that the wage is set by Nash bargaining and was able to express it as a weighted average of the MRS and MPL, as in equation (3.43) for example.

Starting with Shimer (2005) and Hall (2005), a recent body of research has assessed the importance the Nash bargaining assumption by considering the role of wage rigidities in search models.[1] In some sense, one can think of this research as a modern effort to capture certain aspects of disequilibrium macroeconomic models (Barro and Grossman 1971; Benassy 1982; Malinvaud 1977). In particular, a search model with rigid wages provides a way of analyzing "classical unemployment," i.e., unemployment caused by high wages.

It is not easy to model wages that are too high in a competitive framework. Loosely speaking, the equilibrium of a competitive business cycle model like that in chapter 1 is described by κ equations in κ unknown variables, one of which is the wage. Since the wage is an equilibrium object, it does not make sense within the context of the model to ask what happens if it is too high. That is, we know that if the wage is not

[1] Earlier research had found a smaller role for the wage determination mechanism. For example, Mortensen and Pissarides (1999) conclude that, "Although most of the literature on equilibrium unemployment incorporates the Nash bargaining assumption, many of the most salient implications of the theory are robust to the wage mechanism specifically assumed" (p. 2,589). That paper does not allow for aggregate shocks and does not consider rigid-wage models, possibly explaining the different conclusion.

equal to its equilibrium level, one (or more) of the equations describing the equilibrium must be dropped to ensure a solution to the remaining system of $\kappa - 1$ equations in $\kappa - 1$ variables. But a competitive business cycle model provides no guidance about which equation should be dropped, and hence does not inform us about the disequilibrium values of the $\kappa - 1$ other variables.

The search model provides the necessary guidance. In the benchmark model, the wage is a weighted average of the MRS and the MPL, but this restriction is no more plausible than a myriad of other possibilities. Replacing the Nash bargaining solution with an alternative, equally ad hoc, assumption on wage setting substitutes one equation for a different one. I show in this chapter that the model is still well-behaved, and so we can use it to ask what happens if wages are too high, i.e., higher than the wage predicted by the Nash bargaining solution. I find that this goes a long way toward explaining the behavior of the labor wedge.

4.1 Wage Indeterminacy

My starting point is the observation that there is typically a set of wages that a worker is willing to accept, $\tilde{V}_n(s^t, w) \geqslant 0$, and that a firm is willing to pay, $\tilde{J}_n(s^t, w) \geqslant 0$. Take, for example, the model with capital in section 3.2. Using equations (3.38), (3.40), and (3.47), $\tilde{J}_n(s^t, w) \geqslant 0$ if and only if

$$(1-\alpha)z(s^t)\left(\frac{k(s^t)}{n(s^t)-\theta(s^t)(1-n(s^t))}\right)^{\alpha}\left(1+\frac{1-x}{\mu(\theta(s^t))}\right) \geqslant w.$$

The left-hand side is the marginal product of a producer plus the marginal product of the workers freed from recruiting by the possibility of the worker still being around next period: the MPL. The firm will employ a worker as long as this exceeds the wage. Similarly, using equations (3.33), (3.38), (3.42), and (3.43), $\tilde{V}_n(s^t, w) \geqslant 0$ if and only if

$$w \geqslant \frac{\gamma c(s^t)}{1-\tau} - \frac{\phi}{1-\phi}(1-\alpha)z(s^t) \times \left(\frac{k(s^t)}{n(s^t)-\theta(s^t)(1-n(s^t))}\right)^{\alpha}\left(\frac{1-x-f(\theta(s^t))}{\mu(\theta(s^t))}\right).$$

The first term is the marginal rate of substitution between consumption and leisure divided by the share of labor income that the household keeps. The second term incorporates the increase in the probability of employment next period from having a job this period; this drops out if $1 - x = f(\theta(s^t))$, so next period's employment status is independent of this period's. In the calibrated model, $1 - x > f(\theta(s^t))$, meaning that a worker is more likely to be employed next month if she is employed this month. This implies that a worker will accept a job paying an after-tax wage less than $\gamma c(s^t)$, the current MRS between consumption and leisure, in order to increase the likelihood that she has a job next period.

To get a sense of the size of the band of wage indeterminacy, I evaluate these inequalities along a balanced-growth path, as in section 3.2.5, with the usual calibration of model parameters. I find that a worker is willing to work in history s^t if $w > 0.88w(s^t)$, while a firm is willing to employ a worker if $w < 1.12w(s^t)$. This leaves a lot of room for wages to deviate from the equilibrium wage $w(s^t)$ without eliminating the bilateral gains from trade.

Within an employment relationship, the level of the wage does not have any allocational effects and so there is no possibility of a bilateral Pareto improvement for a matched worker and firm. Indeed, since households own the firms, the wage simply affects the distribution of capital and labor income, without altering consumption. But future wages determine whether firms allocate workers to production or recruiting. If they expect wages to be low relative to productivity, they will allocate more workers to recruiting, pulling down the unemployment rate. This is the key reason why the rigid-wage model that I develop in this chapter can significantly affect the unemployment rate.

I start my formal analysis in the next section by extending the benchmark model without capital to allow for rigid wages. There are two ways one could approach this problem. First, one could think hard about why wages are rigid by delving deeper into the wage bargaining problem; recent examples of papers that do that include Hall and Milgrom (2008) and Gertler and Trigari (2009), both of which I discuss in chapter 5. If we can model wage bargaining "correctly," the model may be useful for its out-of-sample predictions and for optimal policy analysis. But while this is undoubtedly a useful research area, it is still unclear which microeconomic model of wage rigidity is correct.

The second approach, the one I adopt here, is admittedly much more ad hoc but has the advantages of transparency and flexibility. I distinguish between a *target wage* $w^*(s^t)$, which is determined by axiomatic Nash bargaining, and the *actual wage* $w(s^t)$, which is a weighted average of the past actual wage adjusted for average productivity growth and the current target wage, $w(s^t) = rw(s^{t-1})e^{\bar{s}} + (1-r)w^*(s^t)$. When $r = 0$, the actual wage and the target wage are equal, as in the benchmark model. When $r = 1$, the actual wage grows with productivity.

I then reintroduce capital into the model. I find that rigid wages significantly amplify employment fluctuations and may be able to explain the behavior of the labor wedge. A transitory increase in productivity growth leads to a persistent increase in employment because wages take some time to catch up with productivity. During much of the adjustment process, the measured labor wedge is negative, which is consistent with the empirical correlation between the labor wedge and employment.

Since there are many alternative models of rigid wages, each of which would potentially give a different prediction for the behavior of employment, it is unclear whether the model's structure puts any restrictions on the data it can generate. Following Hall (2009), I finish this chapter by arguing that it does. I show that rigid wages can make it look as if the elasticity of labor supply is effectively infinite along the extensive margin. That is, the search model with rigid wages can potentially explain why it looks as if the elasticity of labor supply is very high, even though households would prefer a smoother path of employment at the prevailing wage.

4.2 No Capital

I return to the model without capital from section 2.2. The households' and firms' problems are the same, with only the wage-setting procedure having changed. I repeat the main results from those problems here before turning to wages.

4.2.1 Households

I assume that the period utility function is $\log c$ for an unemployed individual who consumes c and $\log c - \gamma$ for an employed individual who consumes c. The household problem then gives three key results. First is the consumption Euler equation with log preferences over consumption:

$$q_t(s^{t+1}) = \beta \frac{\Pi(s^{t+1})c(s^t)}{\Pi(s^t)c(s^{t+1})}. \tag{4.1}$$

Second, the value of having an additional worker employed is equal to her after-tax wage, measured in units of marginal utility, minus the disutility of working, plus the discounted value of having an additional worker employed next period, multiplied by the increase in the probability that the worker is employed next period if she has a job this period:

$$\begin{aligned} V_n(s^t, a(s^t), n(s^t)) \\ &= \frac{(1-\tau)w(s^t)}{c(s^t)} - \gamma \\ &\quad + \beta(1 - x - f(\theta(s^t))) \sum_{s^{t+1}|s^t} \frac{\Pi(s^{t+1})}{\Pi(s^t)} V_n(s^{t+1}, a(s^{t+1}), n(s^{t+1})). \end{aligned} \tag{4.2}$$

Finally, the marginal value of having a worker employed at an arbitrary wage w rather than unemployed is

$$\tilde{V}_n(s^t, w) = \frac{(1-\tau)(w - w(s^t))}{c(s^t)} + V_n(s^t, a(s^t), n(s^t)), \tag{4.3}$$

i.e., the increment in the after-tax wage, measured in utils, plus the marginal value of an employed worker.

4.2.2 Firms

The firm's problem also delivers three key results. First, for firms to be willing to engage in both recruiting and production, the returns from the two activities must be equal. Producing yields output $z(s^t)$ today, while recruiting yields $\mu(\theta(s^t))$ new employees tomorrow, each valued at $\bar{J}(s^{t+1})$, so

$$z(s^t) = \mu(\theta(s^t)) \sum_{s^{t+1}|s^t} q_t(s^{t+1}) \bar{J}(s^{t+1}). \tag{4.4}$$

Second, by employing one more worker today, the firm gets an additional $z(s^t)$ units of output. It may also reallocate $(1 - x)/\mu(\theta(s^t))$ workers from recruiting to production and still have the same expected employment next period, further raising current production. On the other hand, it must pay the wage. Putting this together, when the firm is indifferent between recruiting and producing, the marginal value of employing an additional worker is

$$\bar{J}(s^t) = z(s^t)\left(1 + \frac{1-x}{\mu(\theta(s^t))}\right) - w(s^t). \tag{4.5}$$

Finally, the marginal value of employing a worker at an arbitrary wage w rather than losing the worker is

$$\tilde{J}_n(s^t, w) = w(s^t) - w + \bar{J}(s^t), \tag{4.6}$$

the decrement in the wage plus the marginal value of a job.

4.2.3 Market Clearing

Next there are two market-clearing conditions. The employment level next period is equal to the number of employed workers who keep their job plus the number of unemployed workers who find a job,

$$n(s^{t+1}) = (1-x)n(s^t) + f(\theta(s^t))(1-n(s^t)), \tag{4.7}$$

and consumption is equal to productivity times the number of employed workers who are not recruiters,

$$c(s^t) = z(s^t)(n(s^t) - \theta(s^t)(1-n(s^t))), \tag{4.8}$$

where the number of recruiters is the recruiter–unemployment ratio, θ, times unemployment, $1-n$. Note that this last condition combines equations (2.44) and (2.45).

4.2.4 Wages

I turn now to the new part of the model: backward-looking wage setting. I assume that the target wage solves the Nash bargaining problem,

$$w^*(s^t) = \arg\max_w \tilde{V}_n(s^t, w)^{\phi} \tilde{J}_n(s^t, w)^{1-\phi}, \tag{4.9}$$

while the actual wage is a weighted average of last period's wage, adjusted for productivity growth, and the current target wage,

$$w(s^t) = rw(s^{t-1})e^{\bar{s}} + (1-r)w^*(s^t), \tag{4.10}$$

where $r \in [0,1)$ is a parameter and $\bar{s}$ is long-run average productivity growth:

$$\bar{s} \equiv \lim_{t' \to \infty} \sum_{s^{t'} | s^t} \frac{\Pi(s^{t'})}{\Pi(s^t)} \frac{\log z(s^{t'}) - \log z(s^t)}{t' - t}.$$

This notation and the discussion that follows presumes that $\bar{s}$ is well-defined and independent of the initial history s^t, consistent with either a deterministic or a stochastic trend in productivity. Note that the benchmark model imposes $r = 0$, while $r = 1$ corresponds to wages that do not respond to shocks, in which case the wage path is determined by an exogenous initial condition.

I use these equations to solve for the target wage. First, equations (4.3) and (4.6) imply

$$\frac{\partial \tilde{V}_n(s^t,w)}{\partial w} = \frac{1-\tau}{c(s^t)},$$

$$\tilde{V}_n(s^t,w^*(s^t)) = \frac{(1-\tau)(w^*(s^t)-w(s^t))}{c(s^t)} + V_n(s^t,a(s^t),n(s^t)),$$

$$\frac{\partial \tilde{J}_n(s^t,w)}{\partial w} = -1,$$

$$\tilde{J}_n(s^t,w^*(s^t)) = w(s^t) - w^*(s^t) + \bar{J}(s^t).$$

Use these expressions to write the necessary and sufficient first-order condition from maximizing equation (4.9) as

$$(1-\phi)V_n(s^t,a(s^t),n(s^t))c(s^t) = (1-\tau)(\phi\bar{J}(s^t) + w(s^t) - w^*(s^t)). \tag{4.11}$$

Combining this with equation (4.2) and using the Euler equation (4.1) implies that

$$\begin{aligned}
&(1-\tau)(\phi\bar{J}(s^t) + w(s^t) - w^*(s^t)) \\
&\quad = (1-\phi)(1-\tau)w(s^t) - (1-\phi)c(s^t)\gamma \\
&\qquad + (1-\tau)(1-x-f(\theta(s^t))) \\
&\qquad\qquad \times \sum_{s^{t+1}|s^t} q_t(s^{t+1})(\phi\bar{J}(s^{t+1}) + w(s^{t+1}) - w^*(s^{t+1})).
\end{aligned}$$

Next eliminate $\bar{J}(s^t)$ using equation (4.5) and $\bar{J}(s^{t+1})$ using equation (4.4). After simplifying I obtain an equation for the wage target:

$$\begin{aligned}
w^*(s^t) &= \phi z(s^t)(1+\theta(s^t)) + (1-\phi)\frac{\gamma c(s^t)}{1-\tau} \\
&\quad + (1-x-f(\theta(s^t))) \sum_{s^{t+1}|s^t} q_t(s^{t+1})(w^*(s^{t+1}) - w(s^{t+1})).
\end{aligned} \tag{4.12}$$

The first two terms are the usual weighted average of the current MPL and the current MRS, while the third term is new. The wage rigidity introduces the possibility that the actual and target wages differ: $w(s^{t+1}) \neq w^*(s^{t+1})$. Assuming that $1 - x > f(\theta(s^t))$, so a worker is more likely to be employed next period if she is employed this period, the expectation that the actual wage will be below the target wage next period puts upward pressure on the target wage this period. Nash bargaining automatically compensates for the loss in future wages.

To understand wage dynamics when $r \in (0,1)$, suppose for a moment that productivity, consumption, and the ratio of recruiters to unemployed workers are constant. Also assume that $\bar{s} = 0$. Then equation (4.12) reduces to

$$w_t^* = \phi\bar{z}(1+\bar{\theta}) + (1-\phi)\frac{\gamma\bar{c}}{1-\tau} + \beta(1-x-f(\bar{\theta}))(w_{t+1}^* - w_{t+1}).$$

Together with the wage adjustment equation (4.10), this is a pair of first-order linear difference equations for the actual wage w_t and the target wage w_t^*. The eigenvalues of the resulting system are both positive, with one bigger than unity and one smaller than unity, consistent with saddle path dynamics. Since both eigenvalues are positive, the actual and target wages converge monotonically toward the steady state

$$\bar{w} \equiv \phi\bar{z}(1+\bar{\theta}) + (1-\phi)\frac{\gamma\bar{c}}{1-\tau}.$$

Moreover, along the saddle path, there is a decreasing relationship between w_t and w_t^*. That is, $w_0 \gtrless \bar{w}$ implies $w_t \gtrless \bar{w} \gtrless w_t^*$ for all t. Along the adjustment path, the wage solves $w_{t+1} = \tilde{r}w_t + (1-\tilde{r})\bar{w}$, where

$$\tilde{r} \equiv \frac{1+r\beta(1-x-f(\bar{\theta})) - \sqrt{(1+r\beta(1-x-f(\bar{\theta})))^2 - 4r^2\beta(1-x-f(\bar{\theta}))}}{2r\beta(1-x-f(\theta))}.$$

One can confirm that $0 < \tilde{r} < r$, so the adjustment toward steady state is faster than under the "naive" rule $w_{t+1} = rw_t + (1-r)\bar{w}$. This is because the target wage is forward-looking, rising above steady state when next period's wage is expected to be below next period's target, which pulls the actual wage toward the steady-state wage.

4.2.5 Balanced Growth

Suppose there is deterministic Hicks-neutral productivity growth at rate $\bar{s} > 0$, $\log z(s^{t+1}) = \log z(s^t) + \bar{s}$. There is an equilibrium where consumption and actual and target wages grow at rate $\bar{s}$, while employment and the ratio of recruiters to unemployed are constant. That is, $c(s^t) = \bar{c}z(s^t)$, $w(s^t) = \bar{w}z(s^t)$, $w^*(s^t) = \bar{w}^*z(s^t)$, $n(s^t) = \bar{n}$, and $\theta(s^t) = \bar{\theta}$. The proof of this claim is simple. Under the conjectured functional forms, equation (4.10) implies that actual and target wages are equal, $\bar{w} = \bar{w}^*$, and hence a comparison of equations (2.43) and (4.12) indicates that both are equal to their value in the flexible-wage economy. The remaining equations are therefore also unchanged.

The assumption that the wage is a weighted average of last period's wage *adjusted for productivity growth* and the current target wage is important for this result. Without the adjustment, faster productivity growth would reduce the current wage relative to the target wage. This would act like a reduction in workers' bargaining power, giving firms an incentive to shift workers into recruiting and reducing unemployment along the balanced-growth path. The adjustment for productivity growth keeps a clear distinction between the effects of backward-looking wages and the effects of productivity growth.

4.2.6 Productivity Shocks: Deterministic Trend

Now suppose that $\log z(s^t) = \bar{s}t + s_t$, where s_t follows a stationary first-order Markov process with mean 0. Thus $\bar{s}$ is the deterministic-growth rate while s_t represents a transitory deviation from trend. Let $\pi(s_{t+1}|s_t) \equiv \Pi(s^{t+1})/\Pi(s^t)$ denote the probability of state s_{t+1} next period conditional on state s_t this period. As usual, define consumption, actual wages, and target wages relative to the underlying growth rate as $\tilde{c}(s^t) \equiv c(s^t)e^{-\bar{s}t}$, $\tilde{w}(s^t) \equiv w(s^t)e^{-\bar{s}t}$, and $\tilde{w}^*(s^t) \equiv w^*(s^t)e^{-\bar{s}t}$. I look for an equilibrium where detrended consumption, detrended actual and target wages, and employment and the recruiter-unemployment ratio are stationary.

In the stochastic model, equations (4.1), (4.4), and (4.5) imply

$$e^{s_t} = \beta\mu(\theta(s^t)) \times \sum_{s^{t+1}|s^t} \pi(s_{t+1}|s_t)\frac{\tilde{c}(s^t)}{\tilde{c}(s^{t+1})}\left(e^{s_{t+1}}\frac{1-x+\mu(\theta(s^{t+1}))}{\mu(\theta(s^{t+1}))} - \tilde{w}(s^{t+1})\right).$$

Equation (4.8) implies that $\tilde{c}(s^t) = e^{s_t}(n(s^t) - \theta(s^t)(1-n(s^t)))$. Use this to eliminate $\tilde{c}(s^t)$ from the previous equation:

$$1 = \beta\mu(\theta(s^t)) \sum_{s^{t+1}|s^t} \pi(s_{t+1}|s_t)\frac{n(s^t) - \theta(s^t)(1-n(s^t))}{n(s^{t+1}) - \theta(s^{t+1})(1-n(s^{t+1}))} \times \left(1 + \frac{1-x}{\mu(\theta(s^{t+1}))} - \frac{\tilde{w}(s^{t+1})}{e^{s_{t+1}}}\right). \quad (4.13)$$

Similarly, eliminate $\tilde{c}(s^t)$ from equation (4.12) for the target wage:

$$\begin{aligned}\tilde{w}^*(s^t)e^{-s_t} &= \phi(1+\theta(s^t)) + (1-\phi)\frac{\gamma}{1-\tau}(n(s^t) - \theta(s^t)(1-n(s^t))) \\ &\quad + \beta(1-x-f(\theta(s^t))) \\ &\quad \times \sum_{s^{t+1}|s^t} \pi(s_{t+1}|s_t)\frac{n(s^t) - \theta(s^t)(1-n(s^t))}{n(s^{t+1}) - \theta(s^{t+1})(1-n(s^{t+1}))}\left(\frac{\tilde{w}^*(s^{t+1}) - \tilde{w}(s^{t+1})}{e^{s_{t+1}}}\right).\end{aligned} \quad (4.14)$$

The state variables n and $\tilde{w}$ are in turn governed by equation (4.7), which is unchanged, and by equation (4.10), which reduces to

$$\tilde{w}(s^t) = r\tilde{w}(s^{t-1}) + (1-r)\tilde{w}^*(s^t). \tag{4.15}$$

Equations (4.7) and (4.13)–(4.15) depend only on stationary variables and so admit a solution in which the policy functions and the evolution of employment and wages relative to trend depend only on the current value of the exogenous state variable s_t, the current level of employment $n(s^t)$, and the previous period's wage relative to trend $\tilde{w}(s^{t-1})$. That is, the policy functions take the forms $\theta(s^t) = \Theta(s_t, n(s^t), \tilde{w}(s^{t-1}))$ and $\tilde{w}^*(s^t) = W^*(s_t, n(s^t), \tilde{w}(s^{t-1}))$ and the state variables evolve according to

$$n(s^{t+1}) = N(s_t, n(s^t), \tilde{w}(s^{t-1})) \quad \text{and} \quad \tilde{w}(s^t) = W(s_t, n(s^t), \tilde{w}(s^{t-1})).$$

I log-linearize equations (4.7) and (4.13)–(4.15) around a stochastic steady state for $(s, n, \tilde{w}_{-1})$ and look for policy functions and laws of motion that are linear in the deviation of the state variables from their stochastic steady-state values. The model has one new parameter: the persistence of wages r. I initially set $r = 0.9$, but I consider the sensitivity of my results to that parameter. The remaining parameters are unchanged from their values in table 3.2, except the capital share, which is implicitly $\alpha = 0$, and the value of leisure, which I recalibrate to $\gamma = 0.579$ to ensure a five percent unemployment rate in steady state.

With this calibration, the equilibrium policy functions are

$$\begin{aligned}\log\theta &= \log 0.078 + 24.351s - 0.743(\log n - \log 0.95)\\ &\qquad - 26.034(\log\tilde{w}_{-1} - \log 0.995),\\ \log\tilde{w}^* &= \log 0.995 + 2.471s + 0.476(\log n - \log 0.95)\\ &\qquad - 1.574(\log\tilde{w}_{-1} - \log 0.995),\end{aligned}$$

where $\tilde{w}_{-1}$ is last period's wage, 0.078 is the steady-state recruiter-unemployment ratio, $\bar{n} = 0.95$ is the steady-state employment rate, and $\bar{w} = 0.995$ is the steady-state ratio of wages to productivity. In contrast to the flexible-wage version of this model, where productivity has no real effects, positive productivity shocks now raise the recruiter-unemployment ratio, while high wages have the opposite effect. On the other hand, if last period's wage was above trend, the current target wage will be below trend, helping to pull the actual wage back to trend. This is the saddle path dynamics of the actual and target wages that I discussed before.

The state variables evolve according to

$$n_{+1} = \log 0.95 + 0.414s + 0.307(\log n - \log 0.95) \\ - 0.443(\log \tilde{w}_{-1} - \log 0.995),$$

$$\tilde{w} = \log 0.995 + 0.247s + 0.048(\log n - \log 0.95) \\ + 0.743(\log \tilde{w}_{-1} - \log 0.995).$$

An increase in productivity immediately raises employment and wages. Higher employment continues to put upward pressure on wages, while higher wages are self-reinforcing because of the slow adjustment process. Higher wages eventually start to reduce employment, returning the economy to steady state.

As usual, I can stack the state variables, $m = \{s, \log n - \log \bar{n}, \log \tilde{w}_{-1} - \log \bar{w}\}$, and express the transitional dynamics as $m_{+1} = Am + Dv_{+1}$. The eigenvalues of the matrix A are all positive and less than one, confirming that the equilibrium is locally stable. The largest, 0.980, is equal to the autocorrelation in productivity. The lowest, 0.363, is determined by the rapid adjustment of employment to steady state. The intermediate one, 0.687, reflects the speed of adjustment in wages. Notably this is significantly faster than the naive persistence measure $r = 0.9$ and suggests that the autocorrelation of wages may be low despite their strong backward-looking nature.

Finally, I can compute the unconditional variance–covariance matrix $\Sigma = A\Sigma A' + DD'$. Using this, I find that the unconditional standard deviation of log employment is about fifteen percent of the unconditional standard deviation of the productivity shock, or 0.004. While small, this is an improvement compared with the neutrality result in the flexible-wage model. Conversely, the unconditional standard deviation of log wages falls slightly, from 0.025 in the flexible-wage model ($r = 0$) to 0.023 in the model with rigid wages.

When wage rigidities are more severe, say $r = 0.99$, all the results are amplified. In this case, the linearized state variables satisfy

$$n_{+1} = \log 0.95 + 1.570s + 0.338(\log n - \log 0.95) \\ - 1.822(\log \tilde{w}_{-1} - \log 0.995),$$

$$\tilde{w} = \log 0.995 + 0.066s + 0.006(\log n - \log 0.95) \\ + 0.925(\log \tilde{w}_{-1} - \log 0.995).$$

Compared with the case of $r = 0.9$, employment is more responsive and wages are less responsive to shocks, while both variables respond more to past wages since that state is increasingly relevant. The local dynamics remain stable, with eigenvalues 0.980, 0.906, and 0.356. Although the middle eigenvalue is higher than before, the persistence of the root associated with wage dynamics remains far below unity. Nevertheless, this significantly alters the variance-covariance matrix. The unconditional standard deviation of log employment is slightly larger than the unconditional standard deviation of the productivity shock, 0.025. This still does little to mute the behavior of wages, whose standard deviation falls only slightly more, to 0.020.

These results suggest that rigid wages may significantly amplify productivity shocks without much affecting the behavior of wages. Although it is possible to further explore the model without capital, for example by studying a stochastic trend in productivity, the implications of rigid wages for labor market outcomes are best understood by reintroducing savings and investment. I return to the more general model now.

4.3 Capital

I extend the model with capital in section 3.2 to allow for rigid wages. Once again, the households' and firms' problems are unchanged. I repeat the main results from those problems before describing wage determination.

4.3.1 Households

The implications of household optimization are summarized by equations (3.31)–(3.33), or equivalently equations (4.1)–(4.3). I repeat them for convenience. Consumption satisfies the Euler equation, determining the intertemporal price:

$$q_t(s^{t+1}) = \beta \frac{\Pi(s^{t+1})c(s^t)}{\Pi(s^t)c(s^{t+1})}. \tag{4.16}$$

The marginal value of an additional employed household member is the after-tax wage expressed in units of marginal utility, minus the disutility of work, plus the increase in the probability that the worker is employed the following period, multiplied by the expected marginal value of an employed household member in that period:

$$\begin{aligned} &V_n(s^t, a(s^t), n(s^t)) \\ &\quad = \frac{(1-\tau)w(s^t)}{c(s^t)} - \gamma \\ &\qquad + \beta(1 - x - f(\theta(s^t))) \sum_{s^{t+1}|s^t} \frac{\Pi(s^{t+1})}{\Pi(s^t)} V_n(s^{t+1}, a(s^{t+1}), n(s^{t+1})). \end{aligned} \tag{4.17}$$

Finally, the marginal value of having a worker employed at an arbitrary wage w rather than unemployed is the value of receiving w rather than the equilibrium wage $w(s^t)$, discounting taxes and expressed in units of marginal utility, plus the value of an additional employed household member:

$$\tilde{V}_n(s^t, w) = \frac{(1-\tau)(w - w(s^t))}{c(s^t)} + V_n(s^t, a(s^t), n(s^t)). \tag{4.18}$$

4.3.2 Firms

The implications of firm optimization are given by the four conditions in equations (3.37)–(3.40). Again I repeat them for convenience, eliminating the share of recruiters in employment using the analogue of equation (3.47). First, if firms are at an interior solution for recruiting and production, then

$$(1-\alpha)z(s^t)\left(\frac{k(s^t)}{n(s^t) - \theta(s^t)(1-n(s^t))}\right)^{\alpha} \\ = \mu(\theta(s^t)) \sum_{s^{t+1}|s^t} q_t(s^{t+1}) J_n(s^{t+1}, n(s^{t+1}), k(s^{t+1})). \tag{4.19}$$

The left-hand side is the output generated by a producer in the current period, where $n - \theta(1-n)$ is the number of producers, i.e., workers minus recruiters. The right-hand side is the future value generated by a recruiter.

Second, the marginal value of an employed worker in history s^t is

$$J_n(s^t, n(s^t), k(s^t)) \\ = (1-\alpha)z(s^t)\left(\frac{k(s^t)}{n(s^t) - \theta(s^t)(1-n(s^t))}\right)^{\alpha}\left(1 + \frac{1-x}{\mu(\theta(s^t))}\right) - w(s^t). \tag{4.20}$$

The worker can produce this period. In addition, her potential employment next period frees $(1-x)/\mu(\theta(s^t))$ other workers from having to recruit, while allowing the firm to maintain its size. Finally, she is paid a wage.

Third, the firm must be indifferent about investing:

$$1 = \sum_{s^{t+1}|s^t} q_t(s^{t+1})\left(\alpha z(s^{t+1})\left(\frac{k(s^{t+1})}{n(s^{t+1}) - \theta(s^{t+1})(1-n(s^{t+1}))}\right)^{\alpha-1} + 1 - \delta\right). \tag{4.21}$$

The left-hand side is the cost of buying a unit of capital. The right-hand side is the expected net marginal product of capital next period.

Finally, the marginal profit of employing a worker at an arbitrary wage w in history s^t and at the equilibrium wage thereafter, rather than losing the worker, is equal to the difference between the equilibrium wage and her actual wage plus the marginal value of an employed worker:

$$\tilde{J}_n(s^t, w) = w(s^t) - w + J_n(s^t, n(s^t), k(s^t)). \qquad (4.22)$$

4.3.3 Market Clearing

There are two market-clearing conditions. Employment next period is

$$n(s^{t+1}) = (1 - x)n(s^t) + f(\theta(s^t))(1 - n(s^t)). \qquad (4.23)$$

And the capital stock next period is

$$k(s^{t+1}) = z(s^t)k(s^t)^{\alpha}(n(s^t) - \theta(s^t)(1 - n(s^t)))^{1-\alpha} + (1 - \delta)k(s^t) - c(s^t). \qquad (4.24)$$

Again these are unchanged from the flexible-wage model.

4.3.4 Wages

As in the first part of this chapter, I assume that the target wage solves the Nash bargaining problem,

$$w^*(s^t) = \arg\max_{w} \tilde{V}_n(s^t, w)^{\phi} \tilde{J}_n(s^t, w)^{1-\phi}, \qquad (4.25)$$

while the actual wage is a weighted average of last period's wage adjusted for productivity growth and the current target wage,

$$w(s^t) = rw(s^{t-1})e^{\bar{s}/(1-\alpha)} + (1 - r)w^*(s^t), \qquad (4.26)$$

where $r \in [0, 1)$ and $\bar{s}$ is the average productivity growth rate. Note that if total factor productivity grows at a steady rate $\bar{s}$, consumption, output, and wages all grow at rate $\bar{s}/(1 - \alpha)$, so the adjustment keeps wages in line with average wage growth.

I characterize the target wage using the same approach as in the first part of the chapter. In particular, use equations (4.18) and (4.22) to determine $\tilde{V}_n(s^t, w^*(s^t))$, $\tilde{J}_n(s^t, w^*(s^t))$, and their partial derivatives. Then use these to write the necessary and sufficient first-order condition from maximizing equation (4.25) as

$$\begin{aligned}(1 - \phi)&V_n(s^t, a(s^t), n(s^t))c(s^t) \\ &= (1 - \tau)(\phi J_n(s^t, n(s^t), k(s^t)) + w(s^t) - w^*(s^t)). \qquad (4.27)\end{aligned}$$

Combining this with equation (4.17) and using the Euler equation (4.16) implies

$$\begin{aligned}(1-\tau)(\phi J_n(s^t,n(s^t),k(s^t))+w(s^t)-w^*(s^t))\\ =(1-\phi)(1-\tau)w(s^t)-(1-\phi)\gamma c(s^t)+(1-\tau)(1-x-f(\theta(s^t)))\\ \times\sum_{s^{t+1}|s^t} q_t(s^{t+1})(\phi J_n(s^{t+1},n(s^{t+1}),k(s^{t+1}))+w(s^{t+1})-w^*(s^{t+1})).\end{aligned}$$

Eliminate the current marginal value of a worker $J_n(s^t,n(s^t),k(s^t))$ using equation (4.20) and the expected future marginal value of a worker $\sum_{s^{t+1}|s^t} q_t(s^{t+1})J_n(s^{t+1},n(s^{t+1}),k(s^{t+1}))$ using equation (4.19). This gives an equation for the target wage:

$$\begin{aligned}w^*(s^t)\\ =\phi(1-\alpha)z(s^t)\left(\frac{k(s^t)}{n(s^t)-\theta(s^t)(1-n(s^t))}\right)^{\alpha}(1+\theta(s^t))+(1-\phi)\frac{\gamma c(s^t)}{1-\tau}\\ +(1-x-f(\theta(s^t)))\sum_{s^{t+1}|s^t} q_t(s^{t+1})(w^*(s^{t+1})-w(s^{t+1})).\end{aligned} \tag{4.28}$$

This is a generalization of equation (3.43) to the case where $w(s^t)$ and $w^*(s^t)$ are not necessarily equal, or equivalently a generalization of equation (4.12) to the case where the marginal product of labor is not simply $z(s^t)$.

4.3.5 Balanced Growth

As in the model without capital, rigid wages do not affect the balanced growth path. That is, if productivity grows deterministically at rate $\bar{s}>0$, $\log z(s^{t+1})=\log z(s^t)+\bar{s}$, then there is an equilibrium in which consumption, capital, and actual and target wages grow at rate $\bar{s}/(1-\alpha)$, while employment and the ratio of recruiters to unemployed are constant. To prove this, assume that the actual and target wages both grow at rate $\bar{s}/(1-\alpha)$, $w(s^t)=\bar{w}e^{\bar{s}t/(1-\alpha)}$ and $w^*(s^t)=\bar{w}^*e^{\bar{s}t/(1-\alpha)}$. Then equation (4.26) implies that $\bar{w}=r\bar{w}+(1-r)\bar{w}^*$, or that $\bar{w}=\bar{w}^*$. But if the actual wage is equal to the target wage, which in turn solves the Nash bargaining problem, the actual wage is unchanged from the flexible-wage model. Since nothing else has changed, the entire equilibrium is unchanged.

4.3.6 Productivity Shocks: Deterministic Trend

To introduce shocks into the model, assume first that productivity fluctuates around a deterministic trend, $\log z(s^t)=\bar{s}t+s_t$, where

s_t follows a stationary first-order Markov process with mean 0. Let $\pi(s_{t+1}|s_t) \equiv \Pi(s^{t+1})/\Pi(s^t)$ denote the probability of state s_{t+1} next period conditional on state s_t this period. Define consumption, capital, actual wages, and target wages relative to the underlying growth rate as $\tilde{c}(s^t) \equiv c(s^t)\mathrm{e}^{-\bar{s}t/(1-\alpha)}$, $\tilde{k}(s^t) \equiv k(s^t)\mathrm{e}^{-\bar{s}t/(1-\alpha)}$, $\tilde{w}(s^t) \equiv w(s^t)\mathrm{e}^{-\bar{s}t/(1-\alpha)}$, and $\tilde{w}^*(s^t) \equiv w^*(s^t)\mathrm{e}^{-\bar{s}t/(1-\alpha)}$.

I rewrite the equations in terms of stationary variables. The first two are unchanged from the flexible-wage model. Replace $q_t(s^{t+1})$ in equation (4.21) using equation (4.16) to obtain

$$\mathrm{e}^{\bar{s}/(1-\alpha)} = \beta \sum_{s^{t+1}|s^t} \pi(s_{t+1}|s_t)\frac{\tilde{c}(s^t)}{\tilde{c}(s^{t+1})} \times \left(\alpha \mathrm{e}^{s_{t+1}}\left(\frac{\tilde{k}(s^{t+1})}{n(s^{t+1}) - \theta(s^{t+1})(1-n(s^{t+1}))}\right)^{\alpha-1} + 1 - \delta\right), \tag{4.29}$$

which is identical to equation (3.53). Similarly, eliminate J_n between equations (4.19) and (4.20), giving

$$\begin{aligned}(1-\alpha)\mathrm{e}^{s_t}&\left(\frac{\tilde{k}(s^t)}{n(s^t) - \theta(s^t)(1-n(s^t))}\right)^{\alpha} \\ &= \beta\mu(\theta(s^t)) \sum_{s^{t+1}|s^t} \pi(s_{t+1}|s_t)\frac{\tilde{c}(s^t)}{\tilde{c}(s^{t+1})} \\ &\quad\times \left((1-\alpha)\mathrm{e}^{s_{t+1}}\left(\frac{\tilde{k}(s^{t+1})}{n(s^{t+1}) - \theta(s^{t+1})(1-n(s^{t+1}))}\right)^{\alpha}\left(1 + \frac{1-x}{\mu(\theta(s^{t+1}))}\right) - \tilde{w}(s^{t+1})\right),\end{aligned} \tag{4.30}$$

which is identical to equation (3.54).

The expression for the target wage, equation (4.28), is new to this model. Expressed in terms of stationary variables, it becomes

$$\begin{aligned}\tilde{w}^*(s^t) &= \phi(1-\alpha)\mathrm{e}^{s_t}\left(\frac{\tilde{k}(s^t)}{n(s^t) - \theta(s^t)(1-n(s^t))}\right)^{\alpha}(1+\theta(s^t)) + (1-\phi)\frac{\gamma\tilde{c}(s^t)}{1-\tau} \\ &\quad + \beta(1-x-f(\theta(s^t))) \sum_{s^{t+1}|s^t} \pi(s_{t+1}|s_t)\frac{\tilde{c}(s^t)}{\tilde{c}(s^{t+1})}(\tilde{w}^*(s^{t+1}) - \tilde{w}(s^{t+1})).\end{aligned} \tag{4.31}$$

The state equations (4.24) and (4.26) reduce to

$$\tilde{k}(s^{t+1})\mathrm{e}^{\bar{s}/(1-\alpha)} = \mathrm{e}^{s_t}\tilde{k}(s^t)^{\alpha}(n(s^t) - \theta(s^t)(1-n(s^t)))^{1-\alpha} + (1-\delta)\tilde{k}(s^t) - \tilde{c}(s^t) \tag{4.32}$$

for the capital stock, which is identical to equation (3.56), and

$$\tilde{w}(s^t) = r\tilde{w}(s^{t-1}) + (1-r)\tilde{w}^*(s^t) \tag{4.33}$$

for the actual wage. Equation (4.23) for the employment rate is unchanged.

Equations (4.23) and (4.29)–(4.33) implicitly define the equilibrium policies $\theta(s^t)$, $\tilde{c}(s^t)$, and $\tilde{w}^*(s^t)$ as functions of the state variables s_t, $n(s^t)$, $\tilde{k}(s^t)$, and $\tilde{w}(s^{t-1})$. As usual, I solve the model by looking for a linear approximation to the optimal policy functions in a neighborhood of the steady state. Most of the calibration is standard at this point and uses the values from the flexible-wage model (table 3.2), but there is one new parameter: the extent of wage rigidity r. Since there is no clear empirical counterpart to this, I use the model for two purposes. First, I examine whether wage rigidities help to align the model's predictions with the data. Second, I examine how changes in this parameter affect the behavior of the model. I start by setting $r = 0.95$ and later consider alternative values.

The linear approximation to the equilibrium policy functions are

$$\begin{aligned}
\log\theta &= \log 0.078 + 40.825s - 0.630(\log n - \log 0.95) \\
&\quad + 10.441(\log\tilde{k} - \log 218.2) - 38.184(\log\tilde{w}_{-1} - \log 4.017), \\
\log\tilde{c} &= \log 4.696 + 0.259s + 0.014(\log n - \log 0.95) \\
&\quad + 0.607(\log\tilde{k} - \log 218.2) - 0.023(\log\tilde{w}_{-1} - \log 4.017), \\
\log\tilde{w}^* &= \log 4.017 + 2.974s - 0.215(\log n - \log 0.95) \\
&\quad + 1.146(\log\tilde{k} - \log 218.2) - 2.321(\log\tilde{w}_{-1} - \log 4.017).
\end{aligned}$$

Comparing with equation (3.61), the responses of detrended consumption to the shock, to employment, and to detrended capital are virtually unchanged. On the other hand, the recruiter–unemployment ratio is five times as responsive to the shock in the rigid-wage model. It is somewhat more responsive to employment. And the sign of the response of the recruiter–unemployment ratio to the detrended capital stock is reversed. The explanation for this last result is instructive. In the flexible-wage economy, the wealth effect from a high capital stock puts upward pressure on wages, which discourages firms from recruiting. In the rigid-wage model, the complementarity between capital and labor dominates. When the capital stock is high, the marginal product of labor is high. For a given value of the lagged wage, this encourages firms to recruit more workers.

The policy functions also show that the recruiter–unemployment ratio falls sharply with the lagged wage, while consumption falls modestly.

The response of the recruiter-unemployment ratio reflects the persistence of wages, since high future wages discourage hiring today. Consumption falls with the lagged wage because low wages make it a profitable time to recruit, which comes at the expense of current consumption.

Finally, the third policy function shows that when actual wages are above trend, the target wage is far below trend, helping to realign the two variables. High capital and high productivity each increase the target wage by raising the marginal product of labor, while high employment has the opposite effect.

I turn next to the linear approximation to the state equations:

$$\begin{aligned}
\log n_{+1} &= \log 0.95 + 0.694s + 0.309(\log n - \log 0.95) \\
&\quad + 0.178(\log \tilde{k} - \log 218.2) - 0.649(\log \tilde{w}_{-1} - \log 4.017), \\
\log \tilde{k}_{+1} &= \log 218.2 + 0.018s + 0.019(\log n - \log 0.95) \\
&\quad + 0.990(\log \tilde{k} - \log 218.2) + 0.003(\log \tilde{w}_{-1} - \log 4.017), \\
\log \tilde{w} &= \log 4.107 + 0.149s - 0.011(\log n - \log 0.95) \\
&\quad + 0.057(\log \tilde{k} - \log 218.2) + 0.834(\log \tilde{w}_{-1} - \log 4.017).
\end{aligned}$$

Higher productivity raises employment, capital, and wages. Employment responds five times more to the shock than it does in the flexible-wage model (equation (3.62)), as the recruiter-unemployment ratio policy function suggested would be the case. Employment is persistent, positively influenced by past capital, and negatively influenced by past wages. The response of the capital stock is largely unchanged from the flexible-wage model. Finally, wages fall with employment and rise with capital due to pressure from the marginal product of labor. They are also strongly related to past wages, although the coefficient on $\tilde{w}_{-1}$, 0.83, is significantly below the coefficient in equation (4.33), $r = 0.95$. The forward-looking target wage moderates the exogenous wage rigidity.

I stack the four state variables to compute the eigenvectors, 0.990, 0.980, 0.854, 0.290. As usual, the largest eigenvector corresponds to the persistence of capital, the second to the persistence of productivity shocks, and the smallest to the persistence of employment. The third largest eigenvector represents the new state variable: the lagged wage. Since all the eigenvectors lie in the unit circle, the model exhibits locally stable dynamics.

Table 4.1 shows the comovement of the key detrended economic variables. It is perhaps best read by comparing it with table 3.3, which shows the behavior of the same variables in the flexible-wage model. Looking

Table 4.1. Model with capital and rigid wages ($r = 0.95$), deterministic trend; comovements of variables in an infinite sample.

		$\tilde{y}$	$\tilde{c}$	θ	$\tilde{k}$	n	wn/y	c/y	$\hat{\tau}$	s
Relative standard deviation		1	0.688	11.207	0.962	0.267	0.144	0.559	0.509	0.691
Correlations	$\tilde{y}$	1	0.844	0.514	0.720	0.559	−0.530	−0.750	0.794	0.982
	$\tilde{c}$	—	1	0.068	0.980	0.083	−0.210	−0.278	0.393	0.751
	θ	—	—	1	−0.104	0.856	−0.943	−0.837	0.703	0.596
	$\tilde{k}$	—	—	—	1	−0.088	−0.069	−0.082	0.205	0.603
	n	—	—	—	—	1	−0.663	−0.898	0.690	0.606
	wn/y	—	—	—	—	—	1	0.690	−0.612	−0.590
	c/y	—	—	—	—	—	—	1	−0.938	−0.833
	$\hat{\tau}$	—	—	—	—	—	—	—	1	0.893
	s	—	—	—	—	—	—	—	—	1

at the first row, rigid wages raise the standard deviation of employment and the recruiter–unemployment ratio relative to output by almost a factor of three. This increases the volatility of the labor share wn/y but, perhaps surprisingly, reduces the volatility of the labor wedge $\hat{\tau}$.

Turning to correlations, the rigid-wage model substantially weakens the correlation between employment and the labor wedge, from 0.96 to 0.69. In the data, the correlation is strongly negative. It similarly weakens the correlation between the consumption–output ratio and the labor wedge, from -1.00 to -0.94, while the data indicate that the correlation is close to zero. Thus this wage rigidity reduces but does not eliminate the gap between model and data.

Finally, the model implies that the labor share wn/y is negatively correlated with employment, although less so than in the flexible-wage model. When productivity rises above trend, the rigidity prevents the wage from rising as much as it would in the flexible-wage model, thus driving the negative correlation. Acting against this, employment responds to the low wage, reducing output per worker and keeping the labor wedge relatively constant.

Table 4.2 shows the annual growth rates of the same variables. The basic picture remains the same. For example, rigid wages reduce the correlation between the annual growth rates of the labor wedge and employment and the annual growth rates of the labor wedge and the consumption–output ratio, but do not break or reverse either relationship.

These comovements stand out clearly in figure 4.1, where I again contrast the baseline model, with $\bar{\mu} = 2.32$, with the model with higher search costs, $\bar{\mu} = 1$. Comparing this with figure 3.1, the response of employment to the productivity shock is both larger and faster. Indeed, employment reaches its maximum value in the period immediately after the shock. But while this dampens the response of the labor wedge, it does not reverse it. Indeed, the labor wedge remains positive during most of the subsequent adjustment. This drives the positive correlation between it and employment.

As I mentioned before, the choice of the wage rigidity parameter r was arbitrary. Indeed, the results I have reported are sensitive to this choice. To see this, figure 4.2 shows the correlation between the labor wedge and both employment and the consumption–output ratio as a function of r, both in levels and in annual growth rates. When the rigidity parameter is approximately 0.993, the correlations are negligible, while for higher rigidities, the labor wedge tends to be low when employment is above trend or when the consumption–output ratio is above trend.

Table 4.2. Model with capital and rigid wages ($r = 0.95$), deterministic trend; comovements of annual growth rates in an infinite sample.

		$\tilde{y}$	$\tilde{c}$	θ	$\tilde{k}$	n	wn/y	c/y	$\hat{\tau}$	s
Relative standard deviation		1	0.259	21.884	0.265	0.513	0.300	0.807	0.551	0.717
Correlations	$\tilde{y}$	1	0.804	0.805	0.162	0.888	−0.653	−0.982	0.915	0.982
	$\tilde{c}$	—	1	0.452	0.704	0.497	−0.366	−0.676	0.790	0.816
	θ	—	—	1	−0.252	0.803	−0.960	−0.853	0.750	0.820
	$\tilde{k}$	—	—	—	1	−0.157	0.261	0.025	0.164	0.164
	n	—	—	—	—	1	−0.607	−0.941	0.670	0.806
	wn/y	—	—	—	—	—	1	0.692	−0.671	−0.708
	c/y	—	—	—	—	—	—	1	−0.881	−0.955
	$\hat{\tau}$	—	—	—	—	—	—	—	1	0.972
	s	—	—	—	—	—	—	—	—	1

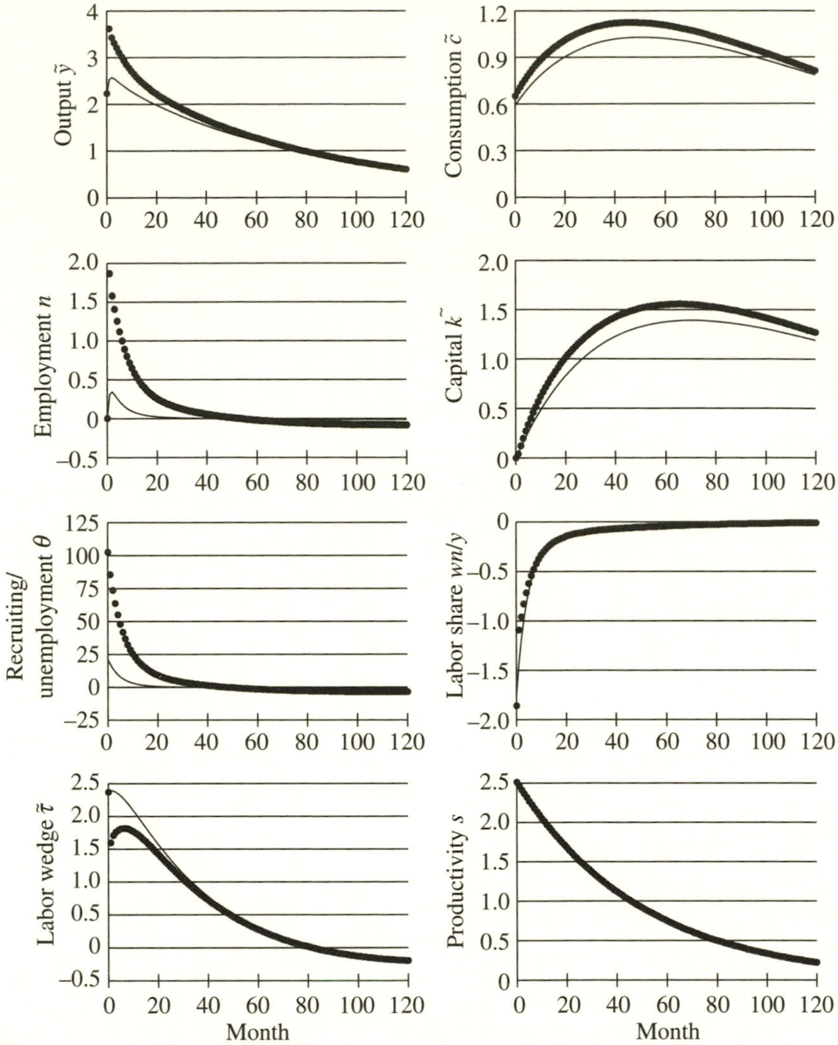

Figure 4.1. Model with capital and rigid wages ($r = 0.95$), deterministic trend. Response to a 2.5 percent increase in productivity at $t = 0$. All variables are expressed as deviations from trend in log points. The thick dots show $\bar{\mu} = 2.32$ and the thin lines show more frictions, $\bar{\mu} = 1$.

To explore the behavior of extreme values of the wage rigidity parameter more carefully, I set $r = 0.993$. Table 4.3 shows the comovements of the variables in this case; the behavior of annual growth rates is similar. Unsurprisingly, more wage rigidity increases the volatility of the recruiter-unemployment ratio and makes employment two-thirds as volatile as output. On the other hand, the increase in wage

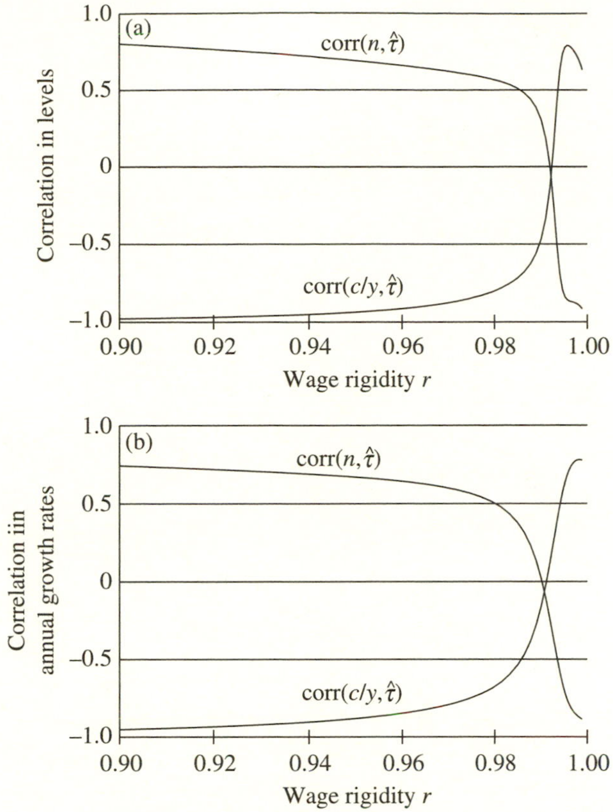

Figure 4.2. Model with capital and rigid wages, deterministic trend. Correlation between the labor wedge, employment, and the consumption-output ratio for various values of the wage rigidity parameter r. (a) Correlations between levels and (b) correlations between annual growth rates.

rigidity substantially reduces the volatility of the labor wedge. This is because employment and the consumption-output ratio are nearly equally volatile and very strongly negatively correlated. In contrast, the data in table A.1 indicate that while employment and the consumption-output ratio are equally volatile, their correlation is only −0.6, and so the labor wedge is in fact more volatile than either of these components. It is also worth noting that the increase in wage rigidity dampens fluctuations in the labor share wn/y, compared with table 4.1. While this calibration is not an unqualified success, it certainly shows that the model can generate extreme volatility in recruiting effort and a negative correlation between employment and the labor wedge without substantially altering the comovement of other variables, e.g., the joint behavior of output, consumption, and capital, as summarized in table 3.3.

Table 4.3. Model with capital and rigid wages ($r = 0.993$), deterministic trend; comovements of variables in an infinite sample.

		$\tilde{y}$	$\tilde{c}$	θ	$\tilde{k}$	n	wn/y	c/y	$\hat{\tau}$	s
Relative standard deviation		1	0.600	26.902	0.912	0.663	0.114	0.643	0.114	0.501
Correlations	$\tilde{y}$	1	0.788	0.735	0.636	0.763	−0.749	−0.819	0.280	0.990
	$\tilde{c}$	—	1	0.188	0.975	0.206	−0.453	−0.293	0.681	0.817
	θ	—	—	1	−0.033	0.954	−0.838	−0.967	−0.131	0.719
	$\tilde{k}$	—	—	—	1	−0.006	−0.276	−0.079	0.727	0.670
	n	—	—	—	—	1	−0.673	−0.994	−0.309	0.708
	wn/y	—	—	—	—	—	1	0.742	−0.417	−0.807
	c/y	—	—	—	—	—	—	1	0.200	−0.777
	$\hat{\tau}$	—	—	—	—	—	—	—	1	0.398
	s	—	—	—	—	—	—	—	—	1

4.3.7 Productivity Shocks: Stochastic Trend

I obtain similar results with a stochastic trend in productivity, so

$$\log z(\{s^t, s_{t+1}\}) = \log z(s^t) + s_{t+1},$$

where s_t follows a stationary first-order Markov process. As usual, I look for an equilibrium where appropriately scaled versions of consumption and wages are stationary when growth is stochastic. Define relative consumption, capital, actual wages, and target wages as

$$\tilde{c}(s^t) \equiv c(s^t)z(s^t)^{-1/(1-\alpha)}, \qquad \tilde{k}(s^t) \equiv k(s^t)z(s^t)^{-1/(1-\alpha)},$$
$$\tilde{w}(s^t) \equiv w(s^t)z(s^t)^{-1/(1-\alpha)}, \qquad \tilde{w}^*(s^t) \equiv w^*(s^t)z(s^t)^{-1/(1-\alpha)}.$$

Similarly, since employment and the share of recruiters in employment are constant along a balanced-growth path, I look for an equilibrium of the stochastic-growth model in which these variables are stationary.

As in the flexible-wage model, replace $q_t(s^{t+1})$ in equation (4.21) using equation (4.16) to obtain

$$1 = \beta \sum_{s^{t+1}|s^t} \pi(s_{t+1}|s_t) \frac{\tilde{c}(s^t)}{\tilde{c}(s^{t+1})} \mathrm{e}^{-s_{t+1}/(1-\alpha)} \times \left(\alpha\left(\frac{\tilde{k}(s^{t+1})}{n(s^{t+1}) - \theta(s^{t+1})(1 - n(s^{t+1}))}\right)^{\alpha-1} + 1 - \delta\right). \tag{4.34}$$

Similarly, eliminate J_n between equations (4.19) and (4.20):

$$(1-\alpha)\left(\frac{\tilde{k}(s^t)}{n(s^t) - \theta(s^t)(1 - n(s^t))}\right)^{\alpha} = \beta\mu(\theta(s^t)) \sum_{s^{t+1}|s^t} \pi(s_{t+1}|s_t) \frac{\tilde{c}(s^t)}{\tilde{c}(s^{t+1})} \times \left((1-\alpha)\left(\frac{\tilde{k}(s^{t+1})}{n(s^{t+1}) - \theta(s^{t+1})(1 - n(s^{t+1}))}\right)^{\alpha}\left(1 + \frac{1-x}{\mu(\theta(s^{t+1}))}\right) - \tilde{w}(s^{t+1})\right). \tag{4.35}$$

The target wage equation (4.28) becomes

$$\tilde{w}^*(s^t) = \phi(1-\alpha)\left(\frac{\tilde{k}(s^t)}{n(s^t) - \theta(s^t)(1 - n(s^t))}\right)^{\alpha}(1 + \theta(s^t)) + (1-\phi)\frac{\gamma\tilde{c}(s^t)}{1-\tau} + \beta(1 - x - f(\theta(s^t))) \sum_{s^{t+1}|s^t} \pi(s_{t+1}|s_t) \frac{\tilde{c}(s^t)}{\tilde{c}(s^{t+1})} (\tilde{w}^*(s^{t+1}) - w(\tilde{s}^{t+1})). \tag{4.36}$$

The state equations (4.24) and (4.26) reduce to

$$\tilde{k}(s^{t+1})e^{s_{t+1}/(1-\alpha)}$$
$$= \tilde{k}(s^t)^{\alpha}(n(s^t) - \theta(s^t)(1 - n(s^t)))^{1-\alpha} + (1-\delta)\tilde{k}(s^t) - \tilde{c}(s^t) \quad (4.37)$$

and

$$\tilde{w}(s^t) = r\tilde{w}(s^{t-1})e^{(\bar{s}-s_t)/(1-\alpha)} + (1-r)\tilde{w}^*(s^t). \quad (4.38)$$

Equation (4.23) for the employment rate is unchanged.

My calibration follows the flexible-wage version of the model in section 3.2.7. In particular, I still set $\bar{s} = 0.0012$, $\rho = 0.4$, and $\varsigma = 0.00325$, where $s_{t+1} = \bar{s} + \rho(s_t - \bar{s}) + \varsigma v_{t+1}$. I again initially set the wage rigidity parameter at $r = 0.95$. The other parameters are unchanged.

I start by reporting the equilibrium policy functions:

$$\begin{aligned}
\log\theta &= \log 0.078 + 81.417(s - 0.0012) - 0.630(\log n - \log 0.95) \\
&\qquad + 10.441(\log\tilde{k} - \log 218.2) - 38.184(\log\tilde{w}_{-1} - \log 4.017), \\
\log\tilde{c} &= \log 4.696 + 0.436(s - 0.0012) + 0.014(\log n - \log 0.95) \\
&\qquad + 0.607(\log\tilde{k} - \log 218.2) - 0.023(\log\tilde{w}_{-1} - \log 4.017), \\
\log\tilde{w}^* &= \log 4.017 + 5.096(s - 0.0012) - 0.215(\log n - \log 0.95) \\
&\qquad + 1.146(\log\tilde{k} - \log 218.2) - 2.321(\log\tilde{w}_{-1} - \log 4.017).
\end{aligned}$$

An increase in the productivity growth rate raises recruiting, consumption, and the target wage on impact. These findings are qualitatively unchanged from the flexible-wage model, although the response of the recruiter-unemployment ratio is about fifty times as large. The responses of the equilibrium policies to the three state variables are unchanged from the case with a deterministic trend, and the interpretation is likewise unaltered.

I turn next to the state equations:

$$\begin{aligned}
\log n_{+1} &= \log 0.95 + 1.384(s - 0.0012) + 0.309(\log n - \log 0.95) \\
&\qquad + 0.178(\log\tilde{k} - \log 218.2) - 0.649(\log\tilde{w}_{-1} - \log 4.017), \\
\log\tilde{k}_{+1} &= \log 218.2 - 0.612(s - 0.0012) + 0.019(\log n - \log 0.95) \\
&\qquad + 0.990(\log\tilde{k} - \log 218.2) + 0.003(\log\tilde{w}_{-1} - \log 4.017), \\
\log\tilde{w} &= \log 4.017 - 1.163(s - 0.0012) - 0.011(\log n - \log 0.95) \\
&\qquad + 0.057(\log\tilde{k} - \log 218.2) + 0.834(\log\tilde{w}_{-1} - \log 4.017).
\end{aligned}$$

An increase in productivity growth raises employment but lowers capital and actual wages relative to trend. The increase in employment reflects the surge in the recruiter-unemployment ratio, while the decline in capital is a consequence of rising interest rates, which encourage current consumption at the expense of investment. The relative wage falls for mechanical reasons: when productivity growth increases, the actual wage cannot keep up because of the wage rigidity. The responses of employment, capital, and wages to each other are unchanged from the model with a deterministic trend. It follows that three of the eigenvalues are unchanged as well, while the fourth, the one associated with the exogenous shock, declines to 0.4.

Table 4.4 shows the comovement of variables in an infinite sample. Table 3.5 shows the behavior of the same variables in the flexible-wage model. The standard deviation of employment and the recruiter-unemployment ratio increase by a factor of eight or nine. Moreover, the correlation between employment and the labor wedge is reversed, falling from 0.97 in the flexible-wage model to −0.45 here. Similarly, the correlation of the consumption-output ratio with the labor wedge rises from −1.00 to 0.04. Table 4.5 shows the corresponding annual growth rates. The conclusions are similar.[2]

Figure 4.3 shows the impulse response to a one-time increase in productivity growth. Recall that this figure shows the behavior of variables in levels, not relative to current productivity, making it easier to interpret the behavior of nonstationary variables like output, consumption, and capital. I find that an increase in the productivity growth rate leads to an immediate increase in consumption and an even larger increase in output. Thus the consumption-output ratio falls upon the impact of the shock before slowly reverting to trend. Since wages are slow to respond to the shock, employment and recruiting also increase strongly before reverting slowly back to their normal levels. The amplification compared with the flexible-wage model in figure 3.2 is clear.

One might expect wage rigidities to create sharp movements in the labor share, but in fact the changes are fairly modest. The labor share falls by −0.2 percent on the impact of this large increase in productivity growth. This reflects the boom in output with fixed employment and rigid wages. As employment starts to grow, the labor share quickly recovers, following a nonmonotonic pattern back to steady state. This observation is important for microeconomic studies that attempt to assess the

[2]The model has some superficially counterfactual predictions, however, such as the negative correlation between employment and detrended consumption or capital. Recall, however, that in the model, I detrended consumption and capital by dividing by actual productivity. When productivity growth increases, consumption and capital increase but decline relative to trend. Thus these results appear to be primarily due to how I measure objects in the model.

Table 4.4. Model with capital and rigid wages ($r = 0.95$), stochastic trend; comovements of variables in an infinite sample.

		$\tilde{y}$	$\tilde{c}$	θ	$\tilde{k}$	n	wn/y	c/y	$\hat{\tau}$	s
Relative standard deviation		1	1.727	83.803	2.944	1.998	0.867	1.787	1.238	0.565
Correlations	$\tilde{y}$	1	0.228	0.497	0.186	0.645	−0.535	−0.339	−0.827	0.097
	$\tilde{c}$	—	1	−0.403	0.988	−0.569	0.295	0.839	−0.437	0.073
	θ	—	—	1	−0.523	0.853	−0.993	−0.668	−0.619	0.702
	$\tilde{k}$	—	—	—	1	−0.625	0.423	0.851	−0.329	−0.076
	n	—	—	—	—	1	−0.810	−0.911	−0.449	0.229
	wn/y	—	—	—	—	—	1	0.584	0.697	−0.750
	c/y	—	—	—	—	—	—	1	0.040	0.016
	$\hat{\tau}$	—	—	—	—	—	—	—	1	−0.591
	s	—	—	—	—	—	—	—	—	1

Table 4.5. Model with capital and rigid wages ($r = 0.95$), stochastic trend; comovements of annual growth rates in an infinite sample.

		$\tilde{y}$	$\tilde{c}$	θ	$\tilde{k}$	n	wn/y	c/y	$\hat{\tau}$	s
Relative standard deviation		1	0.790	88.160	1.273	2.071	0.942	1.559	1.210	0.667
Correlations	$\tilde{y}$	1	−0.510	0.743	−0.654	0.969	−0.707	−0.900	−0.748	0.108
	$\tilde{c}$	—	1	−0.191	0.922	−0.628	0.133	0.834	0.002	0.445
	θ	—	—	1	−0.541	0.807	−0.998	−0.573	−0.965	0.717
	$\tilde{k}$	—	—	—	1	−0.803	0.493	0.887	0.347	0.066
	n	—	—	—	—	1	−0.770	−0.940	−0.751	0.169
	wn/y	—	—	—	—	—	1	0.521	0.970	−0.756
	c/y	—	—	—	—	—	—	1	0.481	0.156
	$\hat{\tau}$	—	—	—	—	—	—	—	1	−0.736
	s	—	—	—	—	—	—	—	—	1

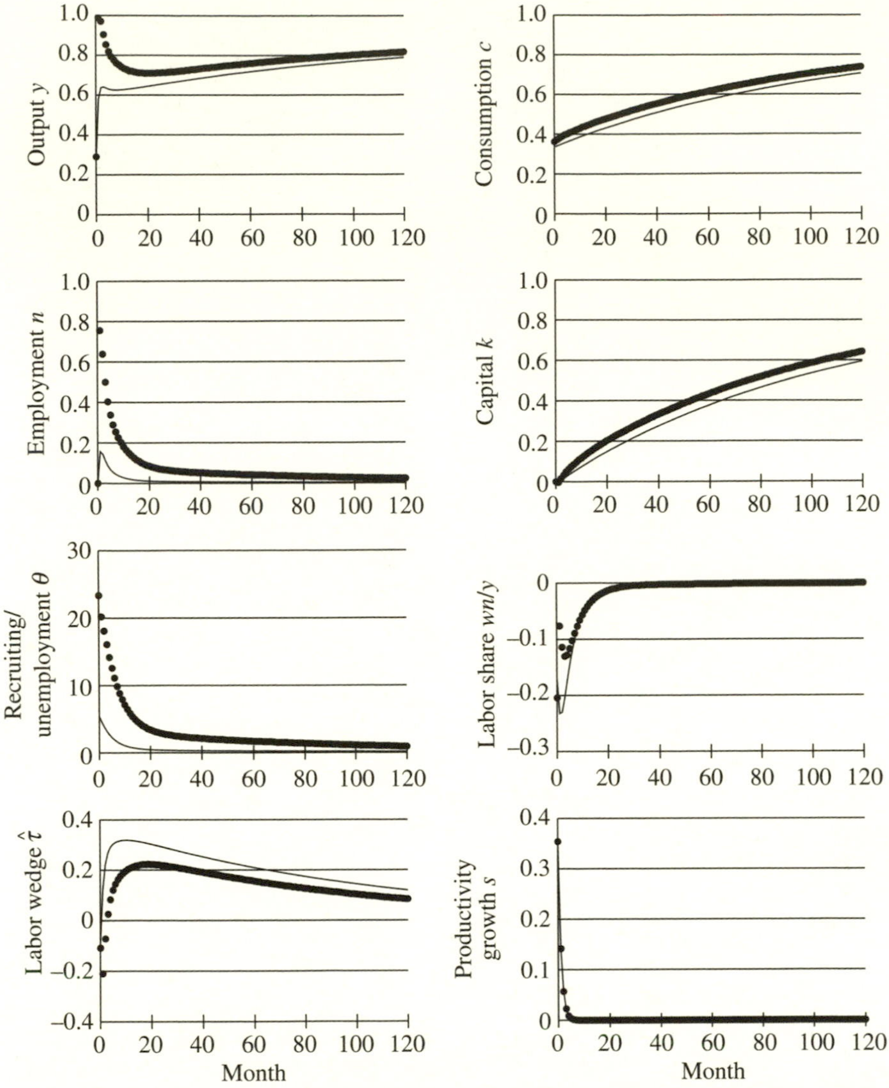

Figure 4.3. Model with capital and rigid wages ($r = 0.95$), stochastic trend. Response to an increase in the productivity growth rate at $t = 0$. All variables are expressed as deviations from initial trend in log points. The dots show $\bar{\mu} = 2.32$ and the lines show more frictions, $\bar{\mu} = 1$.

extent of wage rigidity by directly comparing the behavior of wages and labor productivity (e.g., Haefke et al. 2008; Pissarides 2009). The labor share is the ratio of the wage w to the measured average product of labor y/n. The finding that the labor share declines only modestly during an expansion implies that labor productivity rises by only slightly more

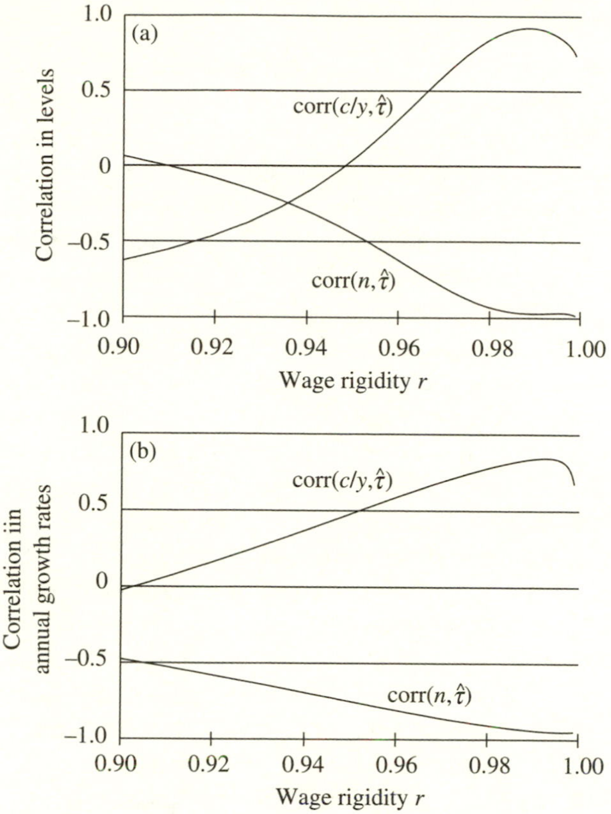

Figure 4.4. Model with capital and rigid wages, stochastic trend. Correlation between the labor wedge, employment, and the consumption–output ratio for various values of the wage rigidity parameter r. (a) Correlations between levels and (b) correlations between annual growth rates.

than wages following an increase in productivity growth. This small gap may be difficult to discern using the best available microeconomic data, and so a failure to observe greater volatility in labor productivity than in wages may say little about the relevance of wage rigidities for labor market fluctuations.

I again explore the role of the wage rigidity parameter r by graphing the correlations between the labor wedge, employment, and the consumption–output ratio as functions of r in figure 4.4. Compared with the version of the model with a deterministic trend, I find less need for an extreme value of this parameter. Indeed, to match the slightly negative correlation between the labor wedge and both employment and the consumption–output ratio, I can allow for values of r even smaller than 0.95.

4.3.8 Evaluation

These experiments help to illustrate the ability of wage rigidities to moderate the gap between model and data, but they are not definitive. As I have emphasized, the level of wage rigidity, r, is a free parameter. One might try to use economic theory to determine its value. In chapter 5, I briefly discuss some efforts in this direction.

A related issue is that the required level of wage rigidity may depend on the nature of shocks hitting the economy. I have argued that the flexible-wage economy cannot match the behavior of the labor wedge regardless of the nature of shocks, e.g., productivity or government spending, aggregate or reallocational. It is conceptually straightforward to introduce these types of shocks into the rigid-wage model. In preliminary research that I do not report here, I find that with different sources of shocks, a different wage rigidity parameter may be necessary to explain the observed comovement of aggregate variables. Certainly one should be cautious of any attempt to identify the value of r from the response of the aggregate variables to productivity shocks.

But the bottom line is that, while wage rigidity may be important for understanding the cyclical behavior of the labor market, it is hard to measure. I close the book with an effort to sidestep this question, asking whether the model has additional restrictions that hold regardless of the true value of r and regardless of the nature of shocks hitting the economy. Following Hall (2009), I tentatively conclude in the next section that it does.

4.4 Using Hours Data to Test the Model

The tenet of the rigid-wage model is that, within the interval of wages that firms are willing to pay and that workers are willing to accept, there is no good reason to predict which wage will be set in equilibrium. The actual wage that will be paid depends on details of wage negotiations between workers and firms. But while this choice does not affect the survival of existing employment relationships, it does affect firms' willingness to recruit, thereby changing the unemployment rate.

Despite this indeterminacy, Hall (2009) argues that a search model with rigid wages makes some predictions about the comovement of the consumption–output ratio and hours worked, at least in an environment in which the number of hours worked per employed worker, $h(s^t)$, is endogenous. Matched workers and firms should agree on a level of hours that maximizes the joint gains from trade, and then use other elements of the wage contract to divide the gains from trade. This insight puts some discipline on the model's predictions.

To be concrete, suppose that a worker's income is linear in her hours worked, $w_0(s^t)+w_1(s^t)h(s^t)$. Workers and firms bargain efficiently over the marginal wage $w_1(s^t)$ and hours worked $h(s^t)$, but I will be deliberately vague about how the fixed component of wages $w_0(s^t)$ is set. Efficient bargaining over the marginal wage and hours ensures that workers' and firms' choice of hours maximizes the joint gains from trade—a prediction that I show has empirical content.

More precisely, I flesh out the details of this model and prove that it is mathematically equivalent to a frictionless one in which workers have a finite elasticity of labor supply along the intensive (hours) margin but an infinite elasticity of labor supply along the extensive (employment) margin. In other words, a search model with rigid wages can potentially explain why it looks as if workers are willing to accept substantial variation in employment over the business cycle, even though in reality the elasticity of labor supply is not large.

4.4.1 Households

I assume throughout this section that the marginal utility of consumption may differ for employed and unemployed workers. The period utility function of a typical household member is

$$\frac{c^{1-\sigma}(1+(\sigma-1)(\gamma\varepsilon/(1+\varepsilon))h^{(1+\varepsilon)/\varepsilon})^{\sigma}-1}{1-\sigma}$$

if she consumes c and is employed for h hours. It is

$$\frac{c^{1-\sigma}-1}{1-\sigma}$$

if she is unemployed. A representative household decides how much each of its members consumes in order to maximize the sum of utilities of its members, acting as if it has utility function

$$\sum_{t=0}^{\infty}\sum_{s^t}\beta^t\Pi(s^t)\bigg(\frac{c_{\mathrm{e}}(s^t)^{1-\sigma}(1+(\sigma-1)(\gamma\varepsilon/(1+\varepsilon))h(s^t)^{(1+\varepsilon)/\varepsilon})^{\sigma}-1}{1-\sigma}n(s^t) + \frac{c_{\mathrm{u}}(s^t)^{1-\sigma}-1}{1-\sigma}(1-n(s^t))\bigg), \tag{4.39}$$

where $c_{\mathrm{e}}(s^t)$ is the consumption of each employed household member and $c_{\mathrm{u}}(s^t)$ is the consumption of each unemployed household member in history s^t.

The household faces a single lifetime budget constraint: that initial assets must be equal to the difference between the present value of consumption and the present value of after-tax labor income plus transfers,

$$a_0 = \sum_{t=0}^{\infty} \sum_{s^t} q_0(s^t)(c(s^t) - (1-\tau)(w_0(s^t) + w_1(s^t)h(s^t))n(s^t) - T(s^t)), \tag{4.40}$$

where

$$c(s^t) \equiv c_e(s^t)n(s^t) + c_u(s^t)(1 - n(s^t))$$

is total consumption. A worker who works for $h(s^t)$ hours in history s^t earns pre-tax income $w_0(s^t) + w_1(s^t)h(s^t)$. In addition, employment is determined by the law of motion

$$n(s^{t+1}) = (1-x)n(s^t) + f(\theta(s^t))(1 - n(s^t)) \tag{4.41}$$

for all $s^{t+1} = \{s^t, s_{t+1}\}$. The household chooses $\{c_e(s^t), c_u(s^t)\}$ to maximize its objective function in equation (4.39) subject to equation (4.40) and equation (4.41), taking as given initial assets a_0, bargained hours $\{h(s^t)\}$, prices $\{w_0(s^t), w_1(s^t), q_0(s^t)\}$, taxes τ, and transfers $\{T(s^t)\}$.

Focus temporarily on the choice of consumption for each employed and unemployed member. Combining the first-order conditions with the definition of total consumption, I obtain

$$c_e(s^t) = \frac{c(s^t)(1 + (\sigma - 1)(\gamma\varepsilon/(1+\varepsilon))h(s^t)^{(1+\varepsilon)/\varepsilon})}{1 + (\sigma - 1)(\gamma\varepsilon/(1+\varepsilon))h(s^t)^{(1+\varepsilon)/\varepsilon}n(s^t)}$$

and

$$c_u(s^t) = \frac{c(s^t)}{1 + (\sigma - 1)(\gamma\varepsilon/(1+\varepsilon))h(s^t)^{(1+\varepsilon)/\varepsilon}n(s^t)}.$$

Substituting this into the utility function equation (4.39) gives

$$\sum_{t=0}^{\infty} \sum_{s^t} \beta^t \Pi(s^t) \frac{c(s^t)^{1-\sigma}(1 + (\sigma - 1)(\gamma\varepsilon/(1+\varepsilon))h(s^t)^{(1+\varepsilon)/\varepsilon}n(s^t))^{\sigma} - 1}{1 - \sigma}, \tag{4.42}$$

so the household chooses total consumption $\{c(s^t)\}$ to maximize this expression subject to equations (4.40) and (4.41), taking as given initial assets a_0, bargained hours $\{h(s^t)\}$, prices $\{w_0(s^t), w_1(s^t), q_0(s^t)\}$, taxes τ, and transfers $\{T(s^t)\}$.

Now let $V(s^t, a, n)$ denote the value of a household with assets a and n employed workers in history s^t. This solves

$$V(s^t, a, n) = \max_{\{a(s^{t+1})\}} \left(\frac{c^{1-\sigma}(1 + (\sigma - 1)(\gamma\varepsilon/(1+\varepsilon))h(s^t)^{(1+\varepsilon)/\varepsilon} n(s^t))^{\sigma} - 1}{1 - \sigma} + \beta \sum_{s^{t+1}|s^t} \frac{\Pi(s^{t+1})}{\Pi(s^t)} V(s^{t+1}, a(s^{t+1}), n') \right), \tag{4.43}$$

where c satisfies the intertemporal budget constraint,

$$c = a + (1 - \tau)(w_0(s^t) + w_1(s^t)h(s^t))n + T(s^t) - \sum_{s^{t+1}|s^t} q_t(s^{t+1})a(s^{t+1}),$$

and next period's employment is determined from current employment and unemployment as

$$n' = (1 - x)n + f(\theta(s^t))(1 - n).$$

As usual, the first-order condition for next period's assets and the envelope condition for current assets yield the Euler equation:

$$q_t(s^{t+1}) = \beta \frac{\Pi(s^{t+1})}{\Pi(s^t)} \left(\frac{c(s^t)(1 + (\sigma - 1)(\gamma\varepsilon/(1+\varepsilon))h(s^{t+1})^{(1+\varepsilon)/\varepsilon} n(s^{t+1}))}{c(s^{t+1})(1 + (\sigma - 1)(\gamma\varepsilon/(1+\varepsilon))h(s^t)^{(1+\varepsilon)/\varepsilon} n(s^t))} \right)^{\sigma}. \tag{4.44}$$

The envelope condition for employment is

$$\begin{aligned} V_n(s^t, a(s^t), n(s^t)) &= \left(\frac{c(s^t)}{1 + (\sigma - 1)(\gamma\varepsilon/(1+\varepsilon))h(s^t)^{(1+\varepsilon)/\varepsilon} n(s^t)} \right)^{-\sigma} \times (1 - \tau)(w_0(s^t) + w_1(s^t)h(s^t)) \\ &\quad - \left(\frac{c(s^t)}{1 + (\sigma - 1)(\gamma\varepsilon/(1+\varepsilon))h(s^t)^{(1+\varepsilon)/\varepsilon} n(s^t)} \right)^{1-\sigma} \times \sigma(\gamma\varepsilon/(1+\varepsilon))h(s^t)^{(1+\varepsilon)/\varepsilon} \\ &\quad + \beta(1 - x - f(\theta(s^t))) \sum_{s^{t+1}|s^t} \frac{\Pi(s^{t+1})}{\Pi(s^t)} V_n(s^{t+1}, a(s^{t+1}), n(s^{t+1})). \end{aligned} \tag{4.45}$$

Also let $\tilde{V}_n(s^t, w_1, h)$ denote the marginal value to a household with the equilibrium level of assets and employment of having a worker employed at an arbitrary hourly wage w_1 and working an arbitrary number of hours h, rather than having that worker unemployed in history s^t. This notation suppresses the fixed component of wages. This solves

$$\begin{aligned}\tilde{V}_n(s^t, w_1, h) = {} & \frac{\gamma\sigma\varepsilon}{1+\varepsilon}(h(s^t)^{(1+\varepsilon)/\varepsilon} - h^{(1+\varepsilon)/\varepsilon}) \\ & \times \left(\frac{c(s^t)}{1 + (\sigma - 1)(\gamma\varepsilon/(1+\varepsilon))h(s^t)^{(1+\varepsilon)/\varepsilon}n(s^t)}\right)^{1-\sigma} \\ & + (1-\tau)(w_1 h - w_1(s^t)h(s^t)) \\ & \times \left(\frac{c(s^t)}{1 + (\sigma - 1)(\gamma\varepsilon/(1+\varepsilon))h(s^t)^{(1+\varepsilon)/\varepsilon}n(s^t)}\right)^{-\sigma} \\ & + V_n(s^t, a(s^t), n(s^t)). \end{aligned} \tag{4.46}$$

The first term is the utility benefit of any reduction in hours of work. The second term is the utility value of the after-tax income generated by a worker employed at (w_1, h) rather than at the equilibrium marginal wage–hour pair $(w_1(s^t), h(s^t))$. The third term is the marginal value of having the worker employed at the equilibrium wage and hours rather than unemployed.

4.4.2 Firms

A representative firm employs $n_0 = n(s^0)$ workers and owns capital $k_0 = k(s^0)$ at time 0. In history s^t, it assigns a fraction $\nu(s^t)$ of its $n(s^t)$ workers to recruiting and the remaining $n(s^t)(1-\nu(s^t))$ workers to production. Each worker works $h(s^t)$ hours. The producers use the capital $k(s^t)$ to generate output $z(s^t)k(s^t)^{\alpha}(h(s^t)n(s^t)(1-\nu(s^t)))^{1-\alpha}$. The single produced good is used both for consumption and for investment. A fraction δ of the capital depreciates during production. The recruiters each attract $h(s^t)\mu(\theta(s^t))$ workers to the firm, while a fraction x of the workers leave the firm, thus determining $n(s^{t+1})$. Finally, the firm can freely buy or sell capital in history s^t, determining $k(s^{t+1})$.

Writing this formally, the firm's value in history s^0 with n_0 workers and capital k_0 is

$$\begin{aligned} J(s^0, n_0, k_0) = \sum_{t=0}^{\infty}\sum_{s^t} q_0(s^t)(z(s^t)k(s^t)^{\alpha}(h(s^t)n(s^t)(1-\nu(s^t)))^{1-\alpha} \\ + (1-\delta)k(s^t) - k(s^{t+1}) - (w_0(s^t) + w_1(s^t)h(s^t))n(s^t)), \end{aligned} \tag{4.47}$$

so flow profit is the sum of output and undepreciated capital minus the cost of new capital and the wage bill. Firm growth satisfies

$$n(s^{t+1}) = n(s^t)(h(s^t)\nu(s^t)\mu(\theta(s^t)) + 1 - x), \tag{4.48}$$

where $s^{t+1} = \{s^t, s_{t+1}\}$. The firm chooses its capital stock $k(s^t)$ and the allocation of workers to recruiting $v(s^t)$ to maximize profits in equation (4.47) subject to the law of motion for employment in equation (4.48), taking as given bargained hours $\{h(s^t)\}$ and wages and prices $\{w_0(s^t), w_1(s^t), q_0(s^t)\}$.

Let $J(s^t, n, k)$ denote the value of a firm that starts history s^t with n workers and k units of capital. The value function satisfies the recursive equation

$$\begin{aligned} J(s^t, n, k) = \max_{v,k'} \Big(& z(s^t)k^{\alpha}(h(s^t)n(1-v))^{1-\alpha} + (1-\delta)k - k' \\ & - n(w_0(s^t) + w_1(s^t)h(s^t)) \\ & + \sum_{s^{t+1}|s^t} q_t(s^{t+1})J(s^{t+1}, n(vh(s^t)\mu(\theta(s^t)) + 1 - x), k')\Big). \end{aligned} \tag{4.49}$$

Assuming an interior solution for the share of recruiters v, I obtain the first-order condition

$$\begin{aligned} (1-\alpha)z(s^t)&\left(\frac{k(s^t)}{h(s^t)n(s^t)(1-v(s^t))}\right)^{\alpha} \\ &= \mu(\theta(s^t)) \sum_{s^{t+1}|s^t} q_t(s^{t+1})J_n(s^{t+1}, n(s^{t+1}), k(s^{t+1})). \end{aligned} \tag{4.50}$$

The left-hand side is the marginal product of an hour of production labor. The right-hand side is the expected value of the additional workers attracted by an hour of recruiting labor. We can also write the envelope condition for employment as

$$\begin{aligned} J_n(s^t, n(s^t), k(s^t)) & \\ = (1-\alpha)z(s^t)&\left(\frac{k(s^t)}{h(s^t)n(s^t)(1-v(s^t))}\right)^{\alpha} h(s^t)(1-v(s^t)) \\ & - (w_0(s^t) + w_1(s^t)h(s^t)) \\ & + (v(s^t)h(s^t)\mu(\theta(s^t)) + 1 - x) \\ & \qquad \times \sum_{s^{t+1}|s^t} q_t(s^{t+1})J_n(s^{t+1}, n(s^{t+1}), k(s^{t+1})). \end{aligned}$$

Eliminate the continuation value using equation (4.50) to obtain

$$\begin{aligned} J_n(s^t, n(s^t), k(s^t)) & \\ = (1-\alpha)z(s^t)&\left(\frac{k(s^t)}{h(s^t)n(s^t)(1-v(s^t))}\right)^{\alpha}\left(h(s^t) + \frac{1-x}{\mu(\theta(s^t))}\right) \\ & - (w_0(s^t) + w_1(s^t)h(s^t)). \end{aligned} \tag{4.51}$$

The value of employing an additional worker is the sum of the worker's marginal product as a producer and the marginal product of the workers who are released from recruiting because of the worker's presence, minus the wage.

Next turn to the first-order condition for next period's capital stock,

$$1 = \sum_{s^{t+1}|s^t} q_t(s^{t+1}) J_k(s^{t+1}, n(s^{t+1}), k(s^{t+1})).$$

Purchasing a unit of capital reduces current profit by 1. This must equal the increase in the continuation value of the firm. The envelope condition for capital is

$$J_k(s^t, n(s^t), k(s^t)) = \alpha z(s^t) \left(\frac{k(s^t)}{h(s^t)n(s^t)(1 - \nu(s^t))} \right)^{\alpha-1} + 1 - \delta.$$

Evaluate this condition in history s^{t+1} and substitute into the first-order condition for next period's capital to get

$$1 = \sum_{s^{t+1}|s^t} q_t(s^{t+1}) \left(\alpha z(s^{t+1}) \left(\frac{k(s^{t+1})}{h(s^{t+1})n(s^{t+1})(1 - \nu(s^{t+1}))} \right)^{\alpha-1} + 1 - \delta \right). \tag{4.52}$$

This ensures that firms are willing to invest in capital, so the cost of capital this period is equal to the net marginal product of capital next period.

Finally, compute the marginal profit of employing a worker at an arbitrary marginal wage w_1 for an arbitrary number of hours h in history s^t and at the equilibrium wage thereafter, rather than losing the worker. For a firm with the equilibrium level of employment $n(s^t)$ and capital $k(s^t)$, this is

$$\begin{aligned} \tilde{J}_n(s^t, w_1, h) = {} & (1 - \alpha) z(s^t) \left(\frac{k(s^t)}{h(s^t)n(s^t)(1 - \nu(s^t))} \right)^{\alpha} (h - h(s^t)) \\ & + (w_1(s^t)h(s^t) - w_1 h) + J_n(s^t, n(s^t), k(s^t)). \end{aligned} \tag{4.53}$$

The first term is the change in output: the marginal product of labor times the change in hours. The second term is the change in the wage bill. The final term is the value of a worker at the equilibrium wage and hours.

4.4.3 Wage Setting and the Labor Wedge

The key assumption is that workers and firms bargain over the marginal wage and hours, satisfying the Nash bargaining procedure:

$$(w_1(s^t), h(s^t)) = \arg\max_{w_1, h} \tilde{V}_n(s^t, w_1, h)^{\phi} \tilde{J}_n(s^t, w_1, h)^{1-\phi}. \tag{4.54}$$

I do not, however, put any restrictions on the base wage $w_0(s^t)$.

Using equations (4.46) and (4.53), the first-order condition of equation (4.54) for the marginal wage evaluated at $(w_1(s^t), h(s^t))$ is

$$\frac{\phi}{V_n(s^t, a(s^t), n(s^t))}(1-\tau)\left(\frac{c(s^t)}{1+(\sigma-1)(\gamma\varepsilon/(1+\varepsilon))h(s^t)^{(1+\varepsilon)/\varepsilon}n(s^t)}\right)^{-\sigma} = \frac{1-\phi}{J_n(s^t, n(s^t), k(s^t))}. \quad (4.55)$$

The same equations imply that the first-order condition for the choice of hours evaluated at $(w_1(s^t), h(s^t))$ is

$$\begin{aligned} &\frac{\phi}{V_n(s^t, a(s^t), n(s^t))} \\ &\quad \times \left(\gamma\sigma h(s^t)^{1/\varepsilon}\left(\frac{c(s^t)}{1+(\sigma-1)(\gamma\varepsilon/(1+\varepsilon))h(s^t)^{(1+\varepsilon)/\varepsilon}n(s^t)}\right)^{1-\sigma}\right. \\ &\qquad \left. -(1-\tau)w_1(s^t)\left(\frac{c(s^t)}{1+(\sigma-1)(\gamma\varepsilon/(1+\varepsilon))h(s^t)^{(1+\varepsilon)/\varepsilon}n(s^t)}\right)^{-\sigma}\right) \\ &\qquad = \frac{1-\phi}{J_n(s^t, n(s^t), k(s^t))} \\ &\qquad\quad \times \left((1-\alpha)z(s^t)\left(\frac{k(s^t)}{h(s^t)n(s^t)(1-\nu(s^t))}\right)^{\alpha} - w_1(s^t)\right). \end{aligned}$$

Eliminating V_n from this expression using the previous one gives us

$$\gamma\sigma h(s^t)^{1/\varepsilon}\left(\frac{c(s^t)}{1+(\sigma-1)(\gamma\varepsilon/(1+\varepsilon))h(s^t)^{(1+\varepsilon)/\varepsilon}n(s^t)}\right) = (1-\tau)(1-\alpha)z(s^t)\left(\frac{k(s^t)}{h(s^t)n(s^t)(1-\nu(s^t))}\right)^{\alpha}. \quad (4.56)$$

The marginal wage $w_1(s^t)$ then determines how those gains are split.

To reinterpret equation (4.56), I write down the monetary gains from trade at an arbitrary wage (w_0, w_1) and hours h. This is the sum of the after-tax value of a job to a firm and the marginal value of having an additional employed worker in the household, evaluated (for expositional convenience only) in units of goods rather than utility:

$$(1-\tau)\tilde{J}_n(s^t, w_1, h) + \tilde{V}_n(s^t, w_1, h)\left(\frac{c(s^t)}{1+(\sigma-1)(\gamma\varepsilon/(1+\varepsilon))h(s^t)^{(1+\varepsilon)/\varepsilon}n(s^t)}\right)^{\sigma}.$$

Now suppose that hours worked maximizes these joint gains from trade. Using equations (4.46) and (4.53) to eliminate $\tilde{V}_n$ and $\tilde{J}_n$, I find that hours worked must maximize

$$(1-\tau)(1-\alpha)z(s^t)\left(\frac{k(s^t)}{h(s^t)n(s^t)(1-\nu(s^t))}\right)^{\alpha}(h-h(s^t))$$
$$+\frac{\gamma\sigma\varepsilon}{1+\varepsilon}(h(s^t)^{(1+\varepsilon)/\varepsilon}-h^{(1+\varepsilon)/\varepsilon})\left(\frac{c(s^t)}{1+(\sigma-1)(\gamma\varepsilon/(1+\varepsilon))h(s^t)^{(1+\varepsilon)/\varepsilon}n(s^t)}\right).$$

But taking the necessary and sufficient first-order condition with respect to h and evaluating at $h = h(s^t)$, I obtain equation (4.56). Thus hours worked maximizes the joint gains from trade, generalizing one of the conclusions from section 2.4.2 to this environment.

I use the insight that hours are chosen to maximize the gains from trade to obtain an expression for the labor wedge. Let

$$y(s^t) \equiv z(s^t)k(s^t)^{\alpha}(h(s^t)n(s^t)(1-\nu(s^t)))^{1-\alpha}$$

denote aggregate output. Then rewrite equation (4.56) as

$$\tau = 1 - \frac{\gamma\sigma((1-\nu(s^t))c(s^t)/y(s^t))h(s^t)^{(1+\varepsilon)/\varepsilon}n(s^t)}{(1-\alpha)(1+(\sigma-1)(\gamma\varepsilon/(1+\varepsilon))h(s^t)^{(1+\varepsilon)/\varepsilon}n(s^t))}. \tag{4.57}$$

This is analogous to equation (1.14) in the frictionless model with nonseparable preferences. There are only two differences. First, there is no analogue of the share of producers $1-\nu(s^t)$ in the frictionless model. With search frictions, measured production only accounts for a fraction $1-\nu(s^t)$ of output; the remaining output is the unmeasured investment in future hiring through recruiting. Thus total (measured and unmeasured) output is $y(s^t)/(1-\nu(s^t))$ and so $(1-\nu(s^t))c(s^t)/y(s^t)$ measures the ratio of consumption to total output.

Second, in the frictionless model, the labor supply elasticity ε governed both the intensive and the extensive hours choice. There was no distinction between hours per worker and the employment–population ratio. With search frictions, the labor supply elasticity governs the choice of hours per worker, but the model behaves as if the elasticity for the employment–population ratio is infinite.

Quantitatively, the first difference between equations (1.14) and (4.57) is likely to be small. In my baseline calibration, a fraction $\nu = 0.004$ of workers are recruiters while the remainder are producers. Even if ν doubles during a boom, this reduces $1-\nu$ from 0.996 to 0.992. From equation (4.57), this scarcely affects the labor wedge.

The second difference is much more significant and suggests a testable implication. Suppose that by varying $w_0(s^t)$ appropriately, I can perfectly match the empirical behavior of the employment rate $n(s^t)$. Equation (4.57) shows that the model still makes predictions about the comovement of employment, the consumption–output ratio, and hours

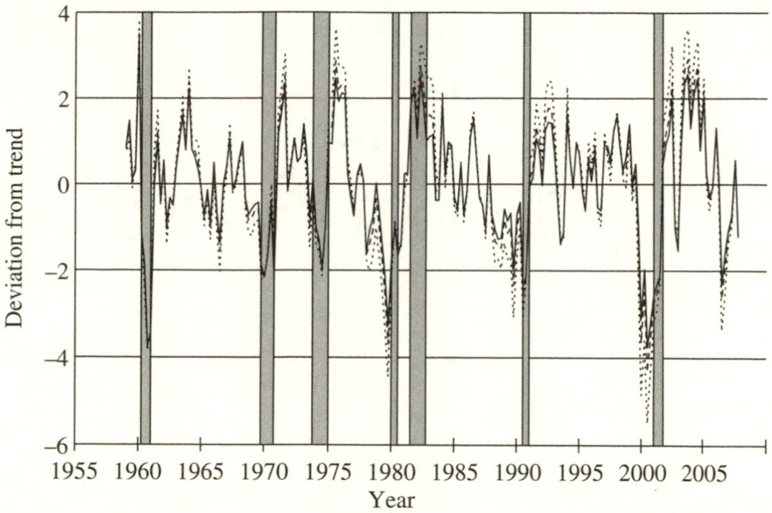

Figure 4.5. The deviation of the labor wedge from log trend, measured as an HP filter with parameter 1,600, using equation (4.57). The dotted line shows $\sigma = 1$, the dashed line shows $\sigma = 2$, and the solid line shows $\sigma = 4$. In each case I set $\varepsilon = 1$ and $\alpha = \frac{1}{3}$ and fix the remaining parameter $\gamma(1 - \nu)$ to ensure that the average labor wedge is 0.40. The gray bands show NBER recession dates.

per employed worker, each of which can be measured in the data. For example, fix the labor supply elasticity at $\varepsilon = 1$ and the capital share at $\alpha = \frac{1}{3}$. For different values of the complementarity parameter σ, I set $\gamma(1 - \nu)$ so that the labor wedge is equal to 0.4 on average.[3] I then use data on the consumption-output ratio $c(s^t)/y(s^t)$, on hours per employed worker $h(s^t)$, and on employment $n(s^t)$ to compute the right-hand side of equation (4.57).[4]

Figure 4.5 shows the results, expressed as deviations from log trend, for three different values of σ. The results are relatively insensitive to the exact choice of σ, although fluctuations are somewhat smaller when σ is larger. The figure shows a significant increase in the labor wedge during all but one of the postwar recessions; however, comparing the magnitude of the increases with the analogous numbers from the frictionless model, it is clear that the search model reduces the extent of the anomalies. For example, the standard deviation of the detrended labor wedge in the rigid-wage model, measured by equation (4.57), with $\varepsilon = 1$ and $\sigma = 2$, is 1.5 percent. The standard deviation of the annual growth rate is

[3] This approach ignores fluctuations in the share of recruiters $\nu(s^t)$. In principle, one could deduce these from the behavior of employment, for example using equation (4.48). As I discussed above, these movements are unlikely to be quantitatively significant and so I ignore them here.

[4] I use data on hours and employment from Prescott et al. (2008).

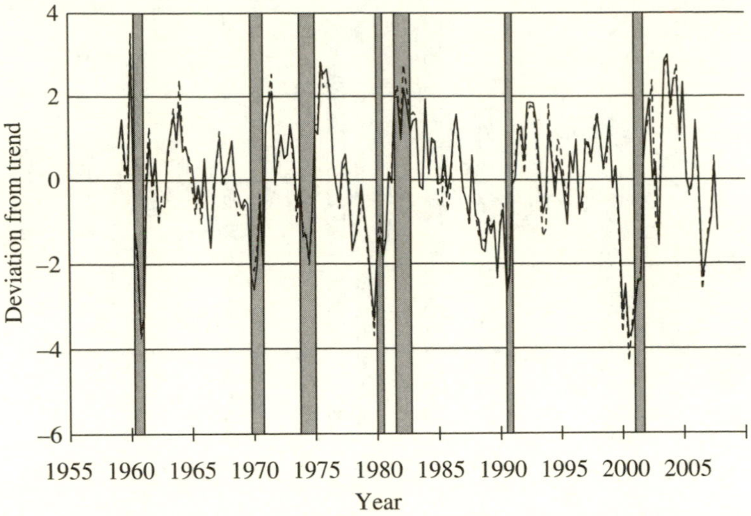

Figure 4.6. The deviation of the labor wedge from log trend, measured as an HP filter with parameter 1,600. Both lines set $\alpha = \frac{1}{3}$. The dashed line shows the rigid-wage model with $\varepsilon = 1$ and $\sigma = 2$, measuring the labor wedge using equation (4.57). The solid line shows the frictionless model with $\varepsilon = \infty$ and $\sigma = 1$, measuring the labor wedge using equation (1.12). The gray bands show NBER recession dates.

2.3 percent. If I measure the labor wedge using the frictionless model (equation (1.12)), with $\varepsilon = \infty$, the standard deviation of the detrended wedge is 1.4 percent and the standard deviation of the annual growth rate is 2.2 percent. Effectively, the search model with rigid wages and a relatively small labor supply elasticity behaves similarly to a frictionless model with an infinite labor supply elasticity. Figure 4.6 displays this point graphically.

This figure does not prove that wage rigidity is important for understanding the behavior of the labor market at business cycle frequencies. It does, however, suggest that the models of wage rigidity can be tested using the same approach that is effective in evaluating both the frictionless model and the flexible-wage model. Obviously, the amount of work is only one margin chosen by matched workers and firms, so the general approach suggested by Hall (2009) and outlined here may yet yield additional predictions.

5
Looking Ahead

My goal throughout this book has been to present an internally consistent model that can help to explain the observed cyclical behavior of the U.S. labor market. I end this book on a more speculative note, conjecturing how this research agenda might continue to progress. I point to some recent theoretical research that provides a better foundation for why wages are rigid and some recent empirical research that uses microeconomic data to assess the extent of wage rigidity. I discuss some of my own research that questions whether the matching function approach that I use throughout this book is the most useful one for understanding why there is unemployment. Finally, I ask whether the indeterminacy that I highlighted in chapter 4 might be relevant in other parts of the economy.

5.1 Theories of Rigid Wages

The theory of wage rigidity that I develop in chapter 4 is admittedly ad hoc, which is unsatisfactory from both an aesthetic and a pragmatic perspective. One would like to use a model like this not only to understand why unemployment is volatile and persistent but also to ask whether policies can and should affect this behavior. But, for example, to understand whether tax cuts will reduce unemployment, one needs to know whether it is pre-tax or after-tax wages that are rigid. If it is the pre-tax wage, then the nature of a tax change determines its incidence. For example, a switch from a payroll tax paid by employers to an income tax paid by employees will reduce firms' labor costs and workers' take-home pay, encouraging firms to recruit more workers. A rigidity in the after-tax wage leaves less latitude for such a simple policy to have real effects.

Similarly, to understand how monetary policy affects the labor market, one needs to know whether it is real or nominal wages that are rigid. Although the model in this book is entirely real, it seems straightforward to extend it to introduce money and to impose that wages are set in terms of this unit of account. An increase in inflation will then depress real wages, putting downward pressure on the unemployment rate. But if it is real wages that are rigid, monetary policy will have no direct impact on labor market outcomes.[1]

To address these questions from a theoretical perspective, we need to understand at a more primitive level why wages are rigid. Some existing papers offer a promising start on this research agenda. Hall and Milgrom (2008) suggest that the problem with flexible-wage models similar to the ones I analyze in chapters 2 and 3 lies not in the Nash bargaining solution per se, but rather in the assumption that if a worker and a firm fail to reach an agreement, their match ends. Following Binmore et al. (1986), they consider a strategic bargaining game between a matched worker and firm. In each period, one of the parties makes a wage offer to the other. If the offer is accepted, output is produced and the worker receives the bargained wage. If it is rejected, the other party may make a counteroffer after some specified delay. While they wait, both the worker and the firm receive a payoff that reflects the cost of bargaining.

In this situation, the relevant threat point may be disagreement, rather than match dissolution. This is important because in their environment, the value of disagreement fluctuates less at business cycle frequencies than does the value of an unemployment worker. Put differently, an important source of the procyclical real wage in chapter 3 comes from endogenous procyclicality in the marginal value of an unemployed worker. By shutting this margin down, Hall and Milgrom (2008) find that the model can generate significantly larger fluctuations in the unemployment rate in response to productivity shocks. Although there are important differences between their framework and mine—they assume linear utility and no capital, and they focus on comparative statics—it seems likely that their insight carries over to my framework as well.

Gertler and Trigari (2009) propose instead that wages are rigid because workers and firms only periodically negotiate, bargaining so as to satisfy the Nash solution and fixing the wage until the next opportunity to renegotiate. Crucially, the negotiated wage applies not only to the firm's existing workers but also to any new workers it might hire. Thus firms that last negotiated their wage prior to an adverse productivity shock will have little incentive to recruit new workers following the shock. This essentially provides a deeper theory for why wages may be backward looking—something I simply imposed in chapter 4.

---

[1] Monetary policy may still have real effects: for example, due to sticky prices. Trigari (2009) develops a model that integrates sticky prices and equilibrium unemployment.

Once one admits that the Nash bargaining solution is ad hoc, the number of alternative bargaining procedures is vast. It is still unclear whether economic theory provides much guidance as to which theories are more acceptable. One promising idea might be to discipline the model by adding more microeconomic structure to it. That is, in the model I use in this book and in the models in Hall and Milgrom (2008) and Gertler and Trigari (2009), all worker–firm matches are identical, producing the same amount of output. Although this abstraction is useful for some purposes, it may be overly simplistic. It seems likely that some matches are highly productive while others are much more marginal, as in Pissarides (1985) and Mortensen and Pissarides (1994). This heterogeneity, together with the requirement that workers and firms exploit all the bilateral gains from trade, may be useful for ruling out some paths for aggregate wages. Careful attention to incentive issues within the employment relationship may similarly provide important discipline for predicted wage behavior. Older research by Gomme (1999) and Alexopoulos (2004), as well as new work by Tawara (2008), are useful steps in this direction.

5.2 Empirical Evidence on Rigid Wages

Another interesting line of work measures the extent of wage rigidity. In Shimer (2004) I argued that the important empirical question for the behavior of a search model was not how rigid wages are for the average worker but rather how rigid they are for newly employed workers. Pissarides (2009) and Haefke et al. (2008) investigate this issue and cannot reject the null hypothesis that wages for new employees are as flexible as productivity.

While this finding is provocative, I stressed in chapter 4 that measured wages need not be much more rigid than measured labor productivity in order for the model to generate significant fluctuations in employment and a negative correlation between employment and the labor wedge. Given the small data sets that these papers use, it appears that they are also unable to reject other interesting hypotheses: for example, that wages are sufficiently rigid to generate significant fluctuations in aggregate employment. As Hall and Milgrom (2008) write, Pissarides (2009) and Haefke et al. (2008) "do not demonstrate that the observed behavior of wages is inconsistent with the limited amount of stickiness needed to explain the observed level of unemployment volatility" (p. 1,670).

Fortunately, it may be possible to address this problem with more data. In a number of European countries, vast data sets record a panel of workers' earnings over long periods of time. In some countries, coverage is nearly universal. Similar microeconomic data exist for some states in the United States as part of the Longitudinal Employer–Household Dynamics program. By looking at workers who switch employers, perhaps after an intervening spell of unemployment, it may be possible to tell whether monthly or quarterly earnings are more rigid than is predicted by the benchmark search model. Still, this approach of confronting the model with data may run into problems. For example, the productivity of newly hired workers need not be the same as the productivity of existing employees—a possibility that Eyigüngör (2008) stresses for a different reason in the context of a vintage capital model with search frictions. Since marginal productivity is even harder to measure than wages, it remains unclear whether this issue can be addressed empirically.

5.3 Alternatives to the Matching Function

Another way to make progress on whether and why wages are rigid may be to rethink the other departure from the competitive model in chapter 1: the assumption that an aggregate matching technology governs how recruiters and unemployed workers generate new matches. One alternative is the Lucas and Prescott (1974) "islands" framework. That paper assumes that workers and firms are located in local labor markets, with many workers and many firms in each. Labor markets are subject to idiosyncratic productivity shocks, which induce workers to switch markets. While there is perfect competition within a labor market, it takes time to switch markets, generating unemployment. In recent research, Alvarez and Shimer (2009) argue that unemployment may also arise because workers prefer the option value of waiting without a job in a particular labor market, rather than paying the cost of moving to a new one.

As in the original Lucas and Prescott (1974) model, Alvarez and Shimer (2009) assume that there are many workers and jobs within a labor market and so competitive forces determine wages. Although perfect competition eliminates any scope for the type of wage rigidity that I have analyzed here, reality may be more complex. For example, in a related model (Shimer 2007a), I focus on indivisibilities in the number of workers and jobs in a local labor market. Wages are determined by the short side of the market, with the long side of the market suffering either unemployment (workers) or vacancies (jobs). With strictly positive probability, however, the number of workers in a market is equal to the number of jobs in that market. In such a situation, any wage in an interval clears the labor market, which is a form of indeterminacy. Although the level of the wage is unimportant for the static equilibrium within a market, it is important for firms' incentives to create jobs, as we saw in chapter 4. This gives enough latitude for a limited amount of wage rigidity, which may have important consequences for unemployment fluctuations.

Ebrahimy and Shimer (2009) encounter a similar issue in a related model, where the ability of workers to match with jobs depends on an idiosyncratic shock. When one worker can take two or more available jobs or one job can be filled by two or more unemployed workers, competitive forces naturally determine wages. But when a single unemployed worker only has one job opportunity and that job can only hire this particular worker, economic theory provides little guidance as to how wages are set. Again this creates the possibility of a limited amount of wage rigidity.

Broadly speaking, careful attention to how a worker's human capital affects the jobs that she can accept gives additional structure to the economic environment. Relative to the model I have studied in this book, the possibility of wage rigidity in an environment without a matching function may be somewhat more limited, but it does not disappear.

5.4 Relevance to Other Markets

Numerous other markets are characterized by time-consuming search and decentralized exchange. An obvious example is, perhaps, the housing market, where search is complicated by heterogeneity in the characteristics of houses and in the tastes of home buyers. In a model where prices are determined by Nash bargaining between buyers and sellers, Wheaton (1990) finds that a search model explains the negative correlation between house prices and the housing vacancy rate. Duffie et al. (2005) and Lagos and Rocheteau (2009) argue that search frictions are also important in over-the-counter asset markets, such as the market for asset-backed securities and corporate bonds. Although the time it takes to find a trading partner is short, these papers conclude that search frictions are useful for understanding trading volume and bid–ask spreads. Again, both these papers assume that asset prices are determined by bargaining between buyers and sellers.

But if prices are determined by bargaining, then the type of rigidities that I emphasized in chapter 4 may be important in these markets as well. The asking price for a house typically reflects the price of recent transactions for comparable properties. Similarly, in financial markets, traders may look at the price of related securities for guidance when they submit their orders. As in the labor market, such rigidities may be innocuous at the individual level, affecting only the division of the gains from trade. Still, they would potentially have important implications for the path of prices, the demand for assets, and the time it takes to trade in the market. This possibility has so far received little attention in the search literature, but, if it is relevant, it may be as important for macroeconomic outcomes as the wage rigidities that I have emphasized in this book. Careful analysis of the implications of wage and price rigidities in search equilibrium should be an important area of research in the years to come.

Appendix A
Data

Although this book focuses on the behavior of the labor wedge, I also discuss the comovement of a number of other macroeconomic time series. Each of these has an empirical counterpart.

Output y**.** I use a quantity-weighted measure of real gross domestic product from National Income and Product Accounts Table 1.1.3, line 1. I express this in per capita terms, dividing by the population series from Prescott et al. (2008).

Consumption c**.** I use a quantity-weighted measure of real consumption of nondurables and services from National Income and Product Accounts Table 1.1.3, lines 5 and 6. I express this in per capita terms, dividing by the population series from Prescott et al. (2008).

Recruiter–unemployment ratio θ**.** I proxy the number of recruiters with the Conference Board monthly help-wanted advertising index, available directly from the Conference Board. I take the quarterly average of this series and divide by the number of unemployed workers from BLS series LNS13000000Q.

Capital stock k**.** I measure the capital stock using the Bureau of Economic Analysis's Fixed Asset Table 1.2, line 1: the chain-type quantity index for the net stock of fixed assets and consumer durable goods. This is an annual series, which I interpolate linearly to obtain a quarterly series. I divide by the population series from Prescott et al. (2008).

Employment n**.** I use the measure of employment from Prescott et al. (2008), divided by population from the same paper.

Labor share wn/y**.** I measure the labor share using National Income and Product Accounts Table 1.10. Labor income is "Compensation of employees, paid" (line 2). Capital income is consumption of fixed capital (line 23) plus net operating surplus of private enterprises (line 11) minus proprietors' income (line 15). Labor share is labor income divided by labor plus capital income. This implicitly assigns the same labor share to proprietors' income and to production and important taxes (line 9).

Consumption–output ratio c/y**.** I measure the nominal consumption–output ratio. Consumption is nondurables and services from National Income and Product Accounts Table 1.1.5, lines 5 and 6. Output is gross domestic product, from line 1 of the same table.

Labor wedge $\hat{\tau}$**.** I measure the labor wedge using equation (1.12), but using data on employment rather than hours. I assume that $\varepsilon = \infty$ and set the disutility of work to ensure that the labor wedge is 0.4 on average.

I construct quarterly data from 1959 to 2007. I detrend the data using an HP filter with parameter 1,600 (table A.1). I also express the data as annual growth rates (table A.2).

Table A.1. Detrended U.S. data, 1959–2007.

		y	c	θ	k	n	wn/y	c/y	$\hat{\tau}$
Relative standard deviation		1	0.589	15.304	0.202	0.655	0.474	0.643	0.832
Correlations	y	1	0.828	0.893	0.379	0.780	−0.177	−0.864	0.050
	c	—	1	0.762	0.312	0.672	−0.079	−0.548	−0.173
	θ	—	—	1	0.452	0.868	−0.097	−0.720	−0.203
	k	—	—	—	1	0.499	0.234	−0.193	−0.339
	n	—	—	—	—	1	0.073	−0.612	−0.460
	wn/y	—	—	—	—	—	1	0.369	−0.420
	c/y	—	—	—	—	—	—	1	−0.388
	$\hat{\tau}$	—	—	—	—	—	—	—	1

Table A.2. Annual growth rates, U.S. data, 1959–2007.

		y	c	θ	k	n	wn/y	c/y	$\hat{\tau}$
Relative standard deviation		1	0.605	14.706	0.242	0.639	0.497	0.664	0.917
Correlations	y	1	0.817	0.876	0.430	0.686	−0.162	−0.835	0.146
	c	—	1	0.699	0.456	0.521	−0.014	−0.490	−0.047
	θ	—	—	1	0.393	0.819	−0.087	−0.705	−0.110
	k	—	—	—	1	0.310	0.279	−0.228	−0.060
	n	—	—	—	—	1	0.045	−0.525	−0.455
	wn/y	—	—	—	—	—	1	0.365	−0.362
	c/y	—	—	—	—	—	—	1	−0.486
	$\hat{\tau}$	—	—	—	—	—	—	—	1

References

Aguiar, M., and E. Hurst. 2005. Consumption versus expenditure. *Journal of Political Economy* 113(5):919–48.

——. 2007. Measuring trends in leisure: the allocation of time over five decades. *Quarterly Journal of Economics* 122(3):969–1,006.

Alexopoulos, M. 2004. Unemployment and the business cycle. *Journal of Monetary Economics* 51(2):277–98.

Alvarez, F., and R. Shimer. 2009. Search and rest unemployment. Mimeo, University of Chicago.

Andolfatto, D. 1996. Business cycles and labor-market search. *American Economic Review* 86(1):112–32.

Barro, R. J. 1977. Long-term contracting, sticky prices, and monetary policy. *Journal of Monetary Economics* 3(3):305–16.

Barro, R. J., and H. I. Grossman. 1971. A general disequilibrium model of income and employment. *American Economic Review* 61(1):82–93.

Becker, G. S. 1965. A theory of the allocation of time. *The Economic Journal* 75(299):493–517.

Benassy, J.-P. 1982. *The Economics of Market Disequilibrium*. New York: Academic Press.

Bils, M., Y. Chang, and S.-B. Kim. 2007. Comparative advantage in cyclical unemployment. NBER Working Paper 13231.

Binmore, K., A. Rubinstein, and A. Wolinsky. 1986. The Nash bargaining solution in economic modeling. *RAND Journal of Economics* 17(2):176–88.

Blanchard, O. J., and P. Diamond. 1989. The Beveridge curve. *Brookings Papers on Economic Activity* 1989(1):1–76.

Blanchard, O. J., and J. Galí. 2006. A new Keynesian model with unemployment. Mimeo, Massachusetts Institute of Technology.

Blanchard, O. J., and R. Perotti. 2002. An empirical characterization of the dynamic effects of changes in government spending and taxes on output. *Quarterly Journal of Economics* 117(4):1,329–68.

Blundell, R., and T. MaCurdy. 1999. Labor supply: a review of alternative approaches. *Handbook of Labor Economics* 3(1):1,559–95.

Chari, V. V., P. J. Kehoe, and E. R. McGrattan. 2007. Business cycle accounting. *Econometrica* 75(3):781–836.

Cole, H. L., and R. Rogerson. 1999. Can the Mortensen-Pissarides matching model match the business-cycle facts? *International Economic Review* 40(4): 933–59.

Cooley, T. F., and E. C. Prescott. 1995. Economic growth and business cycles. In *Frontiers of Business Cycle Research* (ed. T. F. Cooley), pp. 1–38. Princeton University Press.

Costain, J. S., and M. Reiter. 2008. Business cycles, unemployment insurance, and the calibration of matching models. *Journal of Economic Dynamics and Control* 32(4):1,120–55.

Davis, S. J., J. C. Haltiwanger, and S. Schuh. 1996. *Job Creation and Destruction.* Cambridge, MA: MIT Press.

Duffie, D., N. Gârleanu, and L. H. Pedersen. 2005. Over-the-counter markets. *Econometrica* 73(6):1,815–47.

Ebrahimy, E., and R. Shimer. 2009. Stock-flow matching. Mimeo, University of Chicago.

Elsby, M. W., R. Michaels, and G. Solon. 2007. The ins and outs of cyclical unemployment. NBER Working Paper 12853.

Erceg, C. J., D. W. Henderson, and A. T. Levin. 2000. Optimal monetary policy with staggered wage and price contracts. *Journal of Monetary Economics* 46(2): 281–313.

Eyigüngör, B. 2008. Specific capital and vintage effects on the dynamics of unemployment and vacancies. Federal Reserve Bank of Philadelphia Working Paper 08-6.

Farmer, R. E. A., and A. Hollenhorst. 2006. Shooting the auctioneer. NBER Working Paper 12584.

Fisher, J. D. M. 2006. The dynamic effects of neutral and investment-specific technology shocks. *Journal of Political Economy* 114(3):413–51.

Fujita, S., and G. Ramey. 2009. The cyclicality of separation and job finding rates. *International Economic Review* 50(2):415–30.

Galí, J., and P. Rabanal. 2004. Technology shocks and aggregate fluctuations: how well does the RBC model fit postwar U.S. data? *NBER Macroeconomics Annual* 19:225–318.

Galí, J., M. Gertler, and J. D. López-Salido. 2007. Markups, gaps, and the welfare costs of business fluctuations. *Review of Economics and Statistics* 89(1):44–59.

Gertler, M., and A. Trigari. 2009. Unemployment fluctuations with staggered Nash wage bargaining. *Journal of Political Economy* 117(1):38–86.

Gomme, P. 1999. Shirking, unemployment and aggregate fluctuations. *International Economic Review* 40(1):3–21.

Haefke, C., M. Sonntag, and T. van Rens. 2008. Wage rigidity and job creation. IZA Discussion Paper 3714.

Hagedorn, M., and I. Manovskii. 2008. The cyclical behavior of equilibrium unemployment and vacancies revisited. *American Economic Review* 98(4): 1,692–706.

Hall, R. E. 1995. Lost jobs. *Brookings Papers on Economic Activity* 1:221–56.

——. 1997. Macroeconomic fluctuations and the allocation of time. *Journal of Labor Economics* 15(1):223–50.

——. 2005. Employment fluctuations with equilibrium wage stickiness. *American Economic Review* 95(1):50–65.

——. 2009. Reconciling cyclical movements in the marginal value of time and the marginal product of labor. Mimeo, Stanford University.

Hall, R. E., and P. R. Milgrom. 2008. The limited influence of unemployment on the wage bargain. *American Economic Review* 98(4):1,653–74.

Hosios, A. J. 1990. On the efficiency of matching and related models of search and unemployment. *Review of Economic Studies* 57(2):279–98.

Kaldor, N. 1957. A model of economic growth. *The Economic Journal* 67(268): 591–624.

Kennan, J. 2006. Private information, wage bargaining and employment fluctuations. NBER Working Paper 11967.

Krause, M. U., and T. A. Lubik. 2007. The (ir)relevance of real wage rigidity in the new Keynesian model with search frictions. *Journal of Monetary Economics* 54(3):706–27.

Krusell, P., L. E. Ohanian, J. V. Ríos-Rull, and G. L. Violante. 2000. Capital-skill complementarity and inequality: a macroeconomic analysis. *Econometrica* 68(5):1,029–53.

Krusell, P., T. Mukoyama, and A. Şahin. 2007. Labor-market matching with precautionary savings and aggregate fluctuations. Mimeo, Princeton University.

Kydland, F. E., and E. C. Prescott. 1982. Time to build and aggregate fluctuations. *Econometrica* 50(6):1,345–70.

Lagos, R., and G. Rocheteau. 2009. Liquidity in asset markets with search frictions. *Econometrica* 77(2):403–26.

Ljungqvist, L., and T. J. Sargent. 2004. *Recursive Macroeconomic Theory*, 2nd edn. Cambridge, MA: MIT Press.

Lucas Jr., R. E., and E. C. Prescott. 1974. Equilibrium search and unemployment. *Journal of Economic Theory* 7:188–209.

Lucas Jr., R. E., and L. A. Rapping. 1969. Real wages, employment, and inflation. *Journal of Political Economy* 77(5):721–54.

Malinvaud, E. 1977. *The Theory of Unemployment Reconsidered.* New York: Halsted Press.

Mankiw, N. G. 1989. Real business cycles: a new Keynesian perspective. *Journal of Economic Perspectives* 3(3):79–90.

Mertens, K., and M. O. Ravn. 2008. The aggregate effects of anticipated and unanticipated U.S. tax policy shocks: theory and empirical evidence. Mimeo, Cornell University.

Merz, M. 1995. Search in the labor market and the real business cycle. *Journal of Monetary Economics* 36(2):269–300.

Modigliani, F. 1977. The monetarist controversy or, should we forsake stabilization policies? *American Economic Review* 67(2):1–19.

Moen, E. R. 1997. Competitive search equilibrium. *Journal of Political Economy* 105(2):385–411.

Mortensen, D. T. 1982. Property rights and efficiency in mating, racing, and related games. *American Economic Review* 72(5):968–79.

Mortensen, D. T., and É. Nagypál. 2007. More on unemployment and vacancy fluctuations. *Review of Economic Dynamics* 10(3):327–47.

Mortensen, D. T., and C. A. Pissarides. 1994. Job creation and job destruction in the theory of unemployment. *Review of Economic Studies* 61(3):397–415.

——. 1999. New developments in models of search in the labor market. In *Handbook of Labor Economics* (ed. O. Ashenfelter and D. Card), volume 3, chapter 39, pp. 2,567–627. Elsevier.

Mulligan, C. B. 2002. A century of labor-leisure distortions. NBER Working Paper 8774.

Nakajima, M. 2008. Business cycles in the equilibrium model of labor market search and self-insurance. Mimeo, University of Illinois at Urbana-Champaign.

Nash, J. 1953. Two-person cooperative games. *Econometrica* 21(1):128–40.

Parkin, M. 1988. A method for determining whether parameters in aggregative models are structural. *Carnegie-Rochester Conference Series on Public Policy* 29:215–52.

Petrongolo, B., and C. A. Pissarides. 2001. Looking into the black box: a survey of the matching function. *Journal of Economic Literature* 39(2):390–431.

Pissarides, C. A. 1985. Short-run equilibrium dynamics of unemployment, vacancies, and real wages. *American Economic Review* 75(4):676–90.

——. 2000. *Equilibrium Unemployment Theory*, 2nd edn. Cambridge, MA: MIT Press.

——. 2009. The unemployment volatility puzzle: is wage stickiness the answer? *Econometrica* 77(5):1,339–70.

Prescott, E. C. 2004. Why do Americans work so much more than Europeans? *Federal Reserve Bank of Minneapolis Quarterly Review* 28(1):2–13.

Prescott, E. C., A. Ueberfeldt, and S. Cociuba. 2008. U.S. hours and productivity behavior: using CPS hours worked data: 1959-I to 2007-IV. Mimeo, Federal Reserve Bank of Dallas (February).

Pries, M. J. 2004. Persistence of employment fluctuations: a model of recurring job loss. *Review of Economic Studies* 71(1):193–215.

Ramey, V. A., and N. Francis. 2009. A century of work and leisure. *American Economic Journal: Macroeconomics* 1(2):189–224.

Romer, C. D., and D. H. Romer. 2007. A narrative analysis of postwar tax changes. Mimeo, University of California, Berkeley.

Rotemberg, J. J. 2006. Cyclical wages in a search-and-bargaining model with large firms. NBER Working Paper 12415.

Rotemberg, J. J., and M. Woodford. 1991. Markups and the business cycle. *NBER Macroeconomics Annual* 6:63–129.

——. 1997. An optimization-based econometric framework for the evaluation of monetary policy. *NBER Macroeconomics Annual* 12:297–346.

——. 1999. The cyclical behavior of prices and costs. In *Handbook of Macroeconomics* (ed. J. B. Taylor and M. Woodford), volume 1, chapter 16, pp. 1,051–135. Elsevier.

Rudanko, L. 2008. Aggregate and idiosyncratic risk in a frictional labor market. Mimeo, Boston University.

——. 2009. Labor market dynamics under long-term wage contracting. *Journal of Monetary Economics* 56(2):170–83.

Shimer, R. 1996. *Essays in Search Theory.* Ph.D. thesis, Massachusetts Institute of Technology.

——. 2004. The consequences of rigid wages in search models. *Journal of the European Economic Association (Papers and Proceedings)* 2(2–3):469–79.

——. 2005. The cyclical behavior of equilibrium unemployment and vacancies. *American Economic Review* 95(1):25–49.

——. 2007a. Mismatch. *American Economic Review* 97(4):1,074–101.

——. 2007b. Reassessing the ins and outs of unemployment. Mimeo, University of Chicago.

Silva, J., and M. Toledo. 2009. Labor turnover costs and the cyclical behavior of vacancies and unemployment. *Macroeconomic Dynamics* 13(51):76–96.

Smets, F., and R. Wouters. 2003. An estimated dynamic stochastic general equilibrium model of the euro area. *Journal of the European Economic Association* 1(5):1,123–75.

——. 2007. Shocks and frictions in US business cycles: a Bayesian DSGE approach. *American Economic Review* 97(3):586–606.

Tawara, N. 2008. Performance pay, efficiency wages and unemployment fluctuations. Mimeo, Kanto Gakuen University.

Trigari, A. 2009. Equilibrium unemployment, job flows, and inflation dynamics. *Journal of Money, Credit and Banking* 41(1):1–33.

Wheaton, W. C. 1990. Vacancy, search, and prices in a housing market matching model. *Journal of Political Economy* 98(6):1,270–92.

Yashiv, E. 2006. Evaluating the performance of the search and matching model. *European Economic Review* 50(4):909–36.

Author Index